KARL BARTH ON THE FILIOQUE

Despite the burgeoning literature on Karl Barth, his doctrine of the Holy Spirit continues to be under-appreciated by his friends and critics alike. Yet, while Barth's commitment to the doctrine of the procession of the Holy Spirit from the Father and the Son (Filioque) is well-known, many scholars dismiss his stand as ecumenically untenable and few have bothered to subject his stance on the Filioque to close theological analysis. For those interested in this long-standing ecumenical point of contention between Eastern and Western Trinitarian theology, this book will show how Barth's doctrine of the Filioque may still have something to contribute to the debate. The work traces the origin of Barth's commitment to the Filioque in his early career (particularly in *Romans* and the *Göttingen Dogmatics*), and then analyzes how the doctrine functions throughout the *Church Dogmatics*. Guretzki concludes that Barth's doctrine of the Filioque, while clearly standing within the Western Trinitarian tradition, is atypical in that he refuses to speak of a "double-procession" in favour of a "common procession" of the Spirit—a position that has more affinity with the Eastern position than many of Barth's critics may have thought

Barth Studies

Series Editors

The work of Barth is central to the history of modern western theology and remains a major voice in contemporary constructive theology. His writings have been the subject of intensive scrutiny and re-evaluation over the past two decades, notably on the part of English-language Barth scholars who have often been at the forefront of fresh interpretation and creative appropriation of his theology. Study of Barth, both by graduate students and by established scholars, is a significant enterprise; literature on him and conferences devoted to his work abound; the Karl Barth Archive in Switzerland and the Center for Barth Studies at Princeton give institutional profile to these interests. Barth's work is also considered by many to be a significant resource for the intellectual life of the churches.

Drawing from the wide pool of Barth scholarship, and including translations of Barth's works, this series aims to function as a means by which writing on Barth, of the highest scholarly calibre, can find publication. The series builds upon and furthers the interest in Barth's work in the theological academy and the church.

Other titles in this series

Barth, Israel, and Jesus
Karl Barth's Theology of Israel
Mark R. Lindsay

Barth's Theology of Interpretation
Donald Wood

A Shorter Commentary on Romans *by Karl Barth*
With an Introductory Essay by Maico Michielin
Maico M. Michielin

Karl Barth and the Fifth Gospel
Barth's Theological Exegesis of Isaiah
Mark S. Gignilliat

Karl Barth on the Filioque

DAVID GURETZKI
Briercrest College and Seminary, Canada

ASHGATE

Published by
Ashgate Publishing Limited
Wey Court East
Union Road
Farnham
Surrey, GU9 7PT
England

Ashgate Publishing Company
Suite 420
101 Cherry Street
Burlington
VT 05401-4405
USA

www.ashgate.com

British Library Cataloguing in Publication Data
Guretzki, David.
Karl Barth on the Filioque. – (Barth studies)
1. Barth, Karl, 1886–1968. 2. Holy Spirit – Procession – History of doctrines – 20th century.
I. Title II. Series
231'.044–dc22

Library of Congress Cataloging-in-Publication Data
Guretzki, David.
Karl Barth on the Filioque / David Guretzki.
p. cm.—(Barth studies)
Includes bibliographical references and index.
ISBN 978-0-7546-6704-9 (hardcover : alk. paper)
1. Holy Spirit—Procession—History of doctrines—20th century. 2. Barth, Karl, 1886–1968. I. Title.

BT114.G87 2009
231'.3092—dc22

2009007557

ISBN 9780754667049 (hbk)
ISBN 9780754695981 (ebk)

Mixed Sources
Product group from well-managed forests and other controlled sources
www.fsc.org Cert no. SA-COC-1565
© 1996 Forest Stewardship Council
FSC

Printed and bound in Great Britain by
MPG Books Group, UK

To Maureen, Joey, Chiante, and Sierra

Contents

Foreword

Dr Douglas Farrow, McGill University

When I first began to read and ponder Karl Barth, unbidden but not unwarned by my seminary teachers, I had no inkling that I would someday be asked to pen a foreword to a book such as this. Even for a novice, however, it was not difficult to see that Barth opened up a realm of thought that could not quickly be conquered or closed. When I later had the privilege of learning about Barth through encounters with some of his most able interpreters, I did not know, but perhaps began to have an inkling, that I would in turn have the privilege of helping others to read and ponder Barth. Colin Gunton saw to it that I did exactly that while I was still a doctoral student—one of the many things for which I remain grateful to him. While I made no pretence then, and can make none now, at belonging to the guild of dedicated Barth scholars, it greatly pleases me to see one of my own doctoral students, David Guretzki, taking his place in the growing ranks of that guild in North America and, more specifically, in Canada.

This book will appeal very directly to the guild, but also to all who have an interest (as any serious theologian must) in the problem of the filioque. Thanks to Dr Guretzki, we can now see much more clearly than before how the filioque functioned in Barth's thought, and in consequence ask some new questions both about the filioque and about Barth himself. For Guretzki demonstrates that Barth's adherence to the filioque had a different origin, and came to serve greater theological purposes than has commonly been supposed.

Tracing Barth's use of the filioque from the first volume of the *Church Dogmatics* back into the Göttingen period, and then onwards into the final volume of his great project, Guretzki takes stock of the changes and developments that occur along the way. Barth, we discover, begins by embracing the filioque, not uncritically as a theologian content with the Latin tradition, nor yet as one engaged critically with the Greek tradition, but quite self-consciously as a Reformed theologian trying to establish the theological grounds for, and dignity of, the task of preaching. Proclamation is thus drawn into the heart of his theory of revelation, alongside the Incarnation and Holy Scripture, as one form of the threefold Word of God, and this is done by way of analogy with the procession of the Spirit from the Father and the Son. The analogy turns out to be a problematic one, however—more problematic, perhaps, than Barth himself appears to notice when he modifies it at the outset of the *Church Dogmatics*.

Of course there is more to Barth's thinking about the filioque than that, as Guretzki goes on to reveal. The filioque is important to theology proper, and hence to Barth's view of God's self-determination as Father and Son. Here, Guretzki argues that Barth's understanding of the divine modes of being makes it difficult to classify his view as typically Latin, since Barth holds not to a double procession from the persons of the Father and the Son, but to a single procession from the common being of the Father and the Son. This raises a number of interesting questions, I think. Does Barth intend to say something different than Anselm does when the latter speaks of the procession of the Spirit from the Father and the Son *tamquam ab uno principio*? Is it accurate to describe the Western tradition in terms of a double procession? What bearing has the distinction, with which Barth wrestles, between the language of origin or causality and the language of perichoretic relations? And how far does Barth's preference for *Seinsweise* over 'person' affect his handling of the filioque?

These are deep theological waters, not easily plumbed. Guretzki's own contribution is to chart the area in which questions like this must arise. He recognizes that, for Barth, the filioque serves, very much in the Western fashion, to uphold the divinity of each of the three persons or modes of being and to maintain the dialectical unity between Christology and pneumatology. He shows how Barth incorporates the filioque into his cosmology through the rather dubious notion of creation history; into his anthropology through his description of the possibility of human communion with God; and into his soteriology in his treatment of the actuality of reconciliation. He displays Barth's understanding of the Spirit as the living boundary and bond between the Father and the Son, and as the 'power of transition' between God and man, and indeed between man and man. He highlights the connection between Barth's methodological commitment to the priority of the economy and his embrace of the filioque; at the same time he questions the clarity of Barth's distinction between the economic and the immanent Trinity, the adequacy of his reading of the economy, and his consistency in beginning with the economy.

Guretzki's reading of Barth is sympathetic throughout. He defends him from some of the charges that have been leveled against him in respect of the filioque: exaggeration of Christology at the expense of pneumatology, for example, which has as its counterpart Hegel's earlier exaggeration of pneumatology at the expense of Christology. But he also observes that the ambiguities in Barth's procedure produce, if not the collapse of the distinction between the immanent and the economic Trinity, then the appearance of something like the *analogia entis* that Barth himself rejects. More positively, he suggests that Barth on the filioque—in part because that great Reformed theologian doesn't begin by worrying about ecumenicity and in part because his theology raises just this sort of question—is much more ecumenically relevant than is commonly realized. I think readers of this book will come to agree, and I would even go so far as to suggest that the book identifies a new opening for Barth studies. At all events, it marks out its author as an able member of the guild devoted to those studies and as a teacher well worthy of his students.

Douglas Farrow
McGill University

Preface

My own interest in the history and doctrine of the filioque spans nearly a decade and a half prior to writing this book. The initial impetus for studying the filioque controversy first arose for me in 1994 in a historical theology class taken at Briercrest Seminary under Dr Bruce Hindmarsh, who encouraged me to pursue the topic. It was as I researched and wrote a paper on the ante-Nicene precedents to Augustine's doctrine of the "double procession of the Spirit" that I became aware of Karl Barth's twentieth-century defense of the filioque. I found this intriguing, not least because it meant for me that the filioque controversy was far from being a quaint ancient theological problem without any current importance. My interest in Karl Barth's work grew steadily from there, and I eventually completed a doctoral dissertation in 2006 on Karl Barth's doctrine of the filioque under the careful scrutiny and brilliant supervision of Professor Douglas Farrow at McGill University, Montreal, Canada. This book is a revision and update of that dissertation. Thus, I extend my sincere gratitude for the crucial roles that Dr Hindmarsh and Dr Farrow played in my own theological development over the past decade and a half.

I also wish to express my gratitude to the administration of Briercrest College and Seminary where I teach and research for providing a sabbatical leave in 2008 during which I completed the manuscript for this book. I also acknowledge the permission to cite from Karl Barth, *Church Dogmatics* (T & T Clark, 1936-1962). By kind permission of Continuum International Publishing Group.

There are many others, too numerous to mention individually, who should also be thanked, including my extended family, and my friends, colleagues, and students at Briercrest College and Seminary where I teach. I pay particular tribute to my students and colleagues of the Karl Barth Reading Group who have been faithfully meeting weekly with me since 2006 to enjoy fellowship and lively conversation about the work of Karl Barth. Finally, I thank my beautiful wife Maureen, along with my three children, Joey, Chiante, and Sierra, for their undying love, encouragement and support throughout the process. It is to them that I dedicate this book.

David Guretzki, PhD
Briercrest College and Seminary

Introduction

Stephen Sykes has aptly observed that "nothing in the history of the interpretation of Barth hitherto should lead one to suppose that any one scholar has the 'key to Barth' secreted in his robes."[1] The problem of interpreting Barth is exacerbated by the hermeneutical challenge of seeking to understand holistically an unusually massive literary corpus. Consequently, Barth scholars often have to concede to the hermeneutical necessity of making generalizations about Barth's theology as a whole in hopes of making sense of a single part of his massive *Church Dogmatics*. For example, while it is often noted that Barth's theology is consistently "Christocentric,"[2] such generalizations can also have the deleterious effect of steering the interpretation of Barth in directions that may not accurately represent his thinking. Add to this the complicating factor that Barth scholars are increasingly wary of interpreting the *Church Dogmatics* in isolation from his earlier works which are now coming to light in Barth's collected works (*Gesamtausgabe*) and the interpretative challenge might seem to be utterly overwhelming.

Interpretative challenges notwithstanding, this study attempts to contribute to the ongoing scholarly investigation of Barth's work by examining closely a part of his theology that has either been largely neglected or, when given attention, has often been dealt with only in summary fashion. Though it is well known that Barth was a vocal defender of the doctrine of the filioque—the ancient doctrine that asserts that the Holy Spirit proceeds from the Father and the Son—to date there has been no monograph-length study devoted to this aspect of Barth's thought. When Barth's stance on the filioque is examined in shorter works, it has been predominantly assumed that the sum total of what Barth had to say about the doctrine is contained in a section near the end of his first half volume of the *Church Dogmatics*. This study, however, will trace the genesis of Barth's doctrine of the filioque to his earlier thought with the goal of setting his formal defense of the doctrine in the *Church Dogmatics* into the larger context of his thought. It will also be shown how there was a shift in Barth's theological rationale for defending the doctrine between the 1920s and the 1930s and how the doctrine continued to function and develop in the remaining volumes of the *Church Dogmatics*.

The study will proceed straightforwardly. After providing a brief historical overview of the filioque controversy itself, including locating Barth within that

1 S. W. Sykes, "The Study of Barth," in S. W. Sykes (ed.), *Karl Barth: Studies of his Theological Method* (Oxford, 1979), pp. 1-16 at p. 2.

2 For a helpful review of this matter, see Marc Cortez, "What Does It Mean to Call Karl Barth a 'Christocentric' Theologian?", *Scottish Journal of Theology*, 60/2 (2007): 127-43.

historical trajectory, Chapter One surveys the critical scholarship that addresses Barth's doctrine of the filioque.

Recent scholarship has called into question the prevailing understanding of the development of Barth's theology from "dialectical" to "analogical" modes of thinking. Such an understanding has often resulted in isolating Barth's later thinking, as represented in the *Church Dogmatics*, from earlier stages of his work. Consequently, Chapter Two will provide a representational account of the genesis and development of Barth's doctrine of the filioque by examining two of Barth's early major works: *Romans* and the *Göttingen Dogmatics*.

Chapter Three will direct an analytical spotlight on the first half-volume of the *Church Dogmatics* because it is there that Barth provides his fullest and most mature defense of the filioque. Careful attention will be given to laying out the literary/dogmatic context in which the formal defense of the filioque is found, and the theological rationale which Barth provided. The chapter will also include, for the purposes of highlighting important nuances in Barth, a comparison of his theology of the filioque with the views of T. F. Torrance, who happened to believe that Barth could have avoided the necessity of defending the filioque altogether.

In Chapter Four the investigation will be extended to analyze those specific instances in the *Church Dogmatics* beyond the first half-volume where Barth makes material applications of the filioque. A close reading of these selected passages will reveal clues as to how Barth continued to develop his thinking about the systematic function of the filioque for his Trinitarian theology, even years after what appeared to be his definitive statement in the first half-volume. The final chapter follows this up by evaluating Barth's doctrine of the filioque, as well as identifying some of the implications of Barth's doctrine of the filioque both for ecumenical and future theological research.

The significance of this study is that it demonstrates that, despite the fact that Barth's understanding and use of the filioque matures over the course of his career, there is also an element of continuity such that Barth can be characterized both in his earlier and later work as displaying a dialectical filioquist pneumatology. That is to say, a latent dialectical Christocentric pneumatology in the second edition of *Romans* (1921) provides the material theological support for the doctrine, which subsequently appears in a formal discussion of the filioque in the *Göttingen Dogmatics* (1924). There Barth speaks of the filioque as a theological analogy of the structure of his developing doctrine of the threefold Word of God. Barth continues to defend and apply the filioque in the *Church Dogmatics*, though the original connection to the threefold form of the Word of God recedes into the background. Instead, in the *Church Dogmatics* Barth views the systematic function of the filioque as a theological guarantee of the unity of the work of the Son and the Spirit and as a dogmatic means of affirming that the Spirit is the eternal "bond and boundary" of fellowship between the Father and Son, and, by theological analogy, between God and humanity (in the person of Jesus Christ), and between God and the Church (as the earthly form of the body of Christ). Barth's most mature view of the filioque, in consistency with his earlier thought, is therefore construed in dialectical terms whereby the Spirit is understood to be eternally active in uniting and differentiating the Father and the Son.

Beyond showing the broad internal consistency of Barth's earlier and later dialectical filioqust pneumatology, it will also be shown that Barth is atypical in the Western filioquist tradition because he refuses to speak of the filioque in terms of a "double procession"; rather, he views the Spirit as proceeding from the "being-of-the-modes-of-being-of-the-Father-and-the-Son." Consequently, Barth's position on the filioque must be properly understood as actually seeking to account for some of the concerns raised in the Eastern monopatrist tradition, particularly in regard to the Eastern rejection of a "double source" theory of the Holy Spirit.

Chapter One
Karl Barth and the Filioque: History and Literature

During the last quarter of the twentieth century, some significant attempts were made to bring resolution to the centuries-old theological debate concerning the doctrine of the procession of the Holy Spirit, more commonly known as the filioque controversy. For example, in an effort to bring about a healing of the millennium-old schism between Orthodox and Catholics, Pope John Paul II called for a Roman clarification on the filioque clause in 1995. The resulting document provided helpful elucidation of similarities and differences between Catholic and Orthodox positions on the matter.[1] Despite the signs of encouraging ecumenical progress, however, a definitive solution to the filioque controversy that is theologically and ecumenically acceptable to Eastern and Western ecclesiastical parties has not yet been formally reached.

However, the recent Roman clarification on the filioque is illustrative of how even longstanding theological traditions are in need of persistent revisitation in hopes of positive theological advance. Attempts at theological *rapprochement*, as important as they may be, can tend to rush impatiently ahead of the necessary work of clarifying respective theological traditions. By analogy to the Catholic clarification of the filioque, Protestants, who have generally shared the Roman Catholic acceptance of the clause, could potentially benefit from a "clarification" of their own. Few have bothered to ask how a deeply embedded tradition such as the filioque has functioned throughout the rest of Protestant theology. Consequently, this study might be viewed as a preliminary contribution to such a "Protestant clarification" by analyzing and evaluating the doctrine of the filioque as defended by one of the most widely influential Protestant theologians of the twentieth century, the Swiss Reformed theologian Karl Barth (1886-1986). Though it will be necessary to identify when, how, and where Barth adopted his support for the

---

[1] "The Greek and Latin Traditions about the procession of the Holy Spirit," in *L'Osservatore Romano,* 38 (20 September 1995): 3, 6. Response to the document has been generally positive, especially in how the document reinforces the monarchy of the Father in agreement with the Eastern tradition. For an Orthodox response, see John Zizioulas, "One Single Source: An Orthodox Response to the Clarification on the Filioque" (2002), available from: http://www.orthodoxresearchinstitute.org/ articles/dogmatics/john_zizioulas_single_source.htm (accessed 2 December 2008). For a Catholic response, see David Coffey, "The Roman 'Clarification' of the Doctrine of the Filioque," *International Journal of Systematic Theology*, 5/1 (March 2003): 3-21.

filioque and its attendant theology, this study pays special attention to Barth's defense and use of the filioque in the *Church Dogmatics* (*CD*).[2]

Before launching directly into the study, however, it will be helpful to review briefly the history of the filioque controversy. This is especially important because the historical and doctrinal aspects of the filioque are rarely discussed amongst Protestants; indeed, the filioque controversy is often perceived by Protestants as an obscure chapter in Roman Catholic and Eastern Orthodox history. Consequently, the following brief historical overview will serve to set Barth into the context of the debate.

The Filioque Controversy: A Brief History

Early in the fifth century AD, certain Spanish churches began including the word "filioque" [Latin, "and the Son"] in the third article of the Latin text of the Nicæno-Constantinopolitan Creed (AD 381).[3] Whereas the original text of the third article read, "in the Holy Spirit … who proceeds from the Father",[4] the interpolation of "filioque" [*Et in Spiritum Sanctum ... qui ex Patre* (*Filioque*) *procedit*] altered the Creed explicitly to teach a procession of the Holy Spirit from the Father *and* the Son.[5]

Despite the affirmation given to the filioque by the third and fourth Councils of Toledo (AD 589 and 633 respectively), the addition itself remained relatively

---

[2] Karl Barth, *Church Dogmatics*, trans. Geoffrey Bromiley and T.F. Torrance (4 vols in 13 Parts, Edinburgh, 1936-1975). Hereafter, the volume and part of the work will be cited, for example, as follows: *CD* I/1. German: Karl Barth, *Die Kirchliche Dogmatik* (13 vols, Zürich, 1932-70). Hereafter referred to as *KD*.

[3] Hereafter referred to either by the abbreviation NCC or simply as "the Creed." On the history of the filioque controversy, see especially J. N. D. Kelly, *Early Christian Creeds*, 3rd edn (London, 1972), pp. 358-67; Jaroslav Pelikan, *The Christian Tradition*, Vol. 3: *The Growth of Medieval Theology (600-1300)* (5 vols, Chicago, 1978), pp. 229ff.; Gerald Bray, "The *Filioque* Clause in History and Theology," *Tyndale Bulletin* 34 (1983), pp. 91-144; Daniel J. Nodes, "Dual Processions of the Holy Spirit: Development of a Theological Tradition," *Scottish Journal of Theology* 52/1 (1999): 1-18; Brian E. Daley, "Revisiting the 'Filioque': Roots and Branches of an Old Debate, Part One," *Pro Ecclesia* 10/1 (Winter 2001): 31-62; Robert Letham, *The Holy Trinity: In Scripture, History, Theology, and Worship* (Phillipsburg, 2004), pp. 201-20.

[4] "εἰς τὸ πνεύμα τὸ ἅγιον … ἐκ τοῦ πατρός ἐκπορευόμενον." The text of the original Nicene Creed simply reads "I believe … in the Holy Spirit" ["Πιστεύομεν … εἰς τὸ ἅγιον πνεύμα."]. On the important theological developments between the Nicene (AD 325) and Constantinopolitan (AD 381) Councils, see John D. Zizioulas, "The Teaching of the Second Ecumenical Council on the Holy Spirit in Historical and Ecumenical Perspective, Vol. 1," in *Credo in Spiritum Sanctum* (Vatican City, 1983), pp. 29-45.

[5] Text from Philip Schaff (ed.), *The Creeds of Christendom*, Vol. 2: *The Greek and Latin Creeds* (3 vols, Grand Rapids, 1993), vol. 2, p. 59.

uncontroversial for nearly three centuries. It was only in 808 that the theological and ecclesiastical significance of the interpolation first began to be recognized.[6] At that time, some Frankish monks arrived in Jerusalem and innocently recited the Creed with filioque included, just as they had been taught to do so in Emperor Charlemagne's chapel. Shocked by this novelty, the Eastern monks of St Sabas rebuked the alien inclusion as an unauthorized and dangerous teaching. Their opposition, in fact, was so strong that they petitioned Pope Leo III for a judgment on the matter. By 810, he ruled that the filioque should *not* be included in the text of the Creed, despite the fact that he personally appeared to uphold the doctrinal truth which the filioque seemed to uphold. But in order to ensure that his ruling was taken seriously, he ordered the Creed—in the original Greek form—to be engraved upon two silver tables and deposited at St Peter's in Rome.[7]

The real watershed for the emerging filioque controversy, however, was not the Council of Toledo, or resistance to Leo III's ruling against the interpolation. Rather, the point at which the filioque became significant as both a theological and an ecumenical problem was the Photian-Carolingian exchanges in the ninth century.[8] Though several Eastern fathers prior to the ninth century had disputed the dogmatic truth of the filioque, it was Patriarch Photius[9] who was largely responsible for bringing about a clarification and consolidation of the Eastern theological position. Unlike his predecessors, who were content to affirm only what the Nicene Creed itself affirmed—i.e., that the Spirit proceeds from the

[6] Gerald Bray helpfully outlines four stages in the evolution of the filioque question: "At stage One, the problem was not recognized. At stage Two, the problem was recognised but not understood. At stage Three, the problem was recognised, understood, but not thought to be fundamental. At stage Four, the problem was recognised, understood, thought to be fundamental but not fully explained in the context of a systematic theology and spirituality." Bray, "*Filioque* Clause," p. 118.

[7] Dietrich Ritschl, "Historical Development and Implications of the Filioque Controversy," in Lukas Vischer (ed.), *Spirit of God, Spirit of Christ: Ecumenical Reflections on the* Filioque *Controversy* (London, 1981), pp. 46-65 at p. 50.

[8] R. G. Heath has argued that historians of the controversy have too often ignored the consequences of a newly created union in the eighth century between the Franks and the papacy. Consequently, the filioque controversy "may be integrated into the larger historical context from which it sprang and [may be] removed from its confinement to a segmented aspect of the development of ecclesiastical dogma." Given the state of Frankish liturgical reform, imposed as it was by a "liturgical king," Heath concludes that the eventual schism would be better identified in the history books as the "Western schism of the Franks." See R. G. Heath, "The Western Schism of the Franks and the 'Filioque'," *Journal of Ecclesiastical History* 23/2 (April 1972): 97-113.

[9] For assessments of Photius and his contributions, see especially Francis Dvornik, *The Photian Schism: History and Legend* (Cambridge, 1948); Richard Haugh, *Photius and the Carolingians: The Trinitarian Controversy* (Belmont, 1975); and Markos A. Orphanos, "The Procession of the Holy Spirit According to Certain Later Greek Fathers," in Vischer), *Spirit of God*, pp. 21-45.

Father[10]—Photius, in 867, advanced the argument a crucial step (though some judge it to be a fatal step leading to the Great Schism) by affirming that the Spirit proceeds "from the Father *alone*" [ἐκ μόνου τοῦ πατρός]. Spurred on by Photius's treatise against the theology of the filioque,[11] the Eastern resistance to the credal addition began to escalate during the ninth and early tenth centuries. Interestingly enough, Western opinion during this time generally did not approve of a Greek equivalent to "filioque" as an interpolation into the Creed, despite the fact that local Latin liturgies included the filioque and received limited polemical defense from some Western theologians. The force of Western appreciation for the filioque was also reflected in the so-called Athanasian Creed (*Quicumque vult*) which likely appeared in France shortly before or during Charlemagne's (d. 814) reign.[12]

If the contribution of Photius solidified the Eastern theological position, it was Pope Benedict VIII who officially endorsed the filioque clause for use in the Latin liturgy, thus making the filioque a Catholic dogma in 1014. However, it should also be noted that, even in 1014, the filioque clause was still restricted to the liturgical Latin version of the Creed; the Greek version remained untouched.

Unfortunately, by the beginning of the eleventh century, the political and theological positions on both Eastern and Western fronts had hardened to the point where reaching a mutually acceptable resolution would have been nearly impossible.[13] Consequently, on 16 July 1054, three papal legates, led by Cardinal Humbert, entered the Church of the Hagia Sophia in Constantinople and placed a sentence of excommunication against Patriarch Michael Cerularius, after which the legates exited the Church.[14] In an immediate act of ecclesiastical retaliation, Patriarch Cerularius "refused to recognise the credentials of the legates and

---

10 Prior to Photius, the Eastern churches customarily accepted the *theological* formulation of the procession of the Spirit *through the Son* [δία τοῦ ὑιοῦ] though they had consistently resisted the addition of any terminology whatsoever to the ecumenical Creed itself. Karl Barth's own assessment of this formulation will be discussed in Chapter Three below.

11 Photius I, *Mystagogia Spiritus Sanctus* [*On the Mystagogy of the Holy Spirit*], trans. Holy Transfiguration Monastery (Astoria, 1983). For a helpful analysis of the significance of Photius in the controversy, see Despina Stratoydaki-White, "Photios and the Filioque Controversy," *The Patristic & Byzantine Review* 2/2 (1983): 246-50.

12 The text of the 23rd article of the *Quicumque vult* reads: "*Spiritus Sanctus a Patre et Fili*" ["The Holy Spirit is of the Father and of the Son"]. See Schaff, *Creeds of Christendom*, vol. 2, p. 68. For an authoritative history and theological analysis of the *Quicumque*, see J. N. D. Kelly, *The Athanasian Creed* (London and New York, 1964).

13 For an analysis of the political and ecclesiastical situation in the tenth and eleventh centuries, see Steven Runciman, *The Eastern Schism: A Study of the Papacy and the Eastern Churches during the 11th and 12th Centuries* (Oxford, 1955).

14 George S. Hendry, "From the Father and the Son: The *Filioque* after Nine Hundred Years," *Theology Today* 11 (January 1955): 449.

excommunicated them as impostors."[15] Though it is probable that the legates did not intend to excommunicate the entire Eastern Church,[16] the historical consequence was an ecclesiastical break between the Greek and Latin Churches, the formal beginnings of what were to become The Holy Orthodox Church of the East and The Catholic Church of the West.[17] Apart from various attempts at reunification since the Schism—most notably the Councils of Lyons (1274)[18] and Florence (1438-9)[19]—the division between Eastern and Western Christendom formally remains to this day.[20]

Once Photius introduced what is now formally identified as the "monopatrist" position, the Western response to monopatrism was also formalized in the centuries to follow.[21] One of the more notable Western defenses of the double procession came from the pen of St Anselm in his *De Processione Spiritu Sancto*[22] (1102). Anselm's primary argument in favor of the double procession of the Spirit rests on his contention that the Father gives all that is his own to the Son, including the ability to participate in the breathing of the Spirit. Therefore, Anselm reasoned, the Holy Spirit proceeds from the Father and the Son *tamquam ab uno principio* ["as from one principle"]. Berthold also notes that, prior to Anselm's formal written defense

---

[15] Ioannes Metaxas-Mariatos, "The Filioque Controversy: Chapters from the Eastern Orthodox Reaction" (MA thesis, University of Durham, 1988), p. 52.

[16] Indeed, it could be argued that the legates could not have even had the ability to frame such a concept; the popular notion that the West "excommunicated" the East makes sense only as one reads back the historical awareness of the schism that eventually took place upon the intentions of the legates.

[17] Walter F. Adeney, *The Greek and Eastern Churches* (New York, 1939), p. 229.

[18] On the Byzantine repudiation in 1285 of the rulings of the so-called "union council" of Lyons in 1274, see Papadakis' superb study on the theological work of Patriarch Gregory II of Cyprus. Aristeides Papadakis, *Crisis in Byzantium: The* Filioque *Controversy in the Patriarchate of Gregory II of Cyprus (1283-1289)* (rev. edn, Crestwood, 1997).

[19] The authoritative study remains Joseph Gill, *The Council of Florence* (Cambridge, 1959). For an examination of the Council of Florence from the perspective of its relevance to contemporary ecumenical concerns, see Mary Ann Fatula, "The Council of Florence and Pluralism in Dogma," *One in Christ,* 19/1 (1983): 14-27. Fatula argues against those who would see the Council as a model of recognizing dogmatic pluralism, contending that the Council itself "failed to recognize the proper and irreducible distinctiveness of the eastern and western traditions" particularly in reference to the filioque controversy. Ibid., p. 26.

[20] John Meyendorff argues that the final break between East and West did not occur in 1054. Instead, "the true and final rupture only took place as a result of the Crusades." John Meyendorff, *The Orthodox Church: Its Past and its Role in the World Today*, trans. John Chapin (London, 1962), pp. 56ff.

[21] For analysis of medieval arguments in defense of the filioque, see Dennis Ngien, *Apologetic for Filioque in Medieval Theology* (Milton Keynes, 2005).

[22] For a contemporary translation, see Anselm, "The Procession of the Holy Spirit," in Jasper Hopkins and Herbert Richardson (eds), *Anselm of Canterbury* (4 vols, Toronto and New York, 1976), vol. 3.

of the filioque, he was asked by Pope Urban to present the Western arguments in favor of the filioque at the Council of Bari in October 1098. It was there that the Greek bishops present at the council gave their assent to the acceptability of the Western formula as Anselm had presented it.[23]

Thomas Aquinas also articulated a defense of the filioque in the article on the Holy Spirit in his magnificent *Summa Theologica.* Aquinas, in a line of reasoning similar to that of Anselm, contended that the Son shared all with the Father, including the ability to spirate the Spirit. However, Aquinas also argued that it was necessary to understand the Spirit as proceeding from the Father and the Son on the basis of what Aquinas called "relations of opposition." That is, for Aquinas, the Father and the Son, though sharing a common essence, nevertheless are related to one another in an opposing relation—i.e., the Father is not the Son, and the Son is not the Father. However, Aquinas reasoned, if the Son and the Spirit are likewise in a relation of opposition to the Father, then there is no way to distinguish between the Son and the Spirit, for their relation to the Father would be identical. As Aquinas argues,

> If therefore in the Son and the Holy Ghost there were two relations only, whereby each of them were related to the Father, these relations would not be opposite to each other, as neither would be the two relations whereby the Father is related to them. Hence, as the person of the Father is one, it would follow that the person of the Son and of the Holy Ghost would be one, having two relations opposed to the two relations of the Father. But this is heretical since it destroys the Faith in the Trinity. Therefore the Son and the Holy Ghost must be related to each other by opposite relations.[24]

Beyond the faltering efforts at Lyons and Florence, few attempts were made for centuries thereafter to seek reconciliation between the Eastern and Western churches. The Reformers, many of whom simply assumed the theology of the filioque, diverted their theological energies to voicing their disagreements with many of the entrenched practices and doctrines of the medieval Roman Catholic Church, though there were some notable defenses of the filioque by both Lutheran and Calvinist schoolmen even up to the seventeenth century.[25] Nevertheless, as

---

23 See George C. Berthold, "Saint Anselm and the Filioque," in *Faith Seeking Understanding: Learning and the Catholic Tradition* (Manchester, 1991), p. 228. On the problems associated with Anselm's formula of the procession of the Spirit *tamquam ab uno principio,* see Mary Ann Fatula, "A Problematic Western Formula," *One in Christ*, 17/4 (1981): 324-34.

24 Thomas Aquinas, *Summa Theologica,* I. q. 36, art. 2., available from: http://www.newadvent.org/summa/1036.htm (accessed 4 December 2008)

25 Bruce Marshall questions the common assumption that Lutherans in particular either simply echoed the medieval arguments for the filioque or that they ignored it altogether. He shows that a number of seventeenth-century Lutheran theologians such as Dannhauer and

the Western and Eastern parts of Christendom drifted apart culturally, politically, and theologically, the filioque was, at best, conceptually absorbed by Western thinkers,[26] or at worst was considered to be little more than an ancient theological controversy of little or no relevance.

Beginning in the latter part of the nineteenth century, however, conversations among Orthodox, Catholics, Anglicans and Protestants were undertaken in the hope of ecclesiastical reunification of Eastern and Western churches. In many of those conversations, the doctrine of the filioque was commonly cited as one of the remaining theological obstacles preventing full ecclesial union. Though not all Orthodox representatives would have assessed the situation quite as starkly, Lossky nevertheless echoed a common Orthodox sentiment that exists among many Orthodox theologians even to this day, when he said, "whether we like it or not, the question of the procession of the Holy Spirit has been the sole dogmatic grounds for the separation of East and West."[27]

However, there have been signs that the division may not be as insurmountable as some may have thought, since there is renewed interest in the filioque as a topic of ecumenical concern. Perhaps the most significant historical event of the renewal of attention to the problem occurred during the Old Catholic-Orthodox consultations convened at Bonn in 1874-75. It was there that the Old Catholic churches agreed to revert to the older form of the Creed without the filioque.[28] Parallel discussions amongst Anglican and Orthodox Churches between 1875 and

---

Quenstedt did not simply echo the standard Western position, but attempted to respond to theological objections to the doctrine. See Bruce D. Marshall, "The Defense of the *Filioque* in Classical Lutheran Theology: An Ecumenical Appreciation," *Neue Zeitschrift für Systematische Theologie und Religionsphilosophie* 44/2 (2002): 154-73.

26 Alan Olson argues, for example, that Hegel's philosophy of *Geist* is "a uniquely original and highly constructive speculative pneumatology" based on the "submerged legacy of Luther." Alan Olson, *Hegel and the Spirit* (Princeton, 1992), p. 9. The Western adoption of a thoroughly filioquist structure in philosophy was evident in Hegel's concept of *Geist* as "sublation" [*Aufhebung*]—a simultaneous canceling and preserving of subject and object. For an examination of the theological implications of Hegel's thought for contemporary pneumatology, see Amos Yong, "A Theology of the Third Article? Hegel and the Contemporary Enterprise in First Philosophy and First Theology," in Stanley E. Porter and Anthony R. Cross (eds), *Semper Reformandum: Studies in Honour of Clark H. Pinnock* (Carlisle, 2003), pp. 208-31.

27 Vladimir Lossky, *In the Image and Likeness of God* (London and Oxford, 1975), p. 71.

28 For a fuller account of the phases of development of the Old Catholic and Orthodox conversation from 1874 forward, see Kurt Stalder, "The Filioque in the Old Catholic Churches: The Chief Phases of Theological Reflection and Church Pronouncements," in Vischer, *Spirit of God*, pp. 97-109. Interestingly enough, the Joint Orthodox-Old Catholic Commission meeting in Chambésy in 1975 took the conclusion one more radical step and "announced its rejection of the filioque not simply as an uncanonical addition to the Creed but also above all as an erroneous doctrine." See André de Halleux, "Towards an Ecumenical

1976 resulted in the Anglicans reaching a similar conclusion to the Old Catholics.[29] Finally, the controversy reached a climax of ecumenical attention when a study group convened by the Faith and Order Commission of the World Council of Churches (WCC) in 1979 set about to study the filioque question. The resulting document, technically known as "Faith and Order Paper No. 103," included the so-called "Klingenthal Memorandum" which recommended "that the original form of the Creed, without the filioque, should everywhere be recognized as the normative one and restored, so that the whole Christian people may be able ... to confess their common faith in the Holy Spirit."[30] However, despite the promising potential of the Klingenthal Memorandum,[31] nearly a decade after the consultations, the WCC was expressing concern over how few member churches had yet formally to adopt the resolution as their own.[32]

Agreement on the Procession of the Holy Spirit and the Addition of the Filioque to the Creed," in Vischer, *Spirit of God*, p. 70.

29 For the so-called "Moscow Agreed Statement," see K. Ware and C. Davey (eds), *Anglican-Orthodox Dialogue. The Moscow Agreed Statement. Anglican-Orthodox Joint Doctrinal Commission 1976* (London, 1977).

30 "The Filioque Clause in Ecumenical Perspective," in Vischer, *Spirit of God*, p. 18.

31 Some questions pertinent to the ecumenical aspects of the filioque controversy which cannot be dealt with in this study include: 1) Why has ecumenical discussion on the filioque question apparently stalled after the Klingenthal consultation? 2) Why have member churches of the WCC generally been slow in bringing about the recommended changes of the Memorandum? 3) In churches that *have* adopted the recommendation (e.g., The Anglican Communion, how has this affected (if at all) specific instances of dogmatic inquiry into pneumatology?

32 Hans G. Link, *One God, One Lord, One Spirit: On the Explication of the Apostolic Faith Today*, Faith and Order Paper No. 139 (Geneva, 1988), p. 9. The scope of this work prevents recounting a full history of the filioque. However, two monographs deserve mention as "bookends" of modern historical research on the filioque controversy. See H. B. Swete, *On the History of the Doctrine of the Procession of the Holy Spirit from the Apostolic Age to the Death of Charlemagne* (Cambridge, 1876); and a more recent survey of the history of the filioque as an ecumenical problem from the biblical materials through to the twentieth century ecumenical debates by See Bernd Oberdorfer, *Filioque: Geschichte und Theologie eines ökumenisches Problems* (Göttingen, 2001). For a brief Eastern perspective, see Boris Bobrinskoy, *The Mystery of the Trinity: Trinitarian Experience and Vision in the Biblical and Patristic Tradition* (Crestwood, 1999), pp. 279-303. Other noteworthy historical surveys include the following (in chronological order): Dietrich Ritschl, "The History of the Filioque Controversy," in Hans Küng and Jürgen Moltmann (eds), *Conflicts About the Holy Spirit* (New York, 1979), pp. 3-14; Boris Bobrinskoy, "The Filioque Yesterday and Today," in *La Signification et l'Actualité du IIe Concile Oecumenique pour le Monde Chrétien d'Aujourd'hui* (Chambesy, 1982), pp. 275-87; Gordon Watson, "The Filioque—Opportunity for Debate?" *Scottish Journal of Theology* 41 (1988): 313-30; Nodes, "Dual Processions of the Holy Spirit"; Peter Gemeinhardt, *Die Filioque-Kontroverse zwischen Ost- und Westkirche im Frühmittelalter* (Berlin and New York, 2002); Robert M. Haddad, "The Stations of the Filioque," *St. Vladimir's Theological Quarterly*, 46/2-3 (2002):

Karl Barth and Ecumenical Discussion on the Filioque

With the foregoing general sketch of the history of the filioque controversy, it is now possible to situate the figure of whom we are primarily concerned in this study. Where does Karl Barth fit into the history of the filioque controversy?

Chronologically, of course, Karl Barth falls between the Old Catholic-Orthodox conversations of the late nineteenth century, but before the pinnacle of the ecumenical discussions on the filioque convened by the WCC in the mid-1970s. In this regard, Karl Barth's contribution to the filioque debate needs to be understood, at least partially, against the backdrop of the twentieth-century ecumenical movement.

It is well known that Barth was harshly critical, especially earlier in his career, of what he perceived to be the misguided aims of the ecumenical movement,[33] though later in life he admitted to seeing some benefit from the movement. Consequently, during the middle to latter part of the twentieth century Barth's vigorous defense of the filioque (which was firmly in place by the early 1930s) has been perceived, especially by those with ecumenical sensitivities, as being out of step with a large number of theologians from various ecclesiastical traditions, who have favored dropping the filioque from the Creed for use in catechism and liturgy. Thus, it is easy to see why Barth expositors, under increasing ecumenical pressure to excise the filioque, whether before or after the Klingenthal consultation in 1979, have generally tended to be critical of his pro-filioque stance. Such criticism, after all, resonates with the *Geist* of modern ecumenical discussion.

Barth did not, of course, live to read the recommendations of the Klingenthal Memorandum, but it is probable that he would not have approved of the implicit ecumenical strategy driving the Commission. Barth was aware of the precedent-setting conversations that had taken place between the Old Catholic and Orthodox churches in 1874-75, but he was clearly not convinced that the filioque could be dropped so easily without significant theological effect.[34] Thus, he remained one of the filioque's most prominent twentieth-century defenders right through to the end of his career, though even thinkers sympathetic to Barth remain divided amongst themselves on the issue.[35]

209-68. Unfortunately, no monograph-length work devoted to recounting carefully the history of the filioque has appeared in English since Swete. This is an area of research that sorely needs attention.

[33] For Barth's criticism of the ecumenical meetings in 1937 at Oxford, see *CD*, I/2, p. 592. For an "insider's" perspective on Barth's relationship to the ecumenical movement, see especially W. A. Visser 't Hooft, "Karl Barth and the Ecumenical Movement," *Ecumenical Review* 32 (April 1980): 129-51.

[34] *CD* I/1, pp. 478-79.

[35] Alasdair Heron perceives that, toward the latter part of the twentieth century, Reformed theologians were divided into two camps in regard to the filioque—namely, those who were ardently supportive of the doctrine and those who were critical and ready

This leads one to ask: why bother, then, with Barth on the filioque? Why pay attention to an aspect of Barth's theology that ecumenical discussion appears to have been moving beyond? Despite the tremendously growing interest in Barth's theology at the outset of the twenty-first century, might it not be appropriate to assume that this is at least one instance where Barth simply made a mistake and has little to offer, despite the immense respect so often afforded to Barth in the history of twentieth-century theology? Is there any good reason to seek to clarify Barth's stance on the filioque in the present theological milieu where the filioque, it seems, appears continuously to be on the "theological chopping block"?

One could argue that Barth's view of the filioque needs clarification for no other reason than for the sake of the scholarly record. Few have undertaken to study this aspect of Barth's Trinitarian theology, even though many see Barth as being largely responsible for the renewal of Trinitarianism in the twentieth century.[36] To discover the reasons why Barth defended the filioque and what impact it had on his theology would therefore be a legitimate exercise in historical theology. In other words, seeking to gain an accurate portrayal of Barth's theology, regardless of whether a particular aspect of his thought is currently ecumenically fashionable, should be more than sufficient reason to undertake such study. But is the assumption that Barth contributes little to the filioque debate really warranted? Should Barth's well-known criticism of the ecumenical movement be sufficient to disqualify him from making an ecumenical contribution to the filioque debate? It is here that a clarification of what it was that Barth resisted in ecumenical discussion can be helpful.

As already noted above, it is well known that Barth was consistently predisposed to resisting the ecumenical movement that arose in the first quarter of the twentieth century.[37] Early signs of Barth's suspicions concerning the movement were made

to reject it. See Alasdair Heron, "The Filioque in Recent Reformed Theology," in Vischer, *Spirit of God*, pp. 110-17 at pp. 111-13. For other accounts of the filioque in the Reformed tradition, see Josef Smolík, "Filioque in the Reformed Tradition," *Communio viatorum*, XXIV (1981): 219-22; and Gabriel Widmer, "La Théologie Réformée et le 'Filioque,'" in *La Signification et l'Actualité du IIe Concile Oecumenique pour le Monde Chrétien d'Aujourd'hui* (Chambesy, 1982): 319-37.

[36] As Jenson put it: "It is … from Barth that twentieth century theology has learned that the doctrine of the Trinity has explanatory and interpretive use for the whole of theology; it is by him that the current vigorous revival of trinitarian reflection was enabled." R. W. Jenson, "Karl Barth," in D. F. Ford (ed.), *The Modern Theologians* (2 vols, Oxford, 1989), vol.1, pp. 21-36 at p. 42. See also Paul Louis Metzger, "Introduction: What Difference Does the Trinity Make?" in Paul Louis Metzger (ed.), *Trinitarian Soundings in Systematic Theology* (London, 2005), pp. 5ff.

[37] It may be possible to interpret Barth's opposition to the ecumenical movement as further evidence of his already well-known confrontational style, similar to how he consistently appeared to cut himself off from otherwise close colleagues (e.g., Emil Brunner) whose theological positions on issues were only marginally different from his own. However, such an explanation, while possibly giving a *psychological* explanation,

manifest in a 1923 essay delivered to the General Assembly of the Union of Reformed Churches where Barth accused his own ecclesiastical colleagues of being ill-prepared for what was then anticipated as the "coming controversy with Rome." He asked:

> [H]ow can we take issue with "Rome" before we have genuinely taken issue with ourselves as to what we non-Roman Christians are, what we represent, and what we desire? Have we today any vigorous community of purpose in distinction to Catholicism? And if we have *not* or do not rightly know whether we have or not, how can we be worthy participants—to say nothing more—in the ecumenical council planned for 1925?[38]

In other words, the reasons that Barth was suspicious of ecumenical discussion was not because he was opposed in principle to such discussion and debate, but because he was convinced that the Reformed camp, at least, had not yet earned the right to challenge other ecclesiastical traditions (which in this case was Roman Catholicism) on various theological issues, mainly because Reformed thinkers did not have a common understanding of the distinctiveness of their own tradition. As he put it later in the same address, "A will to unite cannot be developed by people who have not yet taken themselves, to say nothing of the others, seriously; the peace of Christendom cannot be served by understandings that lack content."[39]

Barth's stance here, we believe, has not been sufficiently appreciated. In his estimation, ecumenical discussion across Reformed/Catholic borders could not legitimately proceed until both sides had clarified their stance *from within* their own theological tradition. Interestingly, Barth appeared to believe that the Catholics of his own day had a better vision of their own theological position on the items of debate, while the Reformed Churches were languishing in theological ambiguity. Consequently, Barth argued, "One of the few real services which the *German* Reformed churches might perform today for their confessional brethren of the West would be to recall … [that] the Reformed churches are in possession of something peculiarly *their own.*" In contrast to what he saw as the "practical unionizing tendencies of the old Reformed churchmen," Barth argued that providing theological clarification *was* "the doctrinal task of the Reformed churches."[40] As Barth lamented elsewhere, the dogmaticians of "present-day Protestantism … can only surmise that finally the churches do not want any dogmatics."[41]

---

can hardly be called upon as a sufficient explanation for a figure who sought consistently to live and to act upon *theological* grounds.

[38] Karl Barth, *The Word of God and the Word of Man*, trans. Douglas Horton (New York, 1957), p. 224.

[39] Ibid., p. 228.

[40] Ibid., p. 224.

[41] Karl Barth, *The Göttingen Dogmatics*, ed. Hannelotte Reiffen, trans. Geoffrey W. Bromiley (Zürich and Grand Rapids, 1991), p. 40. In a similar vein, Princeton theologian

In recalling the recommendation of the Klingenthal Commission cited above, a major methodological distinction between the approaches of many ecumenists and that of Barth is thereby made evident. Whereas the wording of the Klingenthal Memorandum indicates that *ecclesiastical* concerns take methodological priority (i.e., the original wording of the Creed must be restored *so that* Christians might be able to confess the common faith), Barth was of the mindset that the dogmatic concerns of his own ecclesial, theological tradition (i.e., the Reformed Churches) must take methodological precedence. Whereas the Klingenthal Commission is confident that dogmatic consensus on the doctrine of the Holy Spirit will arise *a posteriori* to a commonly accepted text of the Creed, Barth was concerned that his own ecclesial tradition engage in a vigorous analysis of the "dogmatic content" of its confession before seeking some kind of common ecumenical ground as a means to creating unity. That is to say, for Barth, ecumenical agreement, even on the wording of the Creed, should not be allowed to become a theological *a priori* in the task of dogmatic inquiry. For Barth, Reformed dogmatic inquiry must appeal to Scripture over against whatever else may be agreed upon at the level of formal ecclesiastical documents.

Whatever is said about the relationship of Barth's stance on the filioque to the ecumenical movement must not fail to take into account his fundamentally different starting-point. On Barth's view, real theological differences between the filioquist (i.e., Western) and monopatrist (i.e., Eastern) traditions of interpreting revelation should not be downplayed in favor of an ecumenically agreed upon end-goal of the particular wording of the Creed. In fact, to favor linguistic agreement on the wording of the Creed is already to disadvantage the Reformed emphasis on discerning from Scripture what is to be dogmatically asserted. In the end, the question for Barth is not whether the addition of the word "filioque" to the Creed is ecclesiastically illegitimate, but whether its addition is *faithful* to the apostolic witness of Scripture.

Given this understanding of Barth's view of how ecumenical agreement is arrived at, it is instructive to compare Jürgen Moltmann's 1979 theological proposal toward resolving the filioque controversy[42] with the aforementioned 1995 Roman clarification of the filioque supplied by the Pontifical Council for Promoting Christian Unity. While Moltmann's proposal starts with an appeal to withdraw the filioque from text of the Creed in order to end ecclesiastical controversy and thereby open up the theological inquiry to attain theological

Bruce McCormack has also lamented that Reformed theology is currently suffering theologically under the demise of confessionalism. See Bruce L. McCormack, "The End of Reformed Theology? The Voice of Karl Barth in the Doctrinal Chaos of the Present," in Wallace M. Alston, Jr. and Michael Welker (eds), *Reformed Theology: Identity and Ecumenicity* (Grand Rapids and Cambridge, 2003), pp. 46-64.

[42] Jürgen Moltmann, "Theological Proposals Towards the Resolution of the Filioque Controversy," in Vischer, *Spirit of God*, pp. 164-73.

agreement between "'filioquist' and 'monopatrist' understandings of the Trinity,"[43] the Roman clarification begins by appealing to the agreement that already exists between East and West on the scriptural teaching concerning the relationship between the Son and the Spirit. Though other comparisons and contrasts could be noted, what is important here is that Barth would have been methodologically inclined toward the Catholic strategy of clarifying a received doctrine of the filioque that sought commonalities with the Eastern tradition, rather than to the methodology of Moltmann's Reformed ecumenism that was ready to excise the filioque at the outset for the sake of answering, together with the East, the meaning of the relation of the Son to the Spirit. The main difference, of course, is that the Catholic clarification assumes that the filioque contributes something to the dogmatic task of clarifying pneumatology, whereas Moltmann's proposal assumes that the filioque is already a dogmatic and ecclesiastical hindrance to attaining to a proper pneumatology.

Barth was clearly committed to the filioque. Therefore, it would be theologically counterproductive (even disingenuous) to try to make Barth's position align with what are more the current ecumenically acceptable non-filioquist ways of viewing the matter. This study, therefore, seeks to clarify the "inner theological rationality" of Barth's defense and use of the filioque as if it were in fact theologically advantageous to hold to the filioque, rather than follow the more generally accepted practice of assuming from the outset that the filioque can be viewed *only* as a theological and ecumenical liability. This is, of course, a theological path far less traveled because as a strategy, it potentially highlights ever more sharply the problems that still remain between Eastern and Western pneumatologies. Nevertheless, it is also the assumption of this study that attending to a theologian's actual *use* of the filioque in her or his theology is necessary if, in fact, the real theological differences that remain between East and West are ever to be resolved. That is to say, the debate about the filioque has far too often stalled at the level of providing an account of the theological and scriptural pros and cons of the filioque over against discerning how the filioque actually functions within the broad dimensions of a dogmatic framework. Echoing Barth's own words in his discussion of the filioque, there is "still cause to give some account of the matter."[44]

Assessing Barth on the Filioque

It is likely not an oversimplification to assert that ecumenical pressure has generally turned scholarly opinion against the filioque and therefore specifically against Barth's own defense of the doctrine. This does not mean, however, that Barth's position has been ignored altogether. Though there are, to date, no monographs (and relatively few scholarly articles) on the topic, it is also the case that there has

---

43 Ibid., p. 164.

44 *CD* I/1, p. 479.

been only a small number of shorter works or sections of works and unpublished dissertations which have focused, to varying degrees, upon Barth's theology of the filioque. A survey and analysis of this literature will be necessary to identify how this present study contributes to the critical literature on Barth's view.

Those who have undertaken to assess Barth's doctrine of the filioque to date have tended to do so following three basic approaches: 1) exegetical-theological analysis; 2) comparative analysis; and 3) intrasystemic analysis. Though these approaches overlap to some degree, they are nevertheless helpful in discerning distinct ways in which Barth's doctrine of the filioque has been examined in the literature. As will become evident, the first approach (exegetical-theological analysis) seeks to assess Barth's doctrine of the filioque, either in reference to how well Barth's defense of the filioque is supported by Scripture (exegetical) or as a coherent part of a larger dogmatic system (theological). The comparative approach seeks to clarify Barth's doctrine of the filioque against the backdrop of similar or competing positions for the purpose of bringing into view the axiomatic frameworks on which the positions rest. Finally, the intrasystemic approach seeks to identify the internal systemic connections, logic or outworking of Barth's doctrine of the filioque throughout his theology. The survey will highlight the need for a distinctive approach to Barth's doctrine of the filioque that incorporates insights from the intrasystemic approach, but will also attend to the genesis and development of Barth's thinking on the filioque from the earliest stages of his career. For the purposes of this study, this fourth methodological category will be called a "genetic-intrasystemic" approach.

Exegetical-Theological Approaches

Not surprisingly, the dominant approach to Barth's doctrine of the filioque has rightly sought to assess it on the merit of its exegetical moorings in Scripture and its theological/dogmatic coherence. Three scholars in particular have produced noteworthy explicit analyses and critiques of Barth's adherence to the filioque: George Hendry, Alasdair Heron, and Thomas Smail. Two others, Jürgen Moltmann and Thomas F. Torrance, are also important to this survey, though their contribution is more indirect and implicit.

George Hendry Princeton theologian George Hendry was one of the earliest to engage in a study of Barth's doctrine of the filioque.[45] According to Hendry, Barth was a theologian who wanted "to elevate the filioque to a position of central

[45] Hendry's analysis of Barth's doctrine of the filioque began in an article published in 1955 and was subsequently included and slightly revised in a book published in 1957. See Hendry, "From the Father and the Son," pp. 449-59; and George S. Hendry, *The Holy Spirit in Christian Theology* (London, 1957).

importance in evangelical faith."[46] He identifies two fundamental arguments—one theological and one exegetical—that Barth used to support the doctrine of the filioque. The first, the theological argument, has to do with Barth's insistence on "an exact identity or parallel between the Trinity of essence and the Trinity of manifestation," or what is now more commonly understood as a parallel between the immanent and economic Trinity respectively. The second, the exegetical argument, has to do with Barth's concern to be faithful to what he discerned as the New Testament witness that identified the Holy Spirit simultaneously as the Spirit of God and the Spirit of Christ. If Barth denied either of these points, Hendry explains, it would have the effect of "tending to encourage, in the economic order, a one-sided conception of the Spirit as the Spirit of the Father, having a mission in the world distinct from the mission of Christ."[47] In other words, Hendry is convinced that Barth's doctrine of the filioque rested on an insistence of full correspondence between the economic and immanent Trinity and on his refusal to separate the work of the Spirit of God from the Spirit of Christ, as attested by the New Testament.

Having identified what he felt were Barth's primary concerns, Hendry goes on to contend that both the theological and exegetical arguments adduced by Barth fall under the same criticisms that have always been leveled against supporters of the double procession doctrine. As Hendry argues, Barth was convinced that if the Spirit proceeds from the Father and the Son in accordance with the economy, systematic consistency should require that a double procession of the Son from the Father and the Spirit ought also to be deduced. However, if such systematic consistency is to be maintained, then should one not also consider the fact that the Gospels portray the Son as receiving in some way from the Spirit, such as in his conception and baptism? Thus, one should conclude that not only does the Spirit proceed from the Father and the Son, but it is equally valid, in order to maintain systematic adherence to the correspondence of economic and immanent Trinity, to deduce that the Son proceeds from the Father and the Spirit (*spirituque*). How much more, Hendry asks, would this insure that not only the unity of Father and Son is maintained, but also the unity of the Son and Spirit?[48]

---

[46] Hendry, "From the Father and the Son," p. 450.

[47] Ibid., p. 454.

[48] Moltmann concurs, noting that continued use of the filioque in the manner in which Barth speaks of it would need to be supplemented by saying also that "the Son proceeds from the Father and has the impress of the Spirit. We might say that Christ comes *a patre spirituque,* from the Father and the Spirit." Jürgen Moltmann, *The Spirit of Life: A Universal Affirmation*, trans. Margaret Kohl (Minneapolis, 1992), p. 71. Though neither Hendry nor Moltmann actually favor a *spirituque,* liberation theologian Leonardo Boff has argued for the distinct possibility of *spirituque* in precisely these terms. See Leonardo Boff, *Trinity and Society* (Marknoll, 1988), p. 205.

Barth was not unaware of the argument that acceptance of the filioque should imply, in a systematically consistent fashion, the warranted acceptance of a *spirituque*. He himself summarizes this argument by saying:

> If we apply at this point our rule that material dogmatic statements about the immanent Trinity can and must be taken from definitions of the modes of being of God in revelation, are we not compelled to accept a relationship of origin between the Spirit and Son which is neither begetting nor breathing but a third thing? And one might also wish to add that the circle of mutual relations in which God is one in three modes of being is only then closed and complete, and that already for this reason one should postulate an origin of the Son from both the Father and the Spirit.[49]

For Barth, such a "systematic argument may be dismissed at once." Why? Because he felt that such an argument conflates the otherwise distinct concepts of the "divine origin" of the Persons of the Trinity and the concept of "divine interpenetration" (*perichoresis*). Barth explains:

> … the *perichoresis*, though it is complete and mutual, is not one of origins as such, but a *perichoresis* of the modes of being as modes of being of the one God. It is a further description of the *homoousia* of Father, Son, and Spirit, but has nothing to do with begetting and breathing as such, and therefore needs no supplementation in this direction.[50]

In other words, if the distinct concepts of "divine origin" and *perichoresis* are confused, then not only must one be led to affirm that the Son proceeds from the Father and the Spirit (*spirituque*), but also that there is "an origin of the Father from the Son and from the Spirit."[51] However, this would be *exegetically* difficult, Barth argues, not because there aren't scriptural texts that could be viewed as evidence for there being a flow of divine action in a direction from the Spirit to the Son,[52] but because one would need to adduce evidence from Scripture to support the possibility that such intra-divine action necessarily speaks of multiple origins in God—evidence which Barth thinks is wholly lacking.

Beyond insisting that committing to the filioque logically leads one to also have to commit to a procession of the Son from the Father and Spirit (*spirituque*), Hendry also observes what he sees as the problem of how Barth's principle of the identification of economic and immanent Trinity tends to color his exegesis.

---

[49] *CD* I/1, p. 485.

[50] *CD* I/1, p. 485.

[51] *CD* I/1, p. 485.

[52] Of which Barth includes reference to the conception (Matt. 1:18, 20; Luke 1:35) and the baptism of Jesus (Mark 1:9ff and par.) amongst other New Testament texts. *CD* I/1, p. 485.

That is, the correspondence of economic and immanent Trinity led Barth to make a wholly undifferentiated identification of the Spirit of God in the Old Testament with the Holy Spirit of the New Testament. However, such identification, Hendry argues, is problematic:

> The New Testament is as emphatic as could be on the novelty of the gift of the Spirit and the soteriological-eschatological character of the work of the Spirit. It is difficult to see how this can be combined with the conception of a general presence of the Spirit in a cosmological-anthropological reference.[53]

Yet Barth was able to identify the work of the Spirit of Christ wholly and unreservedly with the work of the Spirit of God that hovered over the surface of the deep in the Creation account.[54] But, as Hendry explains, Barth was able to do this only

> … by strict adherence to the canon of Trinitarian orthodoxy, which lays it down that the external operations of the Trinity are undivided (*opera trinitatis ad extra indivisa sunt*). [Barth] interprets the work of creation accordingly as a work of the whole Trinity, not only of God the Father, but of God the Father with the Son and the Holy Spirit.[55]

In Hendry's view, this leads Barth to a place where it becomes practically impossible to speak about how the three persons of the Trinity are distinct, and adherence to the filioque simply magnifies that problem. For example, "in Barth's anthropology the Spirit reduplicates the role of the Son, and the distinction between them, which underlies his defence of the filioque, disappears. The external operations of the Trinity are not only undivided—they have become indistinguishable."[56] Unfortunately, Hendry's criticism is no more insoluble for Barth than for any other theologian in either Eastern or Western traditions who wished to uphold the unity of divine action even while maintaining a real distinction of divine persons.

In his final evaluation Hendry concludes that Barth, among all other Western defenders of the filioque that went before him, was "right in affirming the existence of the problem [of the relationship between Son and Spirit], but wrong in the solution [he] proposed for it." Yet on the other hand, Hendry asserts, "the Greeks were wrong in denying the existence of the problem, but right in rejecting the

---

53 Hendry, *Holy Spirit*, p. 46.

54 Cf. Gen. 1:2.

55 Hendry, *Holy Spirit*, p. 48.

56 Ibid., p. 52. Though Barth does not appear to have responded directly to this type of criticism, other scholars (such as Alasdair Heron noted below) argued that Hendry's criticism is no more insoluble for Barth than for any other theologian, Eastern or Western, who wishes to uphold both unity and diversity of action in the Trinity.

solution proposed." Thus, for Hendry, Barth joins rank with every other Western theologian who has used the filioque as "a false solution to real problem."[57] Unfortunately, the problem with this criticism—aimed, as it is, at Barth's position on the filioque—is that it says more about Hendry's general problem with the filioque than anything specific or unique about Barth's formulation of the defense. In other words, Hendry is predisposed to see the filioque as problematic and, not surprisingly, sees the same problems in Barth's defense. However, this raises the legitimate question whether such a reading has not already decided that no defense of the filioque will be sufficient to satisfy the theological demand placed upon it, no matter what exegetical or theological evidence is adduced.

Alasdair Heron A second exegetical-theological analysis of Barth's doctrine of the filioque comes from Scottish theologian Alasdair Heron. Unlike Hendry, who sought to identify fundamental axioms upon which Barth deduces the filioque, Heron seeks to assess the progression of Barth's logic that led him to support it. According to Heron, Barth relied on a three-stage logical structure of argumentation to defend the filioque—a logical structure that closely parallels that of St Anselm. Heron delineates Barth's (and Anselm's) three stages as follows:

1. The New Testament witnesses to the Spirit as being the Spirit of both the Father and the Son.
2. We can understand the inner economy of the Trinity only as we see it worked out and made known to us in revelation.
3. The unity of the Father with the Son is ontologically prior to their differentiation.[58]

Heron observes that each of the argumentative stages is qualitatively different from the other two. The first assertion is a statement of biblical theology, derived as a conclusion from exegetical study of Scripture; the second is a principle followed in theological inquiry—an assertion of a theological axiom; and the third is a "key formulation of Trinitarian doctrine—neither a product of biblical theology nor an axiom of theological inquiry, but rather a conclusion hammered out in the fires of long centuries of theological debate."[59]

On the first assertion—that the Spirit is the Spirit of the Father and the Son—Heron is convinced that both Barth's and Anselm's assertions are "obviously true, so far as it goes."[60] Heron's only challenge to this assertion is whether this is *all* that can be said of the Spirit. For example, Heron notes, "the New Testament … also contains a strand which appears to put things the other way round, and defines

[57] Hendry, "From the Father and the Son," p. 458.

[58] Alasdair I. C. Heron, "'Who Proceedeth from the Father and the Son': The Problem of the Filioque," *Scottish Journal of Theology* 24/2 (May 1971): 149-66 at 152.

[59] Ibid.

[60] Ibid., p. 154.

the Person and work of Christ in terms of the Spirit."[61] Barth's and Anselm's reply to such an observation, however, is that "the work of the Spirit in this connexion has to do solely with the humanity of Christ"[62] even if, according to Heron, "this reply carries us out of the area of plain New Testament exegesis into that of Dogmatics."[63] Though Barth's assertion that the work of the Spirit has only to do with Jesus' humanity is problematic,[64] Heron is content to concur with Barth's assertion that the New Testament portrayal of the Spirit is one that sees the Spirit as "associated with and even secondary to the Son, rather than being simply linked to the Father."[65]

Significantly, it is in examining the second assertion that Heron reiterates a version of Hendry's criticism of the filioque (and thereby of Barth). Heron notes that Hendry is uncomfortable with the fact that Barth identifies the Spirit's work in Creation so closely with his work in Redemption. Heron, however, does not agree that this is a problem. As he puts it:

> …[a]lthough Hendry is here ostensibly discussing the "Filioque", it is clear enough that the difficulties he attributes to it do not arise directly from the doctrine of the double procession at all, but rather from the attempt to base the whole doctrine of God on the pattern given in the historical Revelation. That attempt is committed to understanding Creation on the basis of Redemption, and to interpreting the pattern of the divine activity in Creation according to that made known in Redemption.[66]

Hendry's complaint with Barth was certainly curious, Heron notes, for, in making it, Hendry distances himself from what orthodox Christian theologians, whether from the East or West, have always attempted to do—namely, to refuse to separate in a quasi-Nestorian (or perhaps Gnostic) manner the doctrines of Creation from Redemption.[67] Consequently, Heron sees Hendry as insisting that "the historical Revelation, centring on Christ, is not to be taken as supplying the ground-plan of all Christian theology." It is not surprising, then, that Hendry ends up preferring instead to appeal to the works of Tillich and Ferré, who in fact *do* make the separation.[68] Nevertheless, Heron argues, even if Hendry's argument is

---

61 Ibid., p. 155.

62 As Barth put it, "What the Son 'owes' to the Spirit in revelation is His being as a man, the possibility of the flesh existing in Him, so that He, the Word, can become flesh. How could one derive from this that He owes His eternal sonship to the Spirit?" *CD* I/1, p. 486.

63 Heron, "Who Proceedeth," pp. 155-56.

64 This problem will be addressed more thoroughly in Chapter Three below.

65 Heron, "Who Proceedeth," p. 156.

66 Ibid., p. 157.

67 Ibid., p. 158.

68 Ibid., p. 157.

finally accepted, it goes roughly against the grain of the traditional commitment of Christian theology in both East and West. Given the fact that both Eastern and Western conceptions of the Trinity agree that the economy must at least in some way be the "ground-plan" for the doctrine of God, Hendry's own argument "cannot therefore be accepted as valid, or as grounds for rejecting the 'Filioque' directly," Heron says. "Whatever the difficulties involved in this attempt may be, they stem from the nature of the enterprise itself, and it is hardly fair to the 'Filioque' to suggest that it is responsible for them."[69] In other words, Hendry may not like Barth's identification of the Spirit of Creation and the Spirit of Redemption, but, as Heron argues, it is clearly not Barth alone who does this, nor even only those who are committed to the filioque.

Heron moves on to assess the third stage of Barth's argumentation—namely, that the unity of the Father with the Son is ontologically prior to their differentiation. Heron identifies such an approach as going back to the "Neo-Nicene theology of the Cappadocians—Basil and the two Gregories—and their formula 'one *ousia,* three *hypostaseis*'; and beyond them to the formulations in terms of 'one *substantia*, three *personae*' in Tertullian and Novatian."[70] Heron demonstrates that Barth (along with Anselm) moves quite deliberately to this stage of the argument.[71] Nevertheless, it is here that Heron perceives a major problem with the filioque (and therefore, by implication, with Barth's own defense of the doctrine) because of the way in which it "tends to eliminate the distinctions between the Persons in all but theory, submerging all three in a shared divinity."[72] Following the Orthodox axiom here—that the Three Persons of the Trinity are "ontologically as ultimate as their essential unity"[73]—Heron is convinced that the filioque, as Barth and other Western supporters have used it, fails to avoid the Sabellian tendency in Western theology whereby "the distinctions between the Persons, and the relationships linking them [are] played down in the interests of an exclusive emphasis on 'God.'"[74] This is not to say that Heron is altogether satisfied with an Eastern view of the matter either. In Heron's estimation, even the Eastern position that views the Father as the source of divinity for both Son and Spirit tends to "a material, if not a formal, Subordinationism, in which divinity is felt to reside primarily and really in the Father alone."[75]

In the most interesting turn of all, Heron argues that a return to Augustine's doctrine of the Trinity, and most specifically, his doctrine of the Spirit as the "bond

69 Ibid., p. 158.

70 Ibid., p. 159.

71 Ibid., p. 152-53.

72 Ibid., p. 160.

73 Ibid. Heron follows Lossky here.

74 Ibid., p. 161.

75 Ibid., p. 162.

of love" [*vinculum caritatis*] is the way forward on the filioque debate.[76] He even notes that the Augustinian doctrine of the Spirit as the bond of love "cannot be combined with the defence of the 'Filioque' given by Anselm and his Western followers." In fact, such a combination of the *vinculum caritatis* and the traditional Western understanding of the unity of God by a shared *ousia* or *substantia* cannot occur because "that would be to combine two mutually contradictory sets of assumptions about the location of the divine unity."[77] That is to say, if the Spirit is the "bond of love" between Father and Son, then the unity of the Persons resides in the Spirit;[78] but if the Spirit proceeds from the Father and the Son, then the unity of the Persons resides in their common source in the Father.

Thomas Smail A third exegetical-theological examination of Barth's adherence to the filioque comes from Thomas A. Smail. Smail, a scholar and churchman who has been involved in circles of charismatic renewal, has written extensively on Trinitarian theology and pneumatology[79] and, more specifically, on the question of the filioque itself. Though Smail is largely charitable toward Barth,[80] he nevertheless

---

[76] This is a surprising suggestion indeed, considering how often Augustine is understood to be the forefather of the "double procession" pneumatology and considering that Augustine did not appear to believe that these two doctrines were incompatible. Even Wolfhart Pannenberg identifies the filioque as an "Augustinian doctrine" which is "an inappropriate formulation of the fellowship of both Father and Son with the Spirit." See Wolfhart Pannenberg, *Systematic Theology* (3 vols, Grand Rapids, 1991), vol. 1, p. 318. Of course, Heron must deal with the difficulty of how Augustine could simultaneously teach both a material doctrine of the filioque (even if not yet formally included in the Creed) *and* the *vinculum caritatis*. Unfortunately, Heron does *not* deal with this problem, but his options appear to be limited: either this was a theological contradiction within Augustine or there is a significant material difference between the Augustinian teaching of the double procession of the Spirit and the later Western adoption of the filioque as something other than a doctrine of "double procession."

[77] Barth here is clearly implied to be one of those Western followers. Heron, "Who Proceedeth," p. 165. See also Heron's discussion of the filioque in Alasdair I.C. Heron, *The Holy Spirit* (Philadelphia, 1983), pp. 176-79. Ironically, as will be noted later in this review, it is precisely this type of combination of the *vinculum* and the filioque that later interpreters have identified as precisely what Barth was trying to accomplish, even if in the minds of those interpreters such a combination is itself wrought with pneumatological problems.

[78] Interestingly, this appears to be the direction in which Barth leans, as will be discussed in Chapter Four below.

[79] See especially Thomas A. Smail, *The Giving Gift* (London, 1994); and Thomas A. Smail, "The Holy Spirit in the Holy Trinity," in Christopher Seitz (ed.), *Nicene Christianity: The Future for a New Ecumenism* (Grand Rapids, 2001), pp. 149-65.

[80] Smail once quipped that Barth's formal pneumatology had never been written because "the Holy Spirit said his final word about Barth before Barth could say his final word about the Holy Spirit!" Thomas A. Smail, "The Filioque in Recent Theological Discussion" (unpublished manuscript, June 1986), p. 2.

believes that Barth's doctrine of the filioque is an unfortunate consequence of Barth's otherwise necessary Christological protest against liberal subjectivism.[81]

In one of Smail's more important essays on Barth's pneumatology, he devotes a section to Barth's doctrine of the filioque. There Smail lodges two major criticisms against Barth, both of which are exegetical-theological in nature.

First, Smail argues, "Barth fails to give sufficient weight to the priority of the Father as *fons et origio totius divinitatis* ["fount and origin of the complete divinity"], which has its scriptural base in the Fourth Gospel, where the subordination of *both* Son and Spirit to the Father is as strongly emphasized as their co-divinity with him."[82] Second, he insists that the Gospels make it clear that "Christ in his baptism and ministry is not only the donor and sender of the Spirit, but also the recipient of the Spirit, receiving from him both his humanity and his charismatic sonship."[83] The failure to identify the reciprocity of relationship between the Son and the Spirit has meant that the filioque in Barth represents, according to Smail, "an unbiblical onesidedness" that "leads almost inevitably to a depression of the role and person of the Spirit in relation to the role and person of the Son." Such a "tendency to subordinate the Spirit to the Son in a one-sided way is … present right through Barth's theology."[84]

Unfortunately, Smail does not acknowledge Barth's anticipated response to such a criticism. Already in *CD* I/1 Barth had acknowledged that Jesus receives his humanity from the Spirit, but that such a reception does not alter the eternal relationship of divine origin that exists between the Son and the Spirit prior to the Incarnation. As will be argued in Chapter Three, Barth can justifiably be understood to be resisting all forms of theological adoptionism. Though Smail is right to raise the question of the Spirit's action upon the Son, he does so in such a way that he does not acknowledge or assess Barth's response, inadequate as he might ultimately judge it to be. That is, as was already mentioned above, Barth does not deny those elements in the Gospels where there is an action of the Spirit upon Jesus, but understands that these references in the Gospels all have to do with the humanity of Jesus, and not the origin of the second eternal mode of being.

Furthermore there is need to question Smail's addition of the qualifier "charismatic"—never defined—to the word "sonship." Is this to be understood as a different kind of sonship than the eternal Sonship of the second Person of the Trinity? In what way is the eternal Sonship of the Son said to be a "gift" of the

---

[81] Thomas A. Smail, "The Doctrine of the Holy Spirit," in John Thompson (ed.), *Theology Beyond Christendom* (Allison Park, 1986), pp. 87-110 at p. 109.

[82] Ibid., p. 107.

[83] Ibid., p. 107-108.

[84] Ibid., p. 108. Elsewhere, Smail suggests that theologians (such as Hendrikus Berkhof) who tend to link the work of the Spirit with the ongoing work of Jesus Christ are often allied with Barth in their pneumatology and are essentially binitarian. See Smail, *The Giving Gift*, p. 43.

Spirit? And where in the New Testament is such a distinction made? Unfortunately, Smail's own qualification in this regard does not significantly clarify the issue.

T. F. Torrance and Jürgen Moltmann The foregoing review of those engaging in exegetical-theological critiques of Barth's theology of the filioque would be incomplete without reference to two other theologians—namely, T. F. Torrance and Jürgen Moltmann—both of whom were tremendously influenced by Barth's thinking and yet went on to develop creative theologies of their own. However, Torrance and Moltmann pay scant attention to Barth's doctrine of the filioque and instead focus on their own proposals for solutions to the problem and, in so doing, more or less bypass Barth altogether on this question. Clearly, though, by virtue of their alternative proposals, they are critical of Barth's doctrine of the filioque and see it as being a dogmatic hindrance. By virtue of their silence, however, one can only assume that their disagreement with Barth is respectfully muted and implicit rather than voiced and explicit.[85]

Thomas F. Torrance is widely recognized as an editor, translator, and disseminator of Barth's theology in the English-speaking world, but he is also, in many respects, one of the world's pre-eminent theologians of the twentieth century in his own right. Given his own long-term interaction with Barth, both personally and academically, it is unfortunate that he never assessed Barth's theology of the filioque in a more direct manner. To be sure, most of Torrance's comments on the filioque focus less on what Barth actually said and did with the filioque and more on how Torrance felt that Barth could have avoided the filioque altogether.

Fortunately, Torrance did deal extensively with the filioque specifically as an ecumenical and dogmatic problem.[86] To be sure, Torrance's criticism of the filioque is based more on his (re)assessment of the patristic evidence than upon modern proposals, including Barth's. Consequently, when Torrance actually does get around to mentioning Barth, he readily admits (in a way reminiscent of Hendry's critique) that Barth's adoption of the filioque was the wrong answer to the right problem.

---

85 One can only venture a guess about whether Torrance's and Moltmann's "non-critique" of Barth on this fundamental issue is a sign of their deferential respect for Barth, or whether they truly believe that Barth had little to offer on the question. Either way, it is disappointing that neither scholar devoted more effort in interacting specifically with Barth on this issue.

86 Most important in this regard is Thomas F. Torrance, *Theology in Reconciliation* (London, 1975). For a concise review of Torrance's theology of the procession of the Holy Spirit, see Elmer M. Colyer, *How to Read T. F. Torrance* (Downers Grove, 2001), pp. 233-41. For a more general review of Torrance's pneumatology, see Gary Deddo, "The Holy Spirit in T. F. Torrance's Theology," in Elmer M. Colyer (ed.), *The Promise of Trinitarian Theology* (Lanham, 2001), pp. 81-114.

Positively, Torrance believes that "it is in his doctrine of God above all … that Barth's thought towers above modern theology like an alpine massif."[87] As Torrance read Barth, he noted:

> I began to find what I had been looking for, in the doctrines of the *hypostatic union* between the divine and human natures in Christ, and of the *consubstantial communion* between the Persons of the Holy Trinity, but also in Barth's very impressive account of the doctrine of the Holy Spirit as the distinctive Freedom of God to be present to the creature and to realise the direction of the creature to himself as its true end.[88]

This led him to re-examine the patristic Fathers, particularly Athanasius, but now with a new outlook. But, ironically, Torrance also believed it was Barth's pneumatology that led him to question the usefulness of the filioque doctrine altogether. It is worth hearing Torrance at length here:

> So far as the earlier volumes of *Church Dogmatics* are concerned, my chief difference with Barth relates to the element of "subordinationism" in his doctrine of the Holy Trinity, which I regard as a hang-over from Latin theology. … This inevitably effects an approach to the filioque clause in the Western Creed. I agree fully with Barth's claim that the Nicene *homoousion* applied to the doctrine of the Holy Spirit means that we cannot but trace back the historical mission of the Spirit from the incarnate Son to the eternal mission of the Spirit from the Father. But I would argue that the problem of the filioque was created by an incipient subordinationism in the Cappadocian doctrine of the Trinity, which the Eastern Church had to answer in one way and the Western Church in another way. However, if we follow the line established by Athanasius, Gregory Nazianzen and Cyril of Alexandria, who rejected subordinationism in Trinitarian relations, we find ourselves operating on a basis where the theological division between East and West does not arise. In that event the unecumenical western intrusion of the filioque clause into the Nicene-Constantinopolitan Creed simply falls away.[89]

Torrance's observations are especially pertinent because they imply that Barth's Trinitarian doctrine and pneumatology contain within them both the wheat of theological promise and the tares of theological inadequacy. According to Torrance, had Barth paid closer attention to his own theology of the hypostatic union of Christ's natures and the homoousial unity of Father, Son and Spirit, and had Barth developed a theology in which the Spirit was understood to have

---

[87] Thomas F. Torrance, *Karl Barth, Biblical and Evangelical Theologian* (Edinburgh, 1990), p. 19.

[88] Ibid., p. 123.

[89] Ibid., pp. 131-32.

proceeded from the ontic unity of Father and Son,[90] the filioque would have been an unnecessary theological addition. Instead, the filioque becomes a crucial means of distinguishing between the *hypostases* of the Son and the Spirit in Barth's theology and he is forced once again, in Torrance's opinion, into a subordinationist corner.

Torrance's proposals here are promising, though it does not appear that he saw Barth as having taken up the challenge. However, evidence will be presented below to suggest that Barth was indeed already moving in the direction of arguing that the Spirit's procession was from the homoousial unity of the Father and Son. In this regard Torrance and Barth may share more in common than Torrance acknowledges. In fact, it is arguable that Barth's defense of the filioque caused Torrance to overlook an important element in Barth's thinking. Torrance clearly believes that the filioque is unnecessary, and this prevents him from probing far enough into the reasons why Barth continued to hold to it. Consequently, a question that will eventually need to be addressed in Chapter Three below is why Barth felt it necessary to continue to defend the filioque while Torrance held it to be a superfluous doctrine.

A second theologian of note, Jürgen Moltmann, was greatly influenced by the work of Karl Barth. Barth appeared to have high hopes for Moltmann as one who might have carried on his desire for a theology of the third article commensurate with his own lifelong attention to the second Christological article.[91] But like Torrance, Moltmann's interaction with Barth's theology of the filioque is disappointingly minimal; even in those places where one would most expect Moltmann to interact with Barth, he remains silent.[92] At best, Moltmann simply lumps Barth together with Rahner by noting their tendency to modalism because of the logical and epistemological priority given in the West to the doctrine of the unity of the divine being of God.[93]

Yet Moltmann is distinct from Torrance at one significant point. Torrance thought the filioque controversy could have been avoided altogether if only theologians had paid closer attention to Athanasius's treatment of the doctrine of *homoousia*. According to Moltmann, however, the Creed takes a minimalist

---

90 According to Elmer Colyer, Torrance's view of the matter is that "the Holy Spirit coinheres or dwells in the inner life and being of the Holy Trinity and shares in the reciprocal knowing and loving of the Father and the Son." Colyer, *T. F. Torrance*, p. 235.

91 For Barth's assessment of Moltmann's potential to carry out Barth's expectations, see Karl Barth, *Letters 1961-1968*, ed. Jürgen Fangmeir and Hinrich Stoevesandt, trans. Geoffrey W. Bromiley (Grand Rapids, 1981), pp. 174-76.

92 Most significantly, Moltmann never mentions Barth when discussing the state of the question on the filioque in his important book *The Trinity and the Kingdom of God*, preferring instead to highlight Russian theologian Boris Bolotov's celebrated "Theses on the Filioque." See Jürgen Moltmann, *The Trinity and the Kingdom* (Minneapolis, 1983), pp. 178-80.

93 Moltmann, "Theological Proposals," p. 173.

stance on pneumatology, which both East and West later filled out in their own way; unfortunately, the problem is that East and West filled out the pneumatology in distinct ways which now must be reconciled while maintaining the historical development of each tradition.

For Moltmann, the way forward is first of all to recognize that the filioque clause itself is to be judged as theologically "superfluous."[94] He feels that a theology of mutuality between Son and Spirit better corresponds with the teaching of the New Testament. For him, it is "the question of the relation of the Son to the Holy Spirit, and of the Holy Spirit to the Son"[95] that is the most pressing theological question that East and West must answer, not simply whether the Spirit proceeds from the Father alone, or from the Father and the Son; for, no matter how the latter question is answered, the former question will continue to remain unanswered. In this regard Moltmann's own answer to the question of the Son-Spirit relation is that "the Spirit *accompanies* the Son, *rests* in the Son, and *shines* from the Son." For Moltmann, such an answer fills out more fully the Trinitarian picture of mutual divine relations and indeed, in his opinion, "corresponds much better to the Spirit-history of Christ and the Christ-history of the Spirit."[96]

It was on the basis of his argument from the history of Christ and the Spirit in the New Testament that Moltmann presented his constructive proposal to the Klingenthal Consultation on the filioque question.[97] There Moltmann proposed an interpretation of the Creed that could possibly gain ecumenical consensus by both Western and Eastern churches if the appropriate clause in the third article were worded as follows: "*The Holy Spirit, who proceeds from the Father of the Son, and receives his form from the Father and from the Son.*"[98] So, what is Moltmann really proposing here? It may be helpful to examine this sentence in two parts.

In the first clause of the proposed solution to the filioque controversy, Moltmann argues that the Creed could be interpreted in such a way that both East and West could agree that the Spirit proceeds from the Father *of* the Son—a phrase which implies that the Spirit proceeds from the homoousial unity of the Father and Son.[99] Thus, the Spirit is said to proceed from the Father who is not a "'universal Father', like Zeus, Jupiter, Vishnu or Wotan," nor even "because he is the unique cause on whom all things depend"; rather, the Spirit proceeds from the Father who is none other than, and is, "uniquely 'the Father of Jesus Christ.'"[100] In other words, to say that the Spirit proceeds from the Father (as the Creed does without further qualification) is already to imply that *this* Father from whom the Spirit proceeds is

---

94 Moltmann, *Spirit of Life*, p. 306.

95 Moltmann, "Theological Proposals," p. 165.

96 Moltmann, *Spirit of Life,* p. 308.

97 Moltmann, "Theological Proposals," pp. 164-73.

98 Ibid., p. 171.

99 Moltmann, *Trinity and the Kingdom*, p. 182.

100 Moltmann, "Theological Proposals," p. 167.

none other than the Father of the Son. So far, so good. But what about the second clause?

It is in the second clause (i.e., "the Holy Spirit … receives his form from the Father and from the Son") that Moltmann's own original theological contribution comes through. Here, Moltmann argues that "the Holy Spirit receives from the Father his own perfect divine *existence* (ὑπόστασις, ὕπαρξις), and obtains from the Son his relational *form* (*Gestalt*) (εἶδος, πρόσωπον)."[101] Or to put it another way, commensurate with the Eastern emphasis on the Father as the "origin" [*arche*] of deity, Moltmann suggests that the Holy Spirit receives his hypostatic existence from the Father, but that the Spirit's "face" or "form" (or "identity") is jointly "stamped *by the Father and the Son*," explaining why the Spirit is called both the Spirit of God and the Spirit of the Son. Or, as he puts it later, "If ὑπόστασις is an ontological concept, *form* is an esthetic one. They do not compete with or replace each other, but are mutually complementary."[102]

Moltmann's proposal is certainly provocative, and one can only speculate what Barth would have thought of it, though there is good reason to believe (as will be shown throughout this study) that he would likely have no reason to dispute the truth of the first clause, but more than likely would have challenged the second. But, whatever Barth's answer, Moltmann's solution is only half-convincing. Why? Unlike Barth, who consistently accepted the need to distinguish between an economic and immanent Trinity, Moltmann prefers to speak only of "*one* Trinity and of its economy of salvation."[103] Yet, despite his hesitation to distinguish between economic and immanent aspects of the Trinity, he is nevertheless ready to distinguish between the *hypostatic existence* and the *outward form* of particular divine hypostases—which, in this case, is the Holy Spirit. The question is, how does this "being/form" distinction differ from the immanent/economic distinction? Does not Moltmann's distinction between hypostatic *existence* and *form* run contrary to his own maxim that, because of God's self-consistency, that which is true in God's revelation (i.e., his form) must also be true of God's being?[104] Unfortunately, such a distinction serves only to solve one problem while introducing another.[105] That is, Moltmann rejects the filioque in one sense (i.e., the Spirit receives his *hypostasis* from the Father only), but imports the filioque back into the manner by which the Spirit receives his form (i.e., the Spirit receives his form from Father and Son) in revelation, only to create a disjunction, contrary to his own wishes, between the revealed Trinity and the ontological Trinity. Consequently, it is safe to say that Barth surely would not have been satisfied with a solution which not only simultaneously denigrates the theological necessity of having a distinct doctrine

101 Ibid., p. 169.

102 Ibid., p. 170.

103 Ibid., p. 165.

104 Ibid., p. 166.

105 For a similar critique, see John Thompson, *Modern Trinitarian Perspectives* (New York and Oxford, 1994), p. 154.

of the economic and immanent Trinity, but also ends up positing divine form over against divine being.

Assessing Exegetical-Theological Approaches The foregoing review of the so-called "exegetical-theological" studies raises the question of how their criticisms of Barth's doctrine of the filioque should be regarded.

On the one hand, the exegetical-theological studies are an important part of the scholarly investigation of Barth's theology because they properly seek to evaluate Barth's work on the basis of his exegesis of Scripture and his overall theological coherence. Failure to pass either of these tests would most certainly be important reasons to reject Barth's doctrine of the filioque, even if the alternative was not immediately clear (Hendry) or if the problems he sought to address could be better solved through attention to a different theological formulation (e.g., *vinculum caritatis,* as per Heron) or more careful exegesis of principal biblical texts (Smail). In any case, it is mildly disappointing that these critics either did not appear to have noticed that Barth did anticipate and respond to some of the exegetical/theological objections leveled against him, or they have simply assumed that Barth's responses were inadequate.

On the other hand, it is also not at all evident that the exegetical-theological critiques have succeeded in defeating Barth's support of the filioque as soundly or thoroughly as might be expected. This is because Barth's critics have tended to open up even greater problems that are not easily or necessarily answered by recourse to scriptural exegesis or appeals to theological coherence. For example, a definitive statement of the relationship of the doctrines of Creation and Redemption can hardly be called upon to adjudicate between Hendry and Barth, for such a definition is still much debated in Christian theology. Nor can the assertion that the Gospels give an account of Christ being a recipient of the action of Spirit be used in denying Barth's doctrine of the filioque (as Smail argues) because this is to argue against the filioque on the presupposed understanding that such reception *must* be applied not only to Christ's taking on of humanity, but also in regard to his eternal Sonship. But this is precisely the dogmatic crux of the debate—a debate that would require greater attention to the theology of the union of Christ's divine and human natures.

Second, it is notable that the scholars who explicitly attend to Barth's view of the filioque do so not only because of his acknowledged theological stature, but also precisely because he was assumed to be a significant representative of the filioque. We believe this to be a crucial point which has had a significant effect on the assessment of Barth's pneumatology in the critical literature. Of course, it is patently true that Barth does in fact defend the filioque; what is not patently obvious is whether his defense is akin to all other defenses. Indeed, of the two scholars mentioned who did not explicitly engage Barth's doctrine of the filioque (Torrance and Moltmann), both went on implicitly to reject Barth's stance on the filioque because they assumed his position to be a typical manifestation of the Western filioquist tradition. The critical question is: what if it isn't?

Consequently, it is important to note that, while it is self-evident that Barth is fully in favor of the filioque, it is not immediately evident that such formal agreement necessarily implies material agreement with any given Western thinker who has previously defended the filioque, whether Aquinas, Anselm, Augustine or others. Heron, at least, explicitly identifies Barth's formulation of the filioque argument as "Anselmian" (thereby distinguishing it from an Augustinian position) on the basis of a common logical development. Just as there are different reasons given for rejecting the filioque in the Eastern tradition, so, too, are there different reasons adduced for accepting the filioque. Agreement on the theological appropriateness of the filioque is not necessarily agreement on the theological rationale for its support. Unfortunately, none of the scholars reviewed above even entertains the question of whether Barth's theological rationale for the filioque may possibly have been *atypical* in the Western tradition. With the possible exception of Heron (who, in this case, could also be categorized as engaging in a level of comparative work), the scholars who have approached Barth's doctrine of the filioque from an exegetical-theological perspective tend to switch rather easily back and forth between discussing the filioque as a general theological problem and Barth's theology of the filioque in particular. Such a lack of precision can easily assume that Barth's defense of the filioque is automatically subject precisely to the same criticisms that have been lodged against the filioque throughout theological history. In other words, Barth is guilty by association; he is viewed primarily as an exemplar of those who defend the filioque, but not as one who may have made a systematic contribution to the doctrine itself. Not surprisingly, then, the studies noted above all readily see in Barth the same weaknesses that they perceive more broadly in the history of the filioque debate. However, are such broad assumptions warranted? What if Barth's defense of the filioque is *materially* different from others in the Western tradition, even if his formal adherence to traditional filioquist language remains the same? Barth may hold to the formula *ex patre filioque procedit,* but the above-noted scholars do not seek to discover what Barth understands such "procession" to represent.

Furthermore, if one admits even to the possibility of a material difference between Barth's and others' doctrines of the filioque, then one also has to wonder how effectively general criticisms of the filioque can be applied to Barth's particular defense of the filioque. One is also forced to consider whether Torrance and Moltmann alike have ruled out *a priori* the possibility of a fully coherent and exegetically satisfying defense of the filioque that is also ecumenically acceptable. While there are strengths in both Torrance's and Moltmann's attempts to negotiate the filioque controversy, both assume that Barth adds little to the history of dogmatic defense of the filioque. Even Vladimir Lossky (and more recently, John Zizioulas), who is famous for his vigorous rejection of the filioque, was able to conceive of the possibility of an Orthodox interpretation of filioque! An overarching purpose, then, of this study is to provide a clearer portrait of the particularity of Barth's theological rationale for supporting the filioque and its function in his theology.

In the end, the exegetical-theological critiques are important because they help clarify two crucial issues that will need to be addressed at various points throughout the book: 1) the relationship of the economic and immanent Trinity; and 2) the role of the Holy Spirit in the incarnation of the Son. Some of the commentators discussed above rightly perceive the significance of Barth's rule[106] in which the economic Trinity corresponds to the immanent Trinity, but the problem is not whether this rule is acceptable as much as whether Barth limits the rule himself by imposing certain restrictions on what can or cannot be read from the economy into the immanent Trinity. Where this becomes especially significant is in the doctrine of the Incarnation and the Spirit's action upon the Son therein. Several of the theologians discussed above want to posit a reverse relationship between the Spirit and Son such that the Son receives from the Spirit as much as the Spirit receives from the Son, but Barth resists such a move, indicating that such reception has only to do with the humanity of Jesus, and not his eternal status as the eternal second person of the Godhead. Whether this is an appropriate restriction to Barth's rule cannot be answered simply by means of exegesis, but requires a careful analysis of how Barth is able to make apparent limitations in the application of his Trinitarian rule.

Comparative Approaches

The foregoing discussion of the exegetical-theological critiques suggests that it is important to discern how Barth's defense of the filioque might be significantly different from other important defenses in theological history. This is where some scholars have engaged in a comparative approach to Barth's filioquist theology.[107] Even if, in the end, one could conclude that Barth's defense of the filioque is, for all intents and purposes, formally and materially the same as that of his Western forebears' (which would be rather surprising given Barth's unusual ability creatively to rework nearly every Christian doctrine), the comparative approach recognizes that Barth's formulation of the problem in the twentieth century is in response to a significantly different set of historical circumstances and concerns than would have been faced by Augustine, Anselm, or Aquinas, for example. Of the scholars discussed previously, Heron, at least, made a significant step forward by suggesting that Barth's defense of the filioque is closer to that of Anselm than of Augustine. Such a distinction is helpful because it demonstrates how not every proponent of the filioque necessarily supports the doctrine by using the same logic or rationale. Consequently, criticism must be based on and aimed at the particular

---

[106] Barth himself calls it a "rule": "We have consistently followed the rule, which we regard as basic, that statements about the divine modes of being antecedently in themselves cannot be different in content from those that are to be made about their reality in revelation." *CD* I/1, p. 479.

[107] Though restricted to medieval defenses of the filioque, Ngien's book serves as a model of comparative work on the filioque. See Ngien, *Apologetic for Filioque*.

formulation of the filioque represented rather than a *carte blanche* criticism of the filioquist tradition as a whole. Fortunately, a number of works in past years have attempted such comparative studies of Barth's doctrine of the filioque. The work of four scholars in particular will be noted here: Jae-Bum Hwang, Mary Corinne Winter, Duncan Reid, and Alar Laats.

Jae-Bum Hwang A 1998 doctoral dissertation completed at Union Theological Seminary (New York) by Jae-Bum Hwang compares Augustine's Trinitarian logic with Barth's pneumatologies, including their views on the filioque.[108] Central to Hwang's study is his attempt to call into question the generally accepted conclusion of many twentieth-century Trinitarian theologians—Rahner and Moltmann most notably—who assert that Western Trinitarianism begins with God's "Oneness" and only then moves to God's "Threeness."[109] In place of such an assumption, Hwang argues that the commonly accepted contrast between Western and Eastern Trinitarianism (in which Eastern Trinitarianism is said to start with Threeness and move to Oneness and Western Trinitarianism moves from Oneness to Threeness) cannot be sustained. Rather, Hwang perceives in both Augustine and Barth a common Trinitarian logic "moving from the Threeness to the Oneness of God" and that this movement has three distinctive consequences: "emphasizing the Tri-unity, giving priority to the economic Trinity, and preferring the filioque pneumatology."[110]

However, Hwang also argues that, despite the similarities, important differences also emerge. Most significantly, Barth makes repeated use of the notions of the economic and immanent Trinity—a distinction that remained underdeveloped in Augustine. Consequently, Barth, unlike Augustine, distinguished between an ontological priority of the Oneness and the epistemological priority of the Threeness. As Hwang puts it, "Barth at first believed that the Threeness and the Oneness come together simultaneously. … This position, however, in reality, has a two-fold meaning: ontologically the Oneness comes first, while epistemologically

108 Jae-Bum Hwang, "The Trinitarian Logics of St. Augustine and Karl Barth: With Special Reference to their Respective Pneumatologies and Filioque-Positions" (PhD thesis, Union Theological Seminary, 1998).

109 Hwang argues that Moltmann and Rahner have radicalized Barth's economically centered Trinitarian theology by utilizing Théodore de Régnon's hypothesis that the Western tradition is characterized by beginning with an assumption of divine Oneness and then moving to Threeness in contrast to the Eastern tradition that begins with an assumption of divine Threeness and only then moves to Oneness. Hwang argues, following a growing number of theological historians of the patristic period, that such contrasts between Eastern and Western approaches to the doctrine of the Trinity are far less exaggerated than is popularly assumed. Ibid., pp. 272-74. For an illuminating account of the tremendous influence of de Régnon's thesis, despite his relative anonymity, see Michel René Barnes, "De Régnon Reconsidered," *Augustinian Studies* 26/2 (1995): 51-79.

110 Hwang, "Trinitarian Logics," p. 255.

the Threeness comes first."[111] Augustine, of course, never made such a distinction between the ontic and noetic in reference to the revelation of the Trinity.

Hwang goes on to argue that Barth consistently maintains the economic-immanent distinction in contrast to Rahner and Moltmann, who have virtually collapsed the immanent Trinity into the economic Trinity. Moltmann, for example, asserts that "[Rahner's] thesis about the fundamental identity of the immanent and the economic Trinity of course remains open to misunderstanding as long as we cling to the distinction at all, because it then sounds like the dissolution of the one in the other."[112]

Specifically on the question of the filioque, Hwang sees little material difference between Augustine's and Barth's views (contra Heron). Hwang argues that both Augustine and Barth agree that the Spirit is the Spirit of the Father and the Spirit of Christ, and thus both conclude that the Spirit proceeds from the Father and the Son. Furthermore, Hwang argues that Barth concurs with Augustine in understanding the Holy Spirit to be the "love of God" in both subjective and objective senses. That is, the Spirit is the "bond of love" [*vinculum caritatis*] between Father and Son, the objective sense, *and* the means by which humans are able to express love to God [*amor Dei*], the subjective sense.[113] The primary difference that Hwang detects between the two, however, is that where Augustine speaks of the Holy Spirit as the "love of God" (both in the sense of God's love for humanity and humanity's love for God), Barth tends instead to speak of the dialectic of "'God's freedom for humanity' which is realized by 'the incarnation of the Word' and of 'humanity's freedom for God' which is caused by 'the outpouring of the Holy Spirit.'"[114]

Hwang also shows that, despite the general similarities between Augustine's and Barth's positions on the filioque, they applied the doctrine differently in describing the relation of the Spirit to humanity. Augustine, Hwang notes, "tended to think that it is more often the Spirit than the Son that directly relates to humanity," though Augustine does at times recognize that Jesus Christ also relates directly to humanity, albeit mainly in his role as the One Mediator.[115] In contrast, Barth clearly distinguishes between the role of the Son and the Spirit. According to Barth, "Jesus Christ, the incarnation of the eternal Word, has become God's

[111] Ibid., p. 257.

[112] Moltmann, *Trinity*, p. 160. For an assessment of the logical coherence of Rahner's rule, see Randal Rauser, "Rahner's Rule: An Emperor without Clothes?" *International Journal of Systematic Theology* 7/1 (January 2005): 81-94. For a fuller account of the reception, appropriation and modification of Rahner's rule, see Fred Sanders, *The Image of the Immanent Trinity: Rahner's Rule and the Theological Interpretation of Scripture* (New York, 2005).

[113] Hwang, "Trinitarian Logics," pp. 261, 264.

[114] Ibid., pp. 265-66.

[115] Ibid., p. 266. For a study of Augustine's view of Christ as mediator, see David Guretzki, "The Function of 'Mediator' in St. Augustine's *De civitate Dei*, Book IX," *Hirundo: The McGill Journal of Classics*, 1 (Fall 2001): 62-75.

Word; and it is to this Word that the Holy Spirit enlightens humanity."[116] Thus, Barth tended to see in the Holy Spirit the means of relating God's Word, the Son, to humanity.

One last observation of Hwang's is especially important for this study. In his observations concerning the actual function of the filioque in Augustine and Barth, Hwang rightly notes, "the theological problem that the filioque clause implies does not stem only from the clause itself but from each theologian's way of doing theology."[117] This is relevant in any discussion of current ecumenical debate because of the dawning realization that there are no theological conclusions that necessarily *must* appear when working either for or against the filioque, but only those conclusions that *actually* appear in a theologian's thought and work.

Mary Corinne Winter A second comparative study of note, also a doctoral dissertation, was completed by Mary Corinne Winter who takes up a theological analysis of the filioque in respect to ecclesiology. [118] Though Winter does not deal as extensively with Barth as does Hwang, her work nevertheless reaches similar conclusions. In her survey and comparison of representative contemporary theologians from Orthodox, Catholic, Anglican, and Protestant perspectives, Winter places Barth and the late Orthodox theologian, Vladimir Lossky, at "extreme positions" on the theological spectrum from West to East respectively.[119] Winter's exposition of Barth's position is limited to a brief account of the appropriate section in Volume I of the *CD*. Though Barth's position is clearly untenable to her, Winter is at least open to the possibility that it was instrumental in opening up the dialogue in new ways.

More important than her exposition of Barth's defense of the filioque is Winter's general conclusion concerning the systematic implications of the filioque for ecclesiology. As she summarizes it:

> This dissertation does not ... agree with Lossky that a filioquist position leads automatically to the Spirit's subordination to Christ in the constitution and action of the church, nor does it agree with Barth that an anti-filioquist position necessarily implies that the Spirit's work could be disconnected from that of Christ. Rather, the filioque discussion as a whole arises from and reveals a problematic conceptual gap in both Eastern and Western theology between God *in se* (*theologia*) and God's self-revelation in the economy of salvation (*oikonomia*).[120]

---

[116] Hwang, "Trinitarian Logics," p. 267.

[117] Ibid., p. 268.

[118] Mary Corinne Winter, "Ecclesiological Implications of the Current Filioque Discussion," (PhD thesis, University of Notre Dame, 1995). Winter's thesis was completed under the supervision of the Catholic theologian Catherine LaCugna.

[119] Ibid., p. 194.

[120] Ibid., pp. 194-95.

While there is cause to question the accuracy of Winter's exposition of Barth's position as one in which he argued that a "necessary" connection existed between an anti-filioquist position and the disconnection of the Spirit from Christ's work,[121] nevertheless she is right to point out that assertions concerning the necessary relationship between a theologian's position on the filioque and the systematic implications to his or her ecclesiology (or any other aspect of theology) are extremely difficult to make. Indeed, such confident assertions could be misleading. That there *is* a relationship need not be denied, but that such a relationship is one of theological necessity can legitimately be questioned. As the great pneumatologist Yves Congar has argued, "In the final analysis … the quarrel about the ecclesiological consequences of the Filioque is of doubtful value."[122]

Duncan Reid and Alar Laats Two other monographs engaging in comparative study of Barth's doctrine of the filioque are considered together because of their similar findings. Duncan Reid's *Energies of the Spirit* takes up the task of bringing into sharp relief the Trinitarian theologies of two Western (Barth and Rahner) and two Eastern (Lossky and Flovorsky) theologians, while Alar Laats' *Doctrines of the Trinity in Eastern and Western Theologies* takes up a similar task of comparing the theology proper of Barth and Lossky. Restricting the discussion here to the authors' analysis of the question of the filioque, both Reid and Laats agree that there are tremendous difficulties in attempting to pit an Eastern monopatrist position (e.g., Lossky) against a Western filioquist position (e.g., Barth). Such a confrontational approach is highly unlikely to succeed in refuting one or the other. The long history of the filioque debate itself should be enough to demonstrate the truth of this. Rather, both studies point to how monopatrist and filioquist theologies have had similar theological concerns and intentions that were nevertheless dealt with in rather different and, for the most part, irreconcilable ways in Eastern and Western theologies. For example, Laats argues:

> Both Lossky and Barth emphasise the unity of the Trinity. Both have special formulas to express this unity. According to Lossky the guarantee of the unity of the Trinity is the monarchy of the Father. … According to Barth the guarantee

---

[121] In the context of his discussion of whether the denial of the filioque leads to a onesidedness in which the Spirit is exaggerated as the Spirit of the Father only, Barth himself qualifies his own assertions: "We must be very careful here, for this is theoretically contested." He also admits that certain characteristics of Eastern thought, such as the possibility of direct illumination of the Spirit, "may not have anything to do with the omission of the Filioque." Rather, Barth insists that "even if not, one would still have to speak of a remarkable coincidence between this omission and these characteristics, which could be very readily understood as the results or the necessary parallels of this omission." *CD* I/1, p. 481.

[122] See Yves Congar, *I Believe in the Holy Spirit*, trans. David Smith (3 vols, New York, 2001), vol. 3, pp. 210-11.

> of the unity of the Trinity is the Spirit or more precisely the procession of the Holy Spirit from the Father and from the Son. In other words: the filioque is the warrant of the unity.[123]

Laats' point here is that Eastern and Western approaches to unity cannot be simultaneously correct at the same time and in the same way. However, taken from within their respective theological, philosophical, and linguistic traditions, both Barth's and Lossky's approaches may be *internally* valid means of safeguarding the divine unity. Reid, too, asks his readers to consider that:

> … we can take each position as an internally coherent or intra-systematically true teaching. This much can be demonstrated by exposing the inadequacy of attempts from each of the positions to prove the other incoherent. What I hope has now become clear is this: the basis on which each side tries to call the other in question has its own concerns and anxieties, which stand in contrast to the questions and concerns of the other tradition.[124]

In providing an example of this commonality of intention, Reid suggests that both Eastern and Western theologies of the Trinity, as represented by these particular theologians, would agree on an essential point: "*there is nothing behind the three hypostases whose activities are experienced in the history of salvation*."[125] However, both traditions would defend this point in irreducibly different ways.[126] Using Barth and Rahner for his Western models, Reid argues that both hold to a principle of identity in which the hypostases revealed in the economic Trinity are themselves understood to be identical in content to the immanent or eternal Trinity. As he puts it, "God must be *experienced* as trinitarian. It must be asserted, against any modalism, that there is no ultimate, hidden unity *behind* the three hypostases."[127] Likewise in an Eastern context, the intention remains the same, but instead it is the Palamite doctrine of energies (as represented in Lossky and Flovorsky) that "insist[s] that the trinitarian activities of God are experienced in the economy of salvation, and that God is not different from what we experience.

123 Alar Laats, *Doctrines of the Trinity in Eastern and Western Theologies: A Study with Special Reference to K. Barth and V. Lossky*, Studien zur Interkulturellen Geschichte des Christentums, Vol. 114 (Frankfurt and New York, 1999), p. 144.

124 Duncan Reid, *Energies of the Spirit: Trinitarian Models in Eastern Orthodox and Western Theology* (Atlanta, 1997), p. 124.

125 Ibid. Italics in original.

126 Fatula has argued along similar lines, suggesting that Eastern and Western Trinitarian traditions cannot be synthesized. She calls, therefore, for an ecumenical environment in which legitimate theological pluralism in dogmatic formulation is accepted. See Mary Ann Fatula, "The Holy Spirit in East and West: Two Irreducible Traditions," *One in Christ* 19/4 (1983): 379-86.

127 Reid, *Energies of the Spirit*, p. 125.

But here … a social or plurality model of the trinity is presupposed."[128] Thus, both of the above studies are important in reference to Barth's doctrine of the filioque because both recognize not only the need to understand the internal logic of the Trinitarian system but also the external theological concerns to which the theologian is responding.

Assessing Comparative Approaches Comparative studies of Barth's doctrine of the filioque make an important contribution on at least two counts. First, comparative approaches of all kinds highlight that one theologian's use (or non-use) of the filioque should not be mistaken for another's. In this light, comparative studies rightly call into question the practice of making unexamined assertions about how the filioque *necessarily* works its way through the rest of a systematic theology as if the doctrine itself can be abstracted from the overall work of a particular theologian. In other words, it is highly unlikely that the doctrine of the filioque, whether in Barth or any other theologian, can be said *a priori* to have certain necessary systematic consequences without carefully examining the theology to see whether in fact this is so. Thus, it is doubly important to trace how the filioque does (or does not) work its way systematically throughout a theologian's corpus. This requires careful discernment throughout as to whether the filioque functions as an axiomatic *a priori* or a theological *a posteriori.* The implication is that a cautious approach to the study of the filioque in Barth requires that the doctrine be carefully examined in the context of its actual use throughout the *Church Dogmatics* (i.e., how and in what contexts Barth appeals to the filioque to make a theological point), and then, and only then, posit *a posteriori* what the relationship of the doctrine of the filioque to other systematic loci actually is within the framework of his dogmatics. In short, the systematic function of the filioque in Barth's theology must not be assumed, but observed.

Second, comparative studies serve well to highlight the difficulties of pitting Barth's doctrine of the filioque against an Eastern monopatrist view, as if, through sustained confrontation, one would eventually become the victor. On the contrary, comparative studies of Eastern and Western pneumatologies, particularly on the question of the filioque, have shown that *direct* comparison is rarely possible. Indeed, both Reid and Laats have demonstrated that to compare monopatrist and filioquist theologies without careful qualification is to engage in the proverbial comparison of apples and oranges. Consequently, comparative studies such as Reid's and Laats' point to the ongoing need to explicate a theologian's doctrine of the filioque (or lack thereof) from an intrasystemic perspective. As with any doctrine, a defense of the filioque cannot be expected to stand alone apart from its actual use throughout the rest of the systematic endeavor, particularly in a theologian such as Barth where the doctrine of God as Trinity is not simply one of the first doctrines to be dealt with, but a doctrine which structures and shapes the entire systematic theology.

---

[128] Ibid.

Intrasystemic Approaches

The third category of literature on Barth's doctrine of the filioque is, relatively speaking, only recently coming to the fore, though it has already been glimpsed in some of the comparative studies examined above. Unlike the theological-exegetical critiques, the intrasystemic approach to the problem of the filioque in Barth recognizes that different theological solutions can be proposed to explain the same data of Scripture. Consequently, the test of a theological solution is not only whether it is exegetically supported in the Bible, or how it is similar to, or different from, other solutions, but how it works itself out internally (systemically/systematically) within the dogmatic framework in which the solution to a dogmatic problem is posed. For example, the exegetical-theological approach has tended to focus on whether the dogmatic assertion that the Spirit proceeds from the Father and the Son is or is not sufficiently warranted from the biblical teaching on the Holy Spirit. Without obviously denigrating the need for a biblical warrant for doctrines, it has also become increasingly recognized that all theologies arise in a historical context and with differing overarching concerns. Thus, to further aid the theologian in judging the sufficiency of the dogmatic assertion to account for exegesis, it is important to ask how *this* dogmatic assertion may systemically manifest itself in other related (or seemingly unrelated) theological loci or, alternatively, how *this* dogmatic assertion actually affected the systemic structure of the dogmatic framework through and through.

As already noted, the use of comparative approaches has been important in helping to sharpen the exposition of Barth's position along with a better delineation of his internal systematic logic. In this sense, what is being called here the intrasystemic approach works explicitly toward what the comparative approach already has sought implicitly to do (mainly, to insure that an accurate and fair comparison of differing systems was made), but with a different goal in mind. Whereas comparative study might seek the internal structure of Barth's filioquist theology for the purpose of comparison and contrast to other systems, the intrasystemic approach seeks to understand the internal structures of Barth's filioquist theology for the purpose of assessing whether the systemic effects lead to distortions in other theological loci, particularly distortions that are inconsistent with Barth's doctrine of the Trinity.

Relatively speaking, intrasystemic approaches to Barth's theology of the filioque are a new sector of the literature on Barth, and thus only two scholars in particular are chosen here for extensive review: Roman Catholic theologian Philip J. Rosato and Lutheran theologian Robert Jenson.

Philip J. Rosato That Barth's *Church Dogmatics* is dominated by a "Christological concentration" is now accepted as an assured result of Barth scholarship. Such an assessment was supported and affirmed by Barth himself. As he put it, "a church dogmatics must … be christologically determined as a whole and in all its parts" and "in the basic statements of a church dogmatics, Christology must either be dominant and perceptible, or else it is not Christology."[129] Indeed, for Barth, Christology is the "center" or "heart" of a Christian dogmatic enterprise, and the degree of prominence given to Christology within a work of dogmatics reveals more about a theologian's presuppositions than almost anything else. As he declared in his lectures on the Creed, "[Christology] is the touchstone of all knowledge of God in the Christian sense, the touchstone of all theology. 'Tell me how it stands with your Christology, and I shall tell you who you are.'"[130]

Barth's heavy emphasis on Christology often meant that he was charged with being a Christomonist.[131] However, scholars in recent years have recognized the inadequacy of the Christomonist critique. Consequently, criticism has shifted away from the largely unfruitful task of seeking an inherent problem in Barth's Christology in favor of seeking to understand the development of Barth's doctrine of the Trinity as a whole. This shift has meant that the systemic nature of Barth's Trinitarianism is being taken even more seriously without denying what Barth himself called the "Christological concentration" in his work. Thus, it is increasingly recognized that Barth's Christology cannot be understood apart from

---

129 *CD* I/2, p. 123.

130 Karl Barth, *Dogmatics in Outline* (New York, 1959), p. 66.

131 It is difficult to know who first applied the term obviously polemical term "Christomonism" to Barth, even though there never appeared to be a consensus on what the term itself was meant to denote. Two examples here will suffice to demonstrate the divergent meanings of the term.

First, John Cobb, Jr. described Barth's "Christomonism" as the methodological bent by which every doctrine within the traditional systematic *loci* is processed and viewed through the lens of Christology—a *methodological* move, according to Cobb, that eventually suffocates the rest of his theology. John B. Cobb, Jr., *God and the World* (Philadelphia, 1969). A second voice is that of G. C. Berkouwer in his influential book, *The Triumph of Grace in the Theology of Karl Barth.* Though Berkouwer did not deny certain methodological effects of Barth's Christocentrism, he tended to see Barth's theology as "Christomonist" from a more ontological perspective. In Barth's thought, Berkouwer argues, the grace of God in Jesus Christ functions as a theological trump card; all questions of the ultimate state of creation, humanity included, are resolved through the triumphant application of an unbounded grace found in Jesus Christ. Thus, Berkouwer says: "The triumph is so unassailable that [for Barth] it has become *pure* fact." See G. C. Berkouwer, *The Triumph of Grace in the Theology of Karl Barth* (Grand Rapids, 1956), pp. 261, 265.

At his Princeton lectures in 1962, Barth was asked how his theology avoided being "Christomonistic" and his answer is, by all accounts, instructive and representative of his common response: "Sound theology cannot be either dualistic or monistic. The Gospel defies all 'isms,' including dualism and monism. … Christomonism would mean that Christ alone is real and that all other men are only apparently real. But that would be in contradiction with what the name Jesus-Christ means, namely, union between God and man. … Jesus Christ as God's servant is true God and true man, but at the same time also our servant and the servant of all men. Christomonism is excluded by the very meaning and goal of God's and man's union in Jesus Christ." Karl Barth, "A Theological Dialogue," *Theology Today* 19/2 (July 1962): 171-77 at 172.

his doctrine of the Trinity or vice versa. By analogy, the question arises whether Barth's pneumatology (or the lack thereof) must be examined in a similar kind of relationship. So the question has turned away from the non-Trinitarian and fragmentary question of "How does Barth's Christology exclude pneumatology?" to "How is Barth's pneumatology related to his doctrine of the Trinity?"

In this regard, a significant shift in scholarly exploration of Barth's theology took place with the publication in 1981 of Philip Rosato's landmark work on Barth's pneumatology, *The Spirit as Lord.*[132] Resisting the older criticisms that Barth's Christology obliterates pneumatology, Rosato argues that Barth does not so much describe the Holy Spirit as much as he *displays* the Spirit at work within his Christology. Unlike many previous critics who discerned an absence of pneumatology in Barth, Rosato boldly claimed that "Barth's pneumatology is so extensive and so imposing that this comparatively lengthy study cannot possibly encompass it, let alone do it justice."[133] Indeed, Rosato was willing to put forth the radical thesis that "Karl Barth is also, and perhaps first and foremost, a pneumatologist."[134]

One of the most important contributions of Rosato's work is in identifying the relationship of Barth's pneumatology to Friedrich Schleiermacher's anthropocentricism (or "Christianocentrism" as it is often called). A great deal of study has been carried out on how Barth's theology was significantly shaped by his lifelong reaction to neo-Protestantism or, more specifically, that trajectory of neo-Protestantism shaped by the work of Schleiermacher.[135] As is well known, Barth maintained a respectful yet critical relationship to the work of Schleiermacher throughout his entire career. His early theological development was firmly located within the Schleiermacherian tradition, but he began to question that tradition when 93 German intellectuals (a few of whom had been Barth's own teachers) signed a manifesto in support of Kaiser Wilhelm II's war policy at the outset of the Great War. Barth then perceived, in his own words, that "the theology of the nineteenth century had no future."[136]

---

132 Philip J. Rosato, *The Spirit As Lord: The Pneumatology of Karl Barth* (Edinburgh, 1981).

133 Ibid., p. vii.

134 Ibid., p. viii.

135 For various views on the relationship between Barth and Schleiermacher, see James O. Duke and Robert F. Streetman (eds), *Barth and Schleiermacher: Beyond the Impasse?* (Philadelphia, 1988). For a more focused comparison on the doctrine of election, see Matthias Gockel, *Barth and Schleiermacher on the Doctrine of Election: A Systematic-Theological Comparison* (Oxford and New York, 2006).

136 Reflecting on this tumultuous time in his own life, Barth testifies of his lifelong admiration for Schleiermacher while simultaneously pointing out that he had "decisively departed from Schleiermacher's path" even if only "*rebus sic stantibus,* 'for the present,' 'until better instructed.'" See Karl Barth, "Concluding Unscientific Postscript on Schleiermacher," in Dietrich Ritschl and Geoffrey W. Bromiley (eds), *The Theology of*

Though scholarship has typically assumed that Barth sought to correct Schleiermacher's "Christianocentric" approach by favoring a "Christocentric" approach, Rosato argues quite differently:

> While Barth accepts the need for a *Vermittlungsprinzip,* or mediating principle of theological methodology, Schleiermacher's selection of man's consciousness, through which the objective becomes subjective and the historical becomes psychologically possible, strikes Barth as inadequate. Through the filter of man's consciousness Schleiermacher forces the biblical understanding of Christ and the Spirit to pass; in the process both are deformed and robbed of their uniqueness. ... The objectivity of biblical revelation is thus lost, and the exclusive emphasis on man's subjective experience as the locus and object of Christian faith is firmly established... . Barth's main difficulty with Schleiermacher, therefore, is that, where the Holy Spirit should stand as the one true mediator between Christ and the believer, Schleiermacher places man's consciousness, thereby reducing Christ and faith to the two theologically immunized concepts of history and experience.[137]

Significantly, Rosato points out that Barth does not simply replace the dialectical framework of Schleiermacher's scheme, but re-theologizes the categories of the dialectic itself. Thus, whereas Schleiermacher was apt to speak of human consciousness as the mediating principle between history (objective pole) and experience (subjective pole), Barth introduces the activity of the Holy Spirit (*Die Tat des Heiligen Geist*) as the mediating "principle" between God's revelation (*Die Offenbarung Gottes*—the objective pole) and human faith (*Der Glaube des Menschen*).[138] In so replacing the Schleiermachian categories, Rosato argues, "Barth both corrects Schleiermacher's vague christology and pneumatology, and forges his own pneumatic methodology which is original yet clearly indebted to the dialectical structure of Schleiermacher's thought."[139]

Despite Rosato's confession that "admiration rather than reservation"[140] is the mark of his own account of Barth's pneumatology, he ultimately voices some reservation. Not surprisingly, Rosato identifies Barth's adherence to the filioque as a major problem. As Rosato puts it:

Schleiermacher (Grand Rapids, 1982), pp. 261-79 at pp. 271, 274. Such a conflation led to the central problem that Barth detected in an entire tradition spawned by nineteenth-century anthropocentric theology: "that there was no ultimate opposition between God and man, no essential distinction between Christ and the Christian." Philip C. Almond, "Karl Barth and Anthropocentric Theology," *Scottish Journal of Theology* 31/5 (1978): 435-47 at 437.

137 Rosato, *Lord as Spirit*, pp. 18-19.

138 Ibid., p. 19.

139 Ibid.

140 Ibid., p. vii.

> One can recognize the connection between trinitarian formalism and christological bias in Barth's pneumatology. The choice of the Latin model of the Trinity, in which the Spirit confirms God's inner community, instead of the Greek model, in which the Spirit communicates God's love to man, forces Barth to attribute to the Son the function which the Greeks appropriated to the Spirit. Without denying the theological importance of the filioque, one can be justifiably critical of its oversystematization in the *Church Dogmatics*. The equally valid *ex patre* is neglected, and a pervasive narrowness results in Barth's pneumatology.[141]

In Rosato's estimation, the filioque has the unfortunate function in Barth of restricting the Spirit "to an almost exclusively ecclesial understanding of pneumatology." Consequently, this "causes Barth to neglect man's universal search for salvation under the guidance of the Spirit apart from the Christ-event and the Christian Church."[142] But not only pneumatology is restricted; so, too, Christology and eschatology. Christologically, Barth's filioquist pneumatology implies that "the absolute uniqueness of Christ's life, death and resurrection is preserved at the expense of His universality which is yet to be not simply acknowledged but accomplished."[143] In terms of eschatology, "Barth's Spirit theology constantly leads back to the already fulfilled salvific event in Jesus Christ, instead of forwards to the as yet incomplete, but essentially open and available, Kingdom of the Christ who is still to come."[144] Thus, though Rosato is convinced that Barth ought to be understood as a pneumatologist first and foremost, he is also convinced that Barth's pneumatology is unnecessarily restrictive and that such restrictiveness is clearly and unequivocally "caused" by Barth's favoring of the filioque.[145]

Robert Jenson Not all scholars have yet been convinced of Rosato's provocative thesis that pneumatology is central to Barth's thought. For example, Lutheran theologian Robert Jenson, in a playful article on Barth's pneumatology, observes what he sees as the "appearing" and "vanishing" of the Spirit in Barth's *Church Dogmatics*. Jenson is convinced that it was Barth's commitment to the doctrine of the Holy Spirit as "the bond of peace (or love) between Father and Son" [*vinculum pacis (*or *vinculum amoris) inter Patrem et Filium*] and its theological corollary, the

---

141 Ibid., p. 162.

142 Ibid., p. 164. Notice here Rosato's language of necessity: Barth's doctrine of the filioque "causes" a restricted soteriology.

143 Ibid., p. 165.

144 Ibid.

145 For reviews of Rosato's book, see George Hendry, "Review of *The Spirit as Lord: The Pneumatology of Karl Barth* in P.J. Rosato," *Theology Today* 43/3 (October 1986): 419-23; and John Thompson, *The Holy Spirit in the Theology of Karl Barth* (Allison Park, 1991), pp. 197-211.

doctrine of the filioque, which prevented, and would have presumably continued to prevent, Barth from developing a "third article" pneumatology himself.

Jenson begins by noting how the *Church Dogmatics* "presents a smorgasbord of cases in which the doctrine of Trinity, as *used,* seems to be rather a doctrine of binity." He goes on: "In normal Western Trinitarianism, characterization of the Spirit as the *vinculum amoris* between the Father and Son is systematically central. Barth is no innovator or exception at this point. Indeed, his great attachment to this theologoumenon is his stated reason for supporting the filioque."[146] Since the *vinculum* doctrine posits the Holy Spirit as the fellowship of love itself between Father and Son, Jenson points out that Barth describes this inner-divine relationship as "two-sided." Barth sees this inner-divine relationship as the eternal ground for fellowship between God and humanity; thus "each two-sided fellowship is the *archetype* of the thereby next grounded such pairing, so that the two-sidedness reproduces itself at every ontological level."[147] Consequently, "the very reality of the Spirit excludes his appearance as a *party* in the triune actuality."[148]

According to Jenson, the filioque functions for Barth both as the form by which the doctrine of the *vinculum* is upheld *and* as the systematic means of application of the *vinculum* throughout the rest of his theology. In other words, Barth's so-called "binitarian tendency" is the systematic consequence of a formal adherence to the *vinculum* principle and its material outworking in the doctrine of the filioque. Because Barth consistently affirms that the Spirit proceeds from the Father and the Son, the Spirit is consistently submerged beneath the shadows of a God who reveals himself exclusively in Christ. Thus, Jenson is convinced that in Barth, "the filioque is used systematically"[149] and Spirit-avoidance is the unfortunate result.

Jenson extrapolates the systemic critique further by noting specific aspects of Barth's theology in the *Dogmatics* where systematic use of the filioque can be discerned. While he admits that "not every conceptual practice that a theologian finds necessary is fully supported by his/her general system," he does feel that,

---

146 Robert W. Jenson, "You Wonder Where the Spirit Went," *Pro Ecclesia* 2/3 (1993): 301, 300. It is significant that Daniel Migliore, in contrast to Jenson, is willing to assert "Obwohl er von Barth nicht so umfassend entwickelt und angewandt wird wie das chalcedonensiche Paradigma, besitzt dieser Begriff ein größeres Potential für eine christo-pneumatologische Theologie, selbst im Rahmen des filioque, als es in der Kirchlichen Dogmatik realisiert ist." ["Although neither developed nor deployed in the *Church Dogmatics* in as full a manner as is his Chalcedonian paradigm, the doctrine of the *vinculum pacis* possesses more potential for a Christo-pneumatological theology, even within the framework of filioque Trinitarianism, than is actually realized in the *Church Dogmatics*."] Daniel I. Migliore, "Vinculum Pacis: Karl Barths Theologie des Heiligen Geistes," *Evangelische Theologie* 60/2 (2000): 150.

147 Jenson, "Where the Spirit Went," p. 301.

148 Ibid.

149 Ibid., p. 299.

within Barth's system, Western hindrances (i.e., the filioque) may obstruct more mischievously than elsewhere, just on account of his achievements.[150]

Taking his cue from traditional Orthodox criticism of Western Trinitarian thought, Jenson suggests that the outpouring of the Spirit at Pentecost is a genuinely new intervention by the third Person of the Trinity, an intervention in which "an ecclesiology of *communion* ensues."[151] Barth necessarily falters on this ecclesiological point, according to Jenson, because his adherence to the filioque prevents him from seeing the Spirit as an *agent* of the love between the Father and Son rather than as a *modus* only. He argues that if the Spirit were understood as an *agent* of the love between the Father and Son, "immanently and economically, then the church, as the community inspirited by this Agent, would be the active *mediatrix* of faith, in precisely the way demanded by Catholics and resisted by Protestants in every chief dialogue."[152] Instead, Jenson laments, Barth's ecclesiology is dominated by an overbearing Christology instead of a liberating pneumatology—that is, Barth's Christology functions to subvert any notion of the Holy Spirit's personal agency.[153] The irony of this, according to Jenson, is that "[t]he personal agent of this work [of the church] in fact turns out at every step of Barth's argument to be *not* the Spirit, as advertised, but Christ."[154] So, Jenson asks:

> When does the Spirit disappear from Barth's pages? Whenever he would appear as someone rather than as something. We miss the Spirit at precisely those points where Bible or catechism have taught us to expect him to appear as someone *with* capacities, rather than as sheer capacity—in the archetype/image scheme, as himself an archetype.[155]

Jenson also makes some more general observations of the "unsolved problem" of pneumatology that has always been felt in Christian theology. The question is: "how the Spirit can be at once his own person and what all three hypostases actively are together? How is the Spirit at once one who has power and that power itself?" As Jenson rightly notes, "it is no general refutation of Barth that he too has left a few problems unsolved." He goes on to say, however, that "interaction between this unsolved problem and Barth's particular achievements produces an especially painful set of symptoms."[156]

---

150 Ibid.

151 Ibid. Emphasis in original.

152 Ibid., p. 303.

153 Jenson is not alone in criticizing what appears to be a lack of personal agency of the Spirit in Barth. See also R. D. Williams, "Barth on the Triune God," in Sykes, *Karl Barth*, pp. 169, 178.

154 Jenson, "Where the Spirit Went," p. 303.

155 Ibid., p. 304. Emphasis in original.

156 Ibid.

Assessing Intrasystemic Approaches A significant feature of Rosato and Jenson's critiques of Barth's doctrine of the filioque is that both proceed on the basis of the assumption that the filioque functions intrasystemically in a fairly consistent way in Barth's theology. This is to be expected. Though both critiques in this case assess the presence of the filioque as a prime factor contributing to Barth's pneumatological want, their assessments nevertheless resist some of the weaknesses of the aforementioned approaches. Neither Rosato nor Jenson fault Barth for his adoption of the filioque per se (as if it were a "false solution to a real problem"), but both are convinced that, at the very least, it has restricted Barth at various points throughout his theology.

Positively, Jenson and Rosato's intrasystemic critiques have rightly sought to identify whether and how Barth's adoption of a Western pneumatological formulation of the Spirit's procession from Father and Son works its way systematically through the rest of his theology. Given the widespread recognition that Barth managed consistently to question traditional forms of dogmatic statement, one is left wondering, along with Jenson and Rosato, whether in fact the doctrine of the filioque is one instance, at least, where Barth either did not do enough homework or was not sufficiently self-critical.[157] This is a legitimate line of questioning that will be explored through the remainder of this study.

In addition, both Jenson and Rosato suggest that Barth conflates the work of the Spirit with that of the Son and blurs the Spirit's unique role by subordinating him to the Son at best, or making him superfluous at worst. For Rosato, this means that the Spirit's work is overly restricted in drawing humans to God in and through the Church and more universally in the world, while Jenson focuses specifically on how he sees Barth's theology as denigrating the role of the Church itself in the economy of salvation. Thus, it will be an important task of this study to identify how Barth distinguishes between, if at all, the roles of the Spirit and the Son and to what extent Barth understands the Spirit to be an "independent" divine agent on par with the Father and Son. Of course, a larger question that may be even beyond answering is what biblical and theological warrant there is to expect such "pneumatological independence" in the first place.

Rosato's and Jenson's analyses provide promising direction for the present investigation of Barth's doctrine of the filioque, but they are susceptible to criticism on at least two critical points. First, both criticisms of Barth's filioquist pneumatology reflect their own desired pneumatological and ecclesiological outcomes. In Rosato's case, a particular form of pneumatological universality in soteriology and eschatology, for example, becomes the measure against which Barth's pneumatology is found wanting. In Jenson's case, Barth's apparent refusal to view the Church either along the ecumenically driven *communio* ecclesiology[158]

---

[157] One only needs to consider the major shift in his doctrine of baptism as evidenced in *CD* IV/4 to realize how radically Barth could be self-critical.

[158] For a careful consideration of the claims of *communio* ecclesiology, see Nicholas M. Healy, "Communion Ecclesiology: A Cautionary Note," *Pro Ecclesia* 4/4 (Fall 1995): 442-53.

or as an "active *mediatrix* of faith" is identified, in Jenson's estimation, as outcome of a systematized filioque. However, what is most interesting here is that it may not be possible to have it both ways as Rosato and Jenson wish. For if it is true that Barth's pneumatology is ecclesiologically restricted, as Rosato argues, such that the work of the Spirit is aligned most closely with the presence of the Christian Church, then Barth's pneumatology is likely much closer to Jenson's expectations for the Church to be an "active *mediatrix* of faith" than Jenson thinks. But if Jenson's critique is right that Barth's ecclesiology is Christologically restricted rather than pneumatologically liberating, then it appears that Barth's pneumatology is not sufficiently ecclesiologically restricted such that the active agency of the Spirit is most clearly seen in the Christian Church!

Whatever the case, these two analyses of the situation falter because they beg the question whether Barth resisted such definitions of the Church (or of salvation or eschatology) *only* because of his adoption of the filioque or for some other reason or reasons that Jenson and Rosato do not perceive. As previously noted, one must be quite cautious when theological causality is identified all too easily as a single factor, and, in this case, the filioque may be an all-too-easy theological scapegoat. There are simply too many other factors to consider.

Furthermore, both Jenson and Rosato assume that the intrasystemic connection between the filioque and other dogmatic loci necessarily flows from the filioque outward, and not the other way around, or even through an indirect path. It is not difficult to see why Jenson and Rosato could assume that the filioque theologically precedes these other systematic loci, given the fact that Barth's defense of the filioque falls at the beginning of the *Church Dogmatics* and it is only in later volumes that he begins to write extensively about soteriology, ecclesiology, or eschatology. Yet this study will show that the filioque was not a simply a presupposition to the development of Barth's doctrine of God, but was in fact Barth's conclusion to his analysis of God's self-revelation—an analysis that began a decade or more prior to the first volume of the *Church Dogmatics*. The filioque, in other words, was not viewed as a presupposed dogmatic axiom meant to be applied systematically at every step throughout his dogmatics. In other words, the filioque is not a foundational doctrine for Barth, even if he continues to hold to it as a fundamental assertion arising, as it does, from his analysis of God's self-revelation corresponding to God as he is in his own eternal being. Thus, some significant questions need to be raised in any assessment of the doctrine of the filioque in Barth. Has Barth rightly discerned the filioque from revelation in the first place? In "reading back" the filioque from the economy into the eternal Trinity, is Barth able simultaneously to hold to a strict correspondence of economic and immanent Trinity while maintaining their distinctiveness? Or is Barth's adherence to the filioque one instance where economic and immanent Trinity collapse into one another after all?

The intrasystemic analyses of Rosato and Jenson, while right-headed in their approach, are finally limited in that both assume that Barth's doctrine of the filioque and its intrasystemic effects can be understood from within the *CD* itself. While there is a real sense in which it is right and proper to speak of Barth's theology of the filioque in the *Church Dogmatics*, it is also the case that Barth's theology of the *CD* must be understood also as a developmental outworking of the pre-*CD* Barth. In other words, what are not addressed or acknowledged by Rosato's and Jenson's criticism of Barth's doctrine of the filioque are the *genetic* factors by which Barth was first led to conclude in favor of the filioque—factors which lie much earlier in Barth's own theological development. Few, if any, scholars have sought to trace the genesis of the filioque in Barth's thinking before the *CD,* and few have sought to identify and analyze particular passages within the *CD* where Barth explicitly brings the doctrine of the filioque to bear. As important as it is to speak of Barth's doctrine of the filioque synchronically, this study provides a more diachronic analysis of the doctrine. In so doing, one avoids assuming that the filioque functions as a theological axiom for Barth that is subsequently "oversystematized" in the rest of his theology, and allows one to be open to discovering whether in fact Barth has contributed anything new to the Western filioquist tradition.

Analyzing Barth on the Filioque: A Genetic-Intrasystemic Approach

The foregoing survey of the scholarly literature on Barth and the filioque suggests that delineating the intrasystemic shape of Barth's doctrine of the filioque is only at the earliest stages of scholarship. However, the two most significant intrasystemic examinations of Barth's filioquist pneumatology, those of Rosato and Jenson, were undertaken prior to a significant shift in North American Barth studies, especially under the influence of Princeton theologian Bruce McCormack. Indeed, McCormack's work, building, as it does, on the work of Continental Barth scholars, has succeeded in calling into question the highly regarded "von Balthasar thesis" concerning Barth's theological development.

Since the early 1950s one of the dominant interpretations of Barth's theological development was that of the Roman Catholic theologian, Hans Urs von Balthasar. Central to his study is that Barth's theology was marked by "two decisive turning points": first, "his turn from liberalism to radical Christianity," and then "his final emancipation from the shackles of philosophy, enabling him finally to arrive at a genuine, self-authenticating theology."[159] More specifically, von Balthasar identifies a twofold shift of emphasis in Barth from an early dialectical to a later analogical mode of thought *(Denkform)*—a methodological shift occurring in two stages. In the first stage, von Balthasar argues that Barth was compelled to reject his inherited liberal theology in favor of a theology of *Krisis* or *Realdialektik*—a "conversion" manifest particularly in the first (and second) edition of his *Römerbrief.* In the second stage (and this is the stage that is being contested), von Balthasar argues that Barth shifted away from the dialectical mode as evidenced in

159 Hans Urs von Balthasar, *The Theology of Karl Barth: Exposition and Interpretation* (San Francisco, 1992), p. 93.

the *Römerbrief* toward an analogical mode of thinking. This shift was inaugurated in Barth's study of Anselm, *Fides Quaerens Intellectum* (1932), even though it continued to take place right up to the writing of the *CD*. Thus, according to von Balthasar, this second shift is the key to understanding the development of Barth's theology of the *Church Dogmatics*.[160]

The von Balthasar thesis that Barth's most mature mode of thinking began to take shape in his Anselm book has been tremendously influential.[161] Indeed, Barth confirms it himself by noting that the thinking of Anselm had been, as he put it, "absorbed into my own line of thinking."[162] Barth even asserts in the preface to the second edition of the book that the Anselm book was "a vital key, if not *the* key, to understanding the process of thought that has impressed me more and more in my *Church Dogmatics*."[163] In addition, the von Balthasar thesis had been accepted to the point where even T. F. Torrance, arguably one of the most important English-speaking interpreters of Barth, more or less accepts von Balthasar's periodization with only minor modification.[164]

The significance of the near-consensus regarding Barth's theological development began to show signs of erosion in the 1970s and 1980s when German scholars, such as Rendtorff, Meckels, Spieckermann, and Beintker, began to question the discontinuities between the early and later Barth presupposed by the von Balthasar thesis. Then in 1995 Bruce McCormack tipped the scholarly applecart when he released his seminal work on the genesis and development of Barth's early theology—a feat enabled through his extensive work in the Barth archives in Switzerland, which house a great many of Barth's untranslated early writings.[165]

McCormack's work is vitally important because of the way in which he constructs a compelling counterargument to von Balthasar's thesis. Building on, though still moderately critical of, an earlier generation of German scholarship, McCormack argues that Barth's theological development is marked more by continuity than discontinuity, and consists of subtle shifts of emphasis in an otherwise consistent mode of thought. Unlike von Balthasar, McCormack argues that dialectical modes of thinking remained at the heart of Barth's thinking from the earliest stages of his

---

160 Ibid., p. 107.

161 The American theologian Hans Frei, for example, adopted von Balthasar's thesis of a "second shift" and conceived of it as being a complete "revolution" of Barth's theology, even though von Balthasar is himself more cautious indicating the shift was gradual. See Hans Frei, "The Doctrine of Revelation in the Thought of Karl Barth, 1909 to 1922," (PhD thesis, Yale University, 1956), p. 194.

162 Karl Barth, *Anselm: Fides Quaerens Intellectum* (Pittsburgh, 1975), p. 11.

163 Ibid.

164 See Thomas F. Torrance, *Karl Barth: An Introduction to His Early Theology, 1910-1931* (London, 1962).

165 Bruce L. McCormack, *Karl Barth's Critically Realistic Dialectic Theology: Its Genesis and Development, 1909-1936* (Oxford, 1995).

career up to and including the *CD*. In contrast to the reading that sets dialectical and analogical thinking at odds with one another, he claims that "the *Realdialektik* of veiling and unveiling" is the "motor which drives Barth's doctrine of analogy and makes it possible."[166] A failure to perceive this has the unfortunate consequence of "render[ing] Barth's mature theology undialectical."[167] Thus, McCormack argues, Barth was from the time of the first edition of the *Römerbrief* through to the *CD*, a critically realistic dialectical theologian.

The far-reaching implications of McCormack's compelling counterthesis are now increasingly being explored in Barth scholarship. It is difficult to estimate how a (re)reading of Barth's *CD* in greater continuity with his earlier work might alter scholarly interpretation of even some of the more commonly explored doctrinal formulations of Barth, such as his doctrine of Election or his doctrine of Revelation—explorations clearly beyond the scope of this study. However, the particular implication for this study is that reviews of Barth's pneumatology antedating the re-examination of Barth's theological development are prone to criticism in this light. This certainly includes Rosato's work on Barth's pneumatology and Jenson's critique of Barth's *vinculum*-filioque theological matrix, both of which assume von Balthasar's identification of the *CD* as a "post-dialectical" work.[168] That Barth continues to think dialectically in his pneumatology will become evident in Chapter Four below, especially when comparing Barth's implicit filioquist pneumatology in *Romans* with the explicit theology of the filioque as evidenced in the later volumes of the *CD*.

Two fundamental presuppositions that characterize the majority, if not all, of the studies surveyed above, can now also be called into question in light of McCormack's developmental study of Barth. First, it can no longer be assumed that Barth's defense of the filioque in the *CD* can be read in isolation from his earlier theological development. While it is true that the *CD* contains Barth's fullest defense of the doctrine, Barth already held to the filioque at least as early as 1924 in the so-called *Göttingen Dogmatics*. This is not to say that Barth fully

166 Ibid., p. 18.

167 Bruce L. McCormack, "Dankeswort," *The Princeton Seminary Bulletin* 21/2 (2000): 212. McCormack argues elsewhere that von Balthasar's reading of Barth enabled the American reception of Barth's work as a "neo-orthodox" theologian. "Barth's theology was quite simply an alien plant which could not flourish on the soil of an American Protestantism long committed to the experiential in religion." Consequently, von Balthasar's thesis enabled American interpreters to place Barth in "a place of honour alongside other luminaries like Emil Brunner and Reinhold Niebuhr, as one of the founders of that most typically American of all theological movements: neo-orthodoxy. But of course, Barth was no longer Barth once the process of assimilation was complete. Thus, the Barth who exercised an influence on American theology in the middle decades of this century was not the theologian known to Europeans but a caricature." Bruce L. McCormack, "The Unheard Message of Karl Barth," *Word & World* 14/1 (Winter 1994): 59-60.

168 Robert W. Jenson, "Jesus, Father, Spirit. The Logic of the Doctrine of the Trinity," *Dialog* 26/4 (Fall 1987): 249.

understood the issue (he himself admitted in the *GD* that he was unclear on it), but it was the best way known to him at that point to express the doctrine of the Trinity as he had already come to understand it—a doctrine of the Trinity that was dialectically construed in terms of God's revelatory "veiling and unveiling."[169]

Second, it should not be assumed that the filioque was, for Barth, a *dogmatic* presupposition for his subsequent *analogical* reasoning. That is to say, to date no interpreter of Barth has asked whether his doctrine of the filioque was a feature of Barth's early dialecticism rather than a presupposition (critically or uncritically) received and carried systematically through by the later Barth, the dogmatic theologian. How would Barth's adoption of the filioque be understood if it were viewed instead from the standpoint of Barth's early emphasis that it is only by the Spirit that the veiled Father is unveiled in the Son while the Spirit simultaneously remains "the-unveiling-veiled-one" who cannot be captured or identified, somewhat like the impossibility of portraying faithfully a bird in flight?[170] These are the kind of questions that remain to be explored.

In many respects, a great debt is owed to Rosato and Jenson for approaching the question of Barth's pneumatology and, specifically, his doctrine of the filioque from an intrasystemic perspective. Nevertheless, the stated criticisms of Rosato's and Jenson's approaches call for a modification (or more accurately, expansion) to the intrasystemic approach as practiced by both. In order to accomplish this, the next chapter will follow the lead of Bruce McCormack's ground-breaking work on Barth's early theology by attending to the genetic factors which led to Barth's adoption of the filioque prior to his writing of the *Church Dogmatics.* There it will be demonstrated that the filioque arose not as a theological *a priori* in the *CD* that Barth systematically worked out in the rest of the dogmatic enterprise, but as a theological *a posteriori* arrived at through his analysis of revelation and, more specifically, of how revelation is related to the Church's task of preaching the Gospel—an issue first materially raised in *Romans* but dealt with more formally in his *Göttingen Dogmatics.*

169 Barth, *Göttingen Dogmatics*, pp. 129-30.

170 Barth, *Word of God and Word of Man*, p. 282.

Chapter Two
The Genesis and Development of the Filioque in Barth's Earlier Theology

That Barth vigorously defended the filioque in the first half-volume of the *CD* is beyond any meaningful dispute. However, to date there is no scholarly account which has traced the emergence or development of this doctrine prior to the first half-volume of the *CD*. Thus, through careful attention to two important texts written in the decade prior to the beginning of the *CD*, this chapter will identify some of the principal historical and theological factors which contributed to Barth's pro-filioque stance. It will be argued that, in the earliest stages of his career, Barth posited a dialectical and Christocentric pneumatology in which the Spirit is understood to be the divine agent by whom humans are able to apprehend God's own self-revelation of himself in Jesus Christ, all without failing to maintain the infinite qualitative distinction between the human and the divine. On the basis of this revelational pneumatology, Barth then went on to develop a doctrine of the Word of God that is formally filioquist in structure, even though he clearly did not yet understand the material dogmatic significance of the filioque, either for the doctrine of God or for its systematic relationship to the rest of theology.

The main thrust of this chapter will be to bring into relief the pneumatological framework of Barth's early theology antecedent to the *CD*. This is important for two reasons. First, increased scholarly attention to continuities between the early and later Barth force his interpreters to realize that the theology of the *CD* cannot be considered in isolation from Barth's earlier thought. Second, an understanding of Barth's first dogmatic investigations on the doctrine of the filioque is important because it illuminates how he sought to deal with the filioque from a reference point within the doctrine of Revelation rather than primarily as a problem of the doctrine of God as classically understood. An appreciation of how Barth first attempted to defend the filioque clarifies how he eventually came to the point where he was able adamantly to defend and apply the filioque throughout the *CD*. The chapter will conclude by pointing out how Barth's initial thinking on the filioque from the perspective of his doctrine of Revelation placed undue restrictions on Barth's pneumatology which he only realized and began to overcome some years later.

For the purposes of this study, two of Barth's major works produced in the decade prior to the beginning of Barth's writing of the *CD* (i.e., 1921-1931) have been selected for closer examination. They are the second edition of the *Epistle to the Romans* (*Der Römerbrief*, 1921); and the *Göttingen Dogmatics* (*Unterricht in der christlichen Religion*, 1924). Some preliminary comments may be helpful to explain the rationale for choosing these works.

The second edition of *Romans* (*Der Römerbrief*)[1] was chosen because it represents the first major work of the young Barth in which he was sufficiently satisfied that he had reached a position he could genuinely call his own. Consequently, this study will focus on the thoroughly revised second edition rather than the original first edition.

It should also be noted that the genre of *Romans* is such that less attention will be paid to finding a developed doctrine of the filioque (indeed, no such formally doctrine would be found) than to seeking to identify how the pneumatology on display in *Romans* contributed to Barth's eventual adoption of the filioque. Overall, *Romans* is important as the point of origin for Barth's pneumatological trajectory.

The *Göttingen Dogmatics*[2] was selected because it is Barth's first formal dogmatic work and contains his first, albeit brief, examination of the filioque as a dogmatic problem. Though it is clearly evident in the *GD* that Barth had not yet grasped the full significance of the doctrine of the filioque, the *GD* highlights Barth's emerging doctrine of the Word of God in a filioquist framework that would eventually be expanded upon and supported in the *Church Dogmatics*.

The "Spirit of Christ" in *Romans*: A Pneumatological Precursor to the Filioque

Historical Background to the Writing of Romans

Barbour has characterized Barth's commentary on the *Epistle to the Romans—Der Römerbrief*—as "stand[ing] at the head of the theological revolt of the twentieth century against the theology, the religion, and indeed the whole culture and history, of the nineteenth."[3] Even though the first edition of the famous commentary,

---

[1] Karl Barth, *Der Römerbrief* (Munich, 1926); English translation: Karl Barth, *The Epistle to the Romans,* trans. Edwyn C. Hoskyns (6th edn, London, 1933, 1968). All citations hereafter are to Hoskyns' English translation of the second edition unless otherwise noted.

[2] Karl Barth, *The Göttingen Dogmatics*, ed. Hannelotte Reiffen, trans. Geoffrey W. Bromiley (Grand Rapids, 1991). Hereafter referred to as *GD.*

[3] R. S. Barbour, "Biblical Classics: X. Karl Barth: The Epistle to the Romans," *The Expository Times*, 90/9 (June 1978): 264-68 at 264. On theological parallels to *Romans*, see Frank Jehle, *Ever against the Stream: The Politics of Karl Barth, 1906-1968* (Grand Rapids, 2002), p. 37.

published in 1919,[4] was not widely regarded outside of Switzerland,[5] according to McCormack it was "Barth's first major effort at an explication of his new theology."[6]

Several factors led Barth to undertake a thorough revision of *Romans* just over a year after its publication. First, according to the preface to the second edition, Barth wanted to respond to the initial criticisms of the book. With perhaps a touch of irritation, Barth pointed out that his critics (he undoubtedly had Jülicher in mind) should have paid attention to the fact that the first edition was clearly announced as a "preliminary undertaking."[7]

Second, after delivering his famous Tambach lecture,[8] Barth's encounter with new theological acquaintances such as Friedrich Gogarten in Germany gave him access to a broader circle of hearers. Thus, in October 1920, after being inspired by a visit from Gogarten—whom Barth called "a dread-nought on our side and against our opponents"[9]—Barth started work on revising the commentary.

Apart from these historical factors, however, Barth confessed that his own continued study of Paul, Overbeck, Plato, and Kant (under the tutelage of his brother Heinrich), and Dostoevsky and Kierkegaard (encouraged by his close friend Eduard Thurneysen), had convinced him of the need to update the *Romans* commentary.[10] By the time he had finished the revision, he was convinced that the commentary now represented his own thinking and his own distinctive position. As he commented, the second edition was "a bit nearer to the truth of the matter than before" and "the pantheistic tinge [of the first edition had] now been removed."[11] Though Barth recognized both continuity and discontinuity between the first and second editions, he nevertheless announced, "the original position has been completely reformed and consolidated."[12] Thus, he was able confidently to proclaim in the preface to the second edition, published in 1922, that "the first edition can now disappear from the scene."[13] It is on this basis that this analysis of

4 On the historical background leading up to the writing of *Romans*, see Eberhard Busch, *Karl Barth: His Life from Letters and Autobiographical Texts*, trans. John Bowden (Grand Rapids, 1976), pp. 92-109; and Bruce McCormack, *Karl Barth's Critically Realistic Dialectical Theology: Its Genesis and Development, 1909-1936* (Oxford, 1995), pp. 135-38.

5 Only 1000 copies of the first edition were printed by the Berne firm of G. A. Bäschlin. Busch, *Karl Barth*, p. 106.

6 McCormack, *Critically Realistic*, p. 182.

7 Barth, *Romans*, p. 2.

8 Busch, *Karl Barth*, pp. 109ff.

9 Ibid., p. 117.

10 Barth, *Romans*, pp. 3-4.

11 Busch, *Karl Barth*, p. 118.

12 Barth, *Romans*, p. 2.

13 Ibid. McCormack contends that Barth's desire to distance himself from the first edition led him even to "attribute to himself in retrospect positions he had never maintained." In McCormack's view, the rationale for this was "to force the public to concentrate its

Barth's pneumatology will focus on the second edition rather than the untranslated first edition.

Preliminary Observations

Before analyzing the pneumatology of *Romans*, several preliminary observations are in order. First, it is no surprise that Barth did not formally discuss the dogmatic problem of the filioque anywhere in *Romans*—the work, after all, does not purport to be a work in dogmatics, but a biblical commentary. Thus, it would be unfair to fault Barth for failing explicitly to discuss the problem. In fact, it is possible that, at this stage of his theological development, Barth was barely aware of the filioque controversy.[14] Nevertheless, *Romans* is important to consider because it is there that one can discern an emerging Christocentric and dialectically structured pneumatology that would eventually shape Barth's interpretation and use of the filioque. Indeed, it will be argued that Barth's most mature application of the

---

attention solely on the second edition" and "to acquire an independent reading for the revised version." McCormack, *Critically Realistic*, pp. 181-82. Whatever the case, it is the second edition, not the first, which has commonly been referred to as "a bomb bursting in the playground of the theologians"—a description first coined by Roman Catholic theologian Karl Adam. See T. H. L. Parker, *Karl Barth* (Grand Rapids, 1970), p. 56. Cf. Steiner's characterization of the second edition of *Romans* as a "violent" book. George Steiner, *Martin Heidegger* (2nd edn, New York, 1978), p. ix.

Much scholarly discussion has focused on a form of German "expressionism" found in Barth's writings. Von Balthasar notes a literary form of expressionism in the second edition not present in the first. Hans Urs von Balthasar, *The Theology of Karl Barth: Exposition and Interpretation* (San Francisco, 1992), p. 90. Torrance concurs, though he characterizes the shift to an expressionist style in more theological terms than von Balthasar. See Thomas F. Torrance, *Karl Barth, Biblical and Evangelical Theologian* (Edinburgh, 1990), p. 11. Dorrien and McCormack, on the other hand, identify elements of expressionism in both editions. See Gary Dorrien, *The Barthian Revolt in Modern Theology: Theology Without Weapons* (Louisville, 2000), pp. 54-55; and Bruce McCormack, "The Unheard Message of Karl Barth," *Word & World* 14/1 (Winter 1994): 59-66 at 62-63. Webb has attempted to provide a rhetorical analysis of Barth's early theology by exploring the so-called "expressionism" in the second edition of *Romans*. He concludes that the expressionistic form cannot be separated from the content of Barth's early theology and that a fuller understanding of the genesis of Barth's theology must pay closer attention to this relationship. In addition, Webb is convinced that "Barth's later theology can be understood rhetorically as a kind of realism, an attempt to evade his earlier configurations." Stephen H. Webb, *Re-Figuring Theology: The Rhetoric of Karl Barth* (Albany, 1991), p. 149. For a more thorough examination of Barth's relationship to German expressionism, see Ian R. Boyd, *Dogmatics among the Ruins: German Expressionism and the Enlightenment as Contexts for Karl Barth's Theological Development* (Bern, 2004).

[14] Barth likely did not become aware of many of the classical dogmatic problems, the filioque included, until he began preparing to lecture on the Reformed confessions when he became Honorary Professor of Reformed Theology at Göttingen in 1921.

filioque in *CD* IV can be understood as a return to, and material expansion upon, the Christocentric and dialectically shaped pneumatology of the second edition of *Romans*.

Second, it is important to note that Barth's commentary was written in the crucible of the demands of parish ministry in Safenwil.[15] The original context of his writing of *Romans* was marked by Barth's struggle to face up to the troubling social conditions of his day and how to address these conditions in his preaching to his parishioners in the aftermath of the Great War.[16] In retrospect, Barth spoke of his celebrated break with liberalism to a group of Schulpforta ministers in 1922 "not as a result of any desire of ours to form a school or to devise a system; it arose simply out of what we felt to be the '*need and promise of Christian preaching.*'"[17] As Barth described it, "the familiar situation of the minister on Saturday at his desk and on Sunday in his pulpit crystallized in my case into a marginal note to all theology, which finally assumed the voluminous form of a complete commentary upon the Epistle to the Romans."[18] Consequently, in the preface to the first

---

15 As Minear rightly observes, "Let us remember that Barth's Commentary was primarily the work of a young pastor, seeking to meet the needs of his parish." Paul S. Minear, "Barth's Commentary on the Romans, 1922-1972: Or Karl Barth vs. The Exegetes," in Martin Rumscheidt (ed.), *Footnotes to a Theology: The Karl Barth Colloquium of 1972* (Waterloo, 1974), pp. 8-29 at p. 9.

16 As has been well documented, Barth became conscious, when he moved to the village of Safenwil, that modern industrialism had moved the world into a stage of crisis. As a pastor to industrial workers, Barth became interested in the relationship of "Jesus Christ and the Social Movement" and thus became politically involved in the trade union movement while seeking to speak to the industrial workers' situation. See Karl Barth, "Jesus Christ and the Movement for Social Justice," in George Hunsinger (ed.), *Karl Barth and Radical Politics* (Philadelphia, 1976), 19-45. However, acknowledging Barth's populist socialist involvement should not minimize the level of commitment that he displayed in struggling with his ecclesiastical responsibilities behind the pulpit. As Barth delighted in saying, "The best and greatest thing I can bring to you as a pastor will always be Jesus Christ." Ibid., p. 19. For further examination of Barth's involvement in the socialist movement in Safenwil up to and including his celebrated "break with liberalism," see McCormack, *Critically Realistic*, pp. 78-125.

17 Karl Barth, *The Word of God and the Word of Man*, trans. Douglas Horton (New York, 1957), p. 100. Italics in original. Despite the common assumption that Barth's break with liberalism took place at the outset of the Great War, McCormack notes that, even before the war, Barth was already leaving the theological path of his teachers when he "learned to be critical of the religious individualism which was celebrated in Marburg." This occurred as early as July 1911 when he gave "socialist speeches" in Safenwil to the local Workers' Union and in which he criticized the view of religion that was dominant in Germany, namely that religion was a matter between God and the soul only. See McCormack, "Unheard Message," p. 60. Willis sees Barth's move into the ministry as displaying "a continuation of both liberal and Reformation elements." Robert E. Willis, *The Ethics of Karl Barth* (Leiden, 1971), p. 7.

18 Barth, *Word of God*, p. 101.

edition Barth informed his readers that his "whole energy of interpreting has been expended in an endeavour to see through and beyond history into the spirit of the Bible, which is the Eternal Spirit."[19]

Third, there are notable shifts in Barth's own hermeneutical reflections made manifest in the prefaces to *Romans*.[20] When one compares the prefaces of the first and second editions,[21] a significant shift of emphasis can be discerned. In the first preface Barth described his task in strictly pneumatocentric terms as "the labour of apprehending" the "Eternal Spirit" of the Bible. In the second preface his view has taken on a decidedly Christocentric form: the goal of exegesis is that "[t]he Word ought to be exposed in the words,"[22] and it is this Word—Jesus Christ—that is the "inner dialectic of the matter [*die Sache*] in the actual words of the text."[23] By the time Barth wrote the third preface in 1922, he appeared to have

---

19 Barth, *Romans*, p. 1.

20 Richard Burnett provides a major contribution to the study of Barth's hermeneutical and methodological self-awareness by drawing careful attention to previously unpublished drafts (recently discovered in the Barth archives in Switzerland) of Barth's first preface to *Romans*. See Richard E. Burnett, *Karl Barth's Theological Exegesis* (Grand Rapids, 2004), pp. 265-92.

21 The preface to the first edition (1918) is just over one page in the translation; in contrast, the preface to the second edition (1921) is 14 pages long.

22 Barth, *Romans*, p. 8.

23 Ibid., p. 10. In previous years scholars have emphasized that Barth's conversion from liberalism led him to discover a "strange new world in the Bible." See, e.g., Neil B. MacDonald, *Karl Barth and the Strange New World within the Bible: Barth, Wittgenstein, and the Metadilemmas of the Enlightenment* (Carlisle, 2000); and George Lindbeck, "Barth and Textuality," *Theology Today*, 43/3 (October 1986): 361-72. Unfortunately, this has often led to speaking of the world-construct of the Bible as if it were the *Sache* to which Barth pointed. But, as Burnett rightly argues, neither the title nor the text of the famous 1917 essay speaks of the biblical *Sache* as "strange." (The original title of Barth's essay was "Die Neue Welt in der Bibel." Cf. Karl Barth, "The Strange New World Within the Bible," in *Word of God*, pp. 28ff.). Rather, "the real impetus behind Barth's theological conversion was not so much his discovery of a 'new world,' a new perspective, *Weltanschauung*, or way-of-being-in-the-world within the Bible as it was his discovery that the Bible's central subject matter, content, and theme was God." See Burnett, *Barth's Exegesis*, p. 74.

Jüngel's explanation of what Barth meant by the "inner dialectic" is especially helpful: "The phrase, 'the inner dialectic' of the '*Sache*' is intended to express the idea that not only speech about the '*Sache*' but also the '*Sache*' itself should be conceived of as dialectical. Accordingly, we are dealing here not simply with a dialectical knowing of a being which in itself is undialectical; rather, the dialectic in human knowing corresponds to a dialectic in the being to be known. The being to be known is itself dialectical." Eberhard Jüngel, "Von der Dialektik zur Analogie: Die Schule Kierkegaards und der Einspruch Petersons," in *Barth Studien: Ökumenische Theologie* (Zurich, 1982), pp. 127-79 at p. 143, cited and translated by Archibald James Spencer, *Clearing a Space for Human Action: Ethical Ontology in the Theology of Karl Barth* (New York, 2003), p. 45. This "dialectic in the being to be known" is what Jüngel calls the *Realdialektik* in God.

settled more firmly on a Christocentric pneumatological emphasis. In response to Bultmann's criticism that there are other spirits who make themselves heard in Paul's epistle other than the Spirit of Christ, Barth rhetorically asked whether "the Spirit of Christ [can] be thought of as standing in the Epistle side by side with other spirits and in competition to them."[24] Barth saw such a view as "impossible," and he argued that only the "Spirit of Christ" is "the veritable subject-matter [*die wirkliche Sache*] of the Epistle."[25] Indeed, Barth insisted:

> … the extent to which the commentator will be able to disclose the Spirit of Christ in his reading of Paul will not be everywhere the same. But he will know that the responsibility rests on his shoulders, and he will not let himself be bewildered by the voices of those other spirits, which so often render inaudible the dominant tones of the Spirit of Christ. … [A]ll other spirits are seen in some way or other to serve the Spirit of Christ.[26]

If one accepts that Barth's prefaces give insight into his own developing hermeneutical self-understanding,[27] the above noted progression is significant. Should these shifts be viewed as substantial or merely incremental? The conceptual shifts represented in the prefaces might suggest that Barth had a substantial theological change of mind on what the essential subject-matter of the Bible is, but it is highly unlikely that he could have intended to differentiate substantially and sharply between the "Eternal Spirit of the Bible" spoken of in the first preface and "the Spirit of Christ" spoken of in the third preface. More likely, the shifts represented Barth's own sharpening of his original understanding of the very nature of the Eternal Spirit. What started out as an admittedly generic (and possibly anthropologically derived) concept became thoroughly sharpened by Barth's Christological emphasis evident in the second edition. Therefore, Barth did not so much change his mind that the "Eternal Spirit" is the subject-matter of the Bible, as wrestle (between 1918 and 1922) over how consistently to relate pneumatology to what was becoming his Christological centre. Furthermore, though his repeated use of the Pauline phrase "Spirit of Christ" in the third preface need not imply at this early stage that he had already adopted the filioque, Barth's determination to hear no other spirit but the Spirit of Christ suggests that he had set out on a theological trajectory that was eventually favorable to it.

---

24 Barth, *Romans*, pp. 16-17.

25 Ibid., p. 17. Barth uses the phrase "Spirit of Christ" no less than 11 times in the third preface.

26 Ibid.

27 Burnett, *Barth's Exegesis*, p. 8.

The Role of the Holy Spirit in the Theology of Romans

The genre of Barth's *Romans* as a theological commentary makes the task of delineating his pneumatology more difficult than it is in the *Göttingen Dogmatics* if for no other reason than the fact that he was seeking to exegete a biblical text rather than provide a dogmatic exposition on particular theological loci. However, it is possible to outline Barth's view of the Spirit in *Romans* programmatically in the following fourfold description:

> *The Holy Spirit is (1) God himself in infinite qualitative distinction from humanity (2) who freely enables humans, by faith, to apprehend contemporaneously the revelation of God (3) in union with the resurrected Jesus Christ (4) without thereby erasing or diminishing the distinction between divine and human.*

The exposition which follows will seek to unpack the four major elements of this pneumatological description.

The Spirit is God himself in infinite qualitative distinction from humanity It is well known that Barth asserted that if there is a recognized system in *Romans*, it was a system attributed to Kierkegaard:[28] the "infinite qualitative distinction" that exists between God and the world, between eternity and time.[29] Indeed, it is Barth's consistently sharp distinction of the *Krisis* or diastasis between the divine and human that was instrumental in leading commentators to describe the theology of the second edition of *Romans* "dialectical theology."[30]

---

[28] Perhaps it is too easily forgotten that Barth had a longstanding appreciation of Kierkegaard. In an article written in the early 1960s, Barth insisted, "I have remained faithful to Kierkegaard's *reveille*, as we heard it then, throughout my theological life, and I am so today still." Barth went on to say that the lack of reference to Kierkegaard in his later writings is not because of his lack of appreciation for him, but because Kierkegaard's existentialism was too much a product of the nineteenth century. In the end, Barth insisted, "I consider [Kierkegaard] to be a teacher into whose school every theologian must go once. Woe to him who has missed it! So long as he does not remain in or return to it!" Karl Barth, "A Thank You and a Bow: Kierkegaard's Reveille," trans. H. M. Rumscheidt, *Canadian Journal of Theology*, 11 (1965): 3-7 at 5. For further comment on Barth's relationship to Kierkegaard, see Torrance, *Karl Barth, Biblical and Evangelical Theologian*, pp. 44ff.

[29] Barth, *Romans*, p. 10. The paradoxical tension between God and humanity is not a theological *novum* in *Romans*, but is consistent with what Barth had been insisting upon since at least 1915: "The world is the world. But God is God." Karl Barth, "Kriegszeit und Gottesreich," a lecture delivered in Basel on 15 November 1915, cited in Busch, *Karl Barth*, p. 87.

[30] McCormack, *Critically Realistic*, p. 23.

Evidence of the infinite qualitative distinction in *Romans* has been well rehearsed in the literature and need not be repeated here.[31] However, two lines of thinking will briefly illustrate the depth of this theme. First, from the opening pages Barth highlights the altereity both of the Gospel and of the Apostle authorized to deliver it: "The Gospel is not one thing in the midst of other things, to be directly apprehended [*direkt zu verstehendes*] and comprehended [*erfassendes*]."[32] Nor is the Gospel "a religious message to inform mankind of their divinity or to tell them how they may become divine."[33] In stark contrast to all other claims to truth, the Gospel "sets a question-mark against all truths."[34] It is "the victory by which the world is overcome," and it is "by the Gospel the whole concrete world is dissolved and established."[35]

In addition, the sharp distinction also applies to the messenger of the Gospel, the Apostle Paul himself. Only one peculiarly speaking from the side of God can claim to be an apostle of the Gospel, because "the pure non-ecclesiastical Gospel is proclaimed by no human mouth,"[36] even by as great a man as Paul. Paul does not speak from his personal perspective as a mere participant in human history, but as an Apostle, "set apart for the Gospel of God."[37] Barth insists: "[The Apostle] stands in no organic relationship with human society as it exists in history: seen from the point of view of human society, he can be regarded only as an exception [*Ausnahme*], nay rather, as an impossibility [*unmögliche Erscheinung*]."[38] As an Apostle of God, Paul is "in contradiction to himself and in distinction from all others." Consequently, though Paul can be called a Pharisee—"'separated,' isolated and distinct," he is also a "Pharisee of a higher order" and, in his relation to God, "he is unique."[39]

Second, throughout *Romans* Barth made use of several metaphors that point to the diastasis or *Krisis* between God and the world. For example, there is a

---

[31] See especially, Michael Beintker, *Die Dialektik in der "Dialektischen Theologie" Karl Barths* (Munich, 1987); Thomas F. Torrance, *Karl Barth: An Introduction to his Early Theology, 1910-1931* (London, 1962).

[32] Barth, *Romans*, p. 28.

[33] Ibid.

[34] Ibid., p. 35.

[35] Ibid. As will be seen, the juxtaposition of "dissolving" [*aufgehoben*] and "establishing" [*begründet*] will be an important characteristic of Barth's dialectical pneumatology.

[36] Ibid., p. 333.

[37] Rom. 1:1 (NRSV).

[38] Barth, *Romans*, pp. 27-28. The words *unmögliche Erscheinung* might better be translated here as "an impossible appearance." It is not that "Paul" is himself an impossibility, but that his appearing on the scene of human history, in and of himself, as an apostle of God is impossible.

[39] Ibid., p. 27.

"gulf which separates God and man";[40] a "frontier between God and man"; an "inexorable barrier and obstacle";[41] and an "abyss which separates men from God."[42] There is no evidence in *Romans* that Barth ever saw the diastasis being annulled or synthesized. On the contrary, Barth's key note during his *Romans* period is that "God is assuredly not the world,"[43] nor does his distinction from the world stand in a kind of equilibrium with the world.

Since our primary interest is in pneumatology, the question is: how does Barth regard the Spirit in view of the infinite qualitative distinction? There is every indication in *Romans* that the Spirit is to be identified fully with God himself. This is made especially clear, for example, in Barth's exposition on Romans 8. There Barth was explicit that though the Spirit is a paradox, "describable only in negatives," we must nevertheless "worship Him as the third Person of the Godhead, await Him, pray for Him, and, confident in His peculiar and particular and quite definite action, be silent in the presence of His power and take care lest we should cause Him tribulation."[44] In all of this, Barth warned, it must never be forgotten that the Spirit is "completely the Other."[45] Even when the Spirit is said to come "near" to the world, he does so only as one who "touches it as a tangent touches a circle, that is, without touching it."[46] In Barth's mind, there is to be no confusion: "there is no partner or opponent of the Spirit"[47] because the Spirit is none other than God himself.

A fundamental aspect of Barth's pneumatology in *Romans,* then, can be characterized as displaying a Kierkegaardian form of dialectical opposition which was meant "to establish more clearly the absolute distance that separates human beings from God."[48] Though Barth insisted that the "Spirit thinks and acts and works," in saying this we also confess that "He has spoken and acted in direct contradiction of everything that I can say or thou canst hear—He contradicts even our questioning. He is completely the Other. Confronting Him, we are confronted with perfected speech and with perfected action."[49] As completely Other, he is not simply pure negation nor is he known by the *via negativa* alone. Rather he is simultaneously both negation and affirmation. "The Spirit is the 'Yes' from which proceeds the negative knowledge which men have of themselves. As negation,

---

[40] Ibid., p. 31.

[41] Ibid., p. 53.

[42] Ibid., p. 332.

[43] Ibid., p. 83.

[44] Ibid., p. 274.

[45] Ibid., p. 275.

[46] Ibid., p. 30.

[47] Ibid., p. 283.

[48] William McDonald, "Søren Kierkegaard," *The Stanford Encyclopedia of Philosophy (Summer 2005 Edition)*, ed. Edward N. Zalta, available from: http://plato.stanford.edu/archives/sum2005/entries/kierkegaard (accessed 3 December 2008).

[49] Barth, *Romans*, p. 275.

the Spirit is the frontier and meaning and reality of human life: as affirmation, the Spirit is the new, transfigured reality which lies beyond this frontier."[50] Or again, "Spirit means that 'Either-Or' in which all antithesis is already destroyed by the victory of the 'Either' over the 'Or.'"[51] This oppositional dialectic, of seeming Kierkegaardian pedigree, is fundamental to Barth's pneumatology. But, as will be shown shortly, his pneumatology also displays elements of a more Hegelian-like dialectic.

... who freely enables humans, by faith, to apprehend contemporaneously the revelation of God Given Barth's insistence of the permanence of the infinite qualitative distinction, and given the fact that God and Gospel stand on the opposing shore of the divide, the question is: how is it possible for humans to receive this alien Gospel, let alone speak it or proclaim it with any intelligibility? This is a question that Barth had clearly wrestled with in his responsibilities as a pastor who sought to deliver meaningful sermons to his parishioners but found himself frustrated by his inability to carry out the task. Indeed, the altereity of God and the Gospel that Barth discovered in *Romans* constituted for him a crisis of biblical exegesis and was largely responsible for his "departure from accepted hermeneutical practice."[52] Indeed, Barth came to the conclusion that the goal of "genuine exegesis" of Scripture needed to be far more ambitious—more critical[53]—than what he observed in the historical critics of the academy. This already comes through subtly, though recognizably, in the preface to the first edition. There Barth began with a contrast between the historical-critical method of biblical interpretation and the doctrine of Inspiration. He comments:

> Were I driven to choose between [the historical-critical method] and the venerable doctrine of Inspiration, I should without hesitation adopt the latter, which has a broader, deeper and more important justification. The doctrine of Inspiration is concerned with the labour of apprehending [*Verstehens*],[54] without which no technical equipment, however complete, is of any use whatever.[55]

Significantly, Barth aligned the "labour of apprehending" on the side of the doctrine of Inspiration, and therefore in connection with pneumatology, rather

---

50 Ibid., p. 272.

51 Ibid., p. 283. Cf. Kierkegaard's *Either/Or: A Fragment of Life.*

52 J. B. Webster, "'On the Frontiers of What Is Observable': Barth's *Römerbrief* and Negative Theology," *Downside Review* 105 (July 1987): 169-80 at 169.

53 Barth, *Romans*, p. 8.

54 The translator of the *Römerbrief* has fairly consistently (though not completely) rendered the term *verstehen* and its related forms as "apprehend."

55 Barth, *Romans*, p. 1.

than on exegetical technique and therefore in connection with anthropology.[56] This is confirmed throughout the commentary in how Barth regularly speaks of the "apprehension of revelation" being made possible only by the Holy Spirit. As Barth argued early on, critical exegesis, while necessary, can only accomplish so much. Consequently, "the commentator must be possessed of a wider intelligence than that which moves within the boundaries of his own natural appreciation."[57] For Barth, this "wider intelligence" is none other than the Holy Spirit himself who enables the human to apprehend God's own revelation of himself.

So, according to Barth, what occurs when the Spirit enables apprehension of revelation? An important point needs be clarified in this regard —namely that apprehension of revelation, because it is, by definition, revelation *of God*, can never be completely possessed by the human, but comes only as a gift of God received in the "miracle of faith."[58] Barth made it abundantly clear throughout the commentary that all that is available to humans is the "residue" of revelation, which Barth variously identified as an "impress of revelation" [*Eindruck von Offenbarung*],[59] a "burnt-out crater,"[60] or "dry canal" left over from the original revelation of God in his acts in Israel culminating in Jesus.[61] While impressions of

---

[56] It is also understandable why many of Barth's critics accused Barth of engaging in a purely "pneumatic exegesis" that appeared to set aside all human efforts at understanding the Bible text. But what was not understood is that Barth was not less interested in the meaning of the text as the biblical author intended it, but that he wanted to break through the meaning of the biblical text itself to that to which the text pointed—to the "inner dialectic of the matter," as he put it.

[57] Barth, *Romans*, p. 8.

[58] Ibid., p. 121. "The miracle of faith which Abraham encountered was entered in his account as divine righteousness. Contrasted with all human being and having and doing, this transaction is effective and is free, and because it is free, it is the authentic action of God. Through what they are not, men participate in what God is."

[59] E.g., ibid., pp. 65, 72, 74, 78, 79, 87, 90, 129, 133,183, 260. Barth also carried the language of the "impress of revelation" or the "impress of the Word" into the *CD*, but there makes a much more explicit connection to a Christocentric pneumatology: "He is the Spirit of the Word itself who brings to our ears the Word and nothing but the Word. Subjective revelation can be only the repetition, the impress, the sealing of objective revelation upon us; or, from our point of view, our own discovery, acknowledgement and affirmation of it." *CD* I/2, p. 239. See also *CD* II/2, p. 35.

[60] E.g., Barth, *Romans*, pp. 65, 74.

[61] E.g., Ibid., pp. 65, 339, 416. Barth is quick to point out that those who perceive the impressions of revelation yield no greater advantage than those who do not. The Apostle says, "But if thou be a transgressor of the law, thy circumcision is become uncircumcision" (Rom. 2:25). Commenting on this, Barth asserts, "Here bursts upon us the unavoidable relativism. The impress of revelation possessed by the children of God becomes a human worldly factor side by side with other factors. Their claim to absolute superiority over others falls therefore to the ground. … The sign-post has become meaningless." Ibid., p. 74.

revelation are, for Barth, evident in the history of Israel and the Church,[62] as well as in the giving of the Law and of Holy Scripture,[63] the impressions are nevertheless not to be identified wholly with revelation but are only and always "sign-posts" pointing to the original and primal revelation.[64]

What, then, is the revelation of God? Barth's answer is consistently clear: revelation is the disclosure of Jesus as the Christ and corresponds to the years AD 1-30 as the Primal Origin of revelation, the "era of revelation and disclosure,"[65] a unique era that makes "every epoch a potential field of revelation and disclosure."[66] But note well: just as revelation is not to be confused with the history of revelation or even with the Bible, neither is revelation for Barth simply and without qualification identical to the Incarnation of Jesus. Rather, revelation is the *disclosure*, fulfilled and made possible by Jesus' life, death and resurrection, that Jesus *is* the Christ. In other words, revelation is the existential, non-temporal "Moment"[67] when Jesus is correctly identified and acknowledged to be who he really is—the Resurrected Lord and Son of God—through the free and gracious act of the Holy Spirit. "The appointment of Jesus to be the Christ takes place in the Spirit and must be apprehended in the Spirit. It is self-sufficient, unlimited, and in itself true."[68]

The important point to be emphasized here is that Barth's emerging theology of revelation in *Romans* places special weight on the work of the Spirit in making the living and eternal Jesus Christ contemporaneous to humans in history. In other words, it is only by the Spirit that humans come to know of God in the risen Jesus Christ, despite the permanent reality of the infinite qualitative distinction. The gap is not closed or filled in by revelational ballast, as it were, but it is traversed—objectively traversed in the Incarnation, but subjectively apprehended by humans in and through the objective Spirit. To know Christ by the Spirit is both to know clearly of the gap separating God and man and the way by which God in Christ bridges that gap.[69] Without the Spirit objectively enacting this subjective apprehension in the human of the fact of God's initiative in Christ, revelation is incomplete and therefore, by definition, no revelation at all. This is the way in which (objectively) "the Spirit thinks and acts and works" such that humans are (subjectively) "confronted with perfected speech and with perfected

---

62 This comes out especially in Barth's exposition on Romans 9. Ibid., pp. 330-61.

63 "The law is the impression of divine revelation left behind in time, in history, in the lives of men." Ibid., p. 65.

64 Ibid.

65 Ibid., pp. 29-30.

66 Ibid., p. 29.

67 Barth uses the term dozens of times throughout the commentary to designate the point in time, which is paradoxically not in time, of the occurrence of revelation.

68 Barth, *Romans*, p. 36.

69 Ibid., p. 31.

action"[70]—God revealing himself in his Word, Jesus Christ. Put epigrammatically, for Barth apprehension of revelation *is* the moment in which "we are apprehended and known by God."[71]

...in union with the resurrected Jesus Christ Barth's stress upon apprehension of revelation by the Spirit could suggest that, for him, the event of revelation is purely a noetic transaction, as though cognizance of a truth is the extent of revelation. Indeed, this kind of characterization of Barth was and is still common, though misleading. However, the noetic aspect of "spiritual apprehension" does not exhaust Barth's concept of the apprehension of revelation and is complemented by Barth's consistent connection of the Spirit to the resurrection of Jesus Christ as the locus of ontic union with him. As Barth explains:

> In the Resurrection the new world of the Holy Spirit touches the world of the flesh, but touches it as a tangent touches a circle, that is, without touching it. … The Resurrection is therefore an occurrence in history which took place outside the gates of Jerusalem in the year A.D. 30, inasmuch as it there "came to pass," was discovered and recognized. But inasmuch as the occurrence was conditioned by the Resurrection, in so far, that is, as it was not the "coming to pass," … the Resurrection is not an event in history at all. Jesus is declared to be the Son of God wherever He reveals Himself and is recognized as the Messiah, before the first Easter Day and, most assuredly, after it.[72]

One should take note of the twosideness inherent in Barth's entire description of the Resurrection. In the Resurrection by the Spirit, the new world and old world touch, but do not touch; the Resurrection of Jesus that "came to pass" by the Spirit makes possible the "coming to pass" of our Resurrection in the Spirit; in the Resurrection of Jesus, the "historical" comes together with that which is "not historical"; and in the Resurrection, "before Easter" is brought together with "after Easter." Yet, as will be explored further below, in each instance, the distinction between the pairs is not erased or synthesized, but upheld, not in symmetrical equilibrium, to be sure, but in an asymmetrical union.

What should be made of the fact that Jesus is bodily resurrected from the dead while humans—even humans who, in the Spirit, have apprehended the resurrected Christ—have not yet received this resurrection? It is here that Barth sounded the eschatological note: the Resurrection has first and foremost to do with hope. "Hope is the solution of the riddle of our 'As though.' We do see. Existentially we see what to us is invisible, and therefore we wait. … We can then, if we understand

[70] Ibid., p. 275.

[71] Ibid., p. 282.

[72] Ibid., p. 30. For a definitive account of Barth's doctrine of the Resurrection, see R. Dale Dawson, *The Resurrection in Karl Barth* (Aldershot, 2006).

ourselves aright, be none other than they who wait."[73] Indeed, Barth insists, "If Christianity be not altogether thoroughgoing eschatology, there remains no relationship whatever with Christ. … Redemption is invisible, inaccessible, and impossible, for it meets us only in hope."[74]

However, Barth warned against making the mistake of confusing the temporal future with the eschatological hope of the Resurrection. This would be to blur the distinction between time and eternity. On the contrary, "the Gospel of the Resurrection of our body … cannot refer to any past or present or future, but only to the all-embracing Futurum resurrectionis: *He shall quicken*."[75] In other words, the "shall" of the confession points to a "Beyond that is beyond 'Here and There.'" The hope of the Resurrection in the Spirit is a binding relation of union, constituted in hope, to God in Jesus Christ by the Spirit. This union is "our hope, our undying portion, and our indestructible relation with God."[76] In essence, "The Futurum resurrectionis reminds us that we have been speaking of God and not of some human possibility."[77]

For Barth, then, the biblical phrase, "walking in the Spirit," refers most specifically to the Moment of revelation when the human simultaneously receives, understands, and apprehends the contradiction of his existence against God, *and* when he is joined in union with Jesus Christ by the power of the Spirit. This is the "eternal turning-point and decision." Barth explained:

> At the incredible point where we discover the question-mark which is set against us—set against us manifestly by One that we are not—we encounter eternity; united with Christ, we are apprehended and known by God, and we possess the possibility which is beyond all possibility, the impossible possibility of walking *after the Spirit*. ... Our whole behaviour, the course of our existence, is lived after the Spirit and is defined by the knowledge of the Son of God. The Son of God, the Lord, in whom we recognize ourselves to be united to Him in the likeness of His death—that is to say, in our death (vi.5)—is the turning-point, the decision, the divine Victory; He is the wholly Other of God; He is—the Spirit (2 Cor. iii.17).[78]

Herein lies the second foci of Barth's dialectical pneumatology, a dialectical form more akin to Hegel's dialectical *Aufhebung* than Kierkegaard's dialectic of opposition.[79] For though Barth maintains the Otherness of God and his Spirit, there

---

73 Ibid., pp. 314-15. Cf. Rom. 8:24 (NRSV) "Hope that is seen is not hope."

74 Ibid., p. 314.

75 Ibid., p. 289. Emphasis in original.

76 Ibid., p. 288.

77 Ibid., p. 306.

78 Ibid., p. 282. Emphasis in original.

79 For a careful examination of the relation of Hegel and Kierkegaard, see Jon Stewart, *Kierkegaard's Relations to Hegel Reconsidered* (Cambridge, 2003).

is a simultaneous unification with God in Jesus Christ. This, then, leads us to the final aspect of the programmatic statement.

... Without thereby erasing or diminishing the distinction between divine and human This final aspect of our working description of Barth's pneumatology in *Romans* is also, in certain respects, its linchpin. For, though the Spirit is the one by which humans apprehend the revelation of God in the resurrected Christ, such apprehension never succumbs to a form of spiritual synthesis in which the human is made divine or the divine is made human. Rather, it is in the Spirit and in the light of God's knowledge of the resurrection in Christ that the contrast between God and humanity is made all the more apparent. Nevertheless, Barth insisted, "by the same illumination the contrast is overcome and dissolved."[80] Is this not a contradiction? Barth admitted that speaking in a way in which contrast between God and the world is both highlighted *and* overcome is problematic. This is because, in reality, even the concept of "contrast" must be understood as only a figure of speech. Normally, when one speaks of a "contrast" between two things there needs to be some similarity or some shared element for the contrast to be meaningful. The contrast between white and black, for example, is possible only on the basis that both black and white are what they are relative to their respective reflection or absorption of light. However, in the theological realm, such an "analogical" contrast between divine and human are spoken of only provisionally and metaphorically. Here it is helpful to hear Barth at length:

> Only in parable can we represent what is finite as though it were a thing contrasted with what is infinite. Only in a parable can we contrast the death of our body with the life of the Spirit of God in us. According to the reality which is beyond our observation, what is finite is not set over against what is infinite, but rather by [*sic*] it is wholly dissolved and therefore wholly established [*sondern es ist in jenem schlechthin aufgehoben,*[81] *aber auch begründet*]. Its dissolution is that by which it is established [*daß seine Aufgehoben seine Begründung ist*]. Thus, according to the unobservable reality, our body is no second, other thing, existing side by side with the Spirit of God that dwelleth in us: the Spirit is rather the altogether restless death of the body, and as such is also its altogether restless life.[82]

---

[80] Ibid., p. 288.

[81] The term here, clearly echoing Hegel, is problematic for translation because *aufgehoben* could also be translated as "reversed" or "abolished." For an especially helpful examination of Hegel's doctrine of the Trinity and his concept of *Aufgehoben*, see Dale M. Schlitt, "The Whole Truth: Hegel's Reconceptualization of Trinity," *The Owl of Minerva*, 15/2 (Spring 1984): 169-82.

[82] Barth, *Romans*, pp. 288-89.

This passage provides further evidence of what was alluded to earlier, namely that Barth viewed the principal role of the Spirit as holding together that which is qualitatively distinct—the divine and the human—but not in order to form a *tertium quid* or higher synthesis, nor even to bring between two things in a kind of symmetrical equilibrium. On the contrary, the Spirit brings and holds the two into an asymmetrical union in which the "lower" is first of all "dissolved" but then "established" or transformed by the "higher."[83] That is to say, Barth posited a "dialectical" pneumatology in which the Spirit is understood as simultaneously highlighting the infinite qualitative distinction between God and humanity (i.e., the Kierkegaardian dialectic) while binding together these same infinitely and qualitatively distinct entities, including eternity and time, divinity and humanity, the eschatological and the historical (i.e., the *Aufhebung* or Hegelian-like dialectic). But in Barth's dialectic, the Spirit binds the infinitely and qualitatively distinct together in such a way that the "lower" of the dialectical pair is taken up and transformed by the "higher" without changing its essential nature.[84] This is, for Barth, the meaning of the work of the Spirit in "redemption"—the redemption of time and humanity, without their erasure or disintegration, what could be called a union-in-distinction and a distinction-in-union of eternity and time, divinity and humanity.

In another important passage, Barth described this union-in-distinction as the essence of what it means to live in the "newness of the Spirit." For Barth, the work of the Spirit is the dissolution of pure differentiated duality and the establishment of differentiated union. Again, Barth needs to be heard at length:

---

[83] The terms "lower" and "higher" are used here not in an essentialist or Platonic manner, but more metaphorically to indicate priority. In addition, McCormack, drawing on Michael Beintker's terminology, describes two basic types of dialectic in the early Barth as "supplementary" and "complementary." In "complementary" dialectic "two members stand over against each other in a relation of open contradiction or antithesis" (what we are calling here the Kierkegaardian form) whereas in "supplementary" dialectic "one member of a pair predominates in value and potency over the other" but "gives way to reconciliation" (which is closer to the Hegelian form). The pneumatological dialectic described here as an "asymmetrical union" is an example of what Beintker calls a "supplementary" dialectic. See McCormack, *Critically Realistic*, p. 163.

[84] This type of dialectic also anticipates Barth's rediscovery of the Reformed doctrine of an anhypostatic Christology (during his time at Göttingen) which, analogously, reflects this asymmetrical relationship. That is, God became incarnate in human flesh, but not in a particular pre-existing human individual. In this way, the human flesh—though really and veritably human—is created and transformed to become human in the fullest sense of the term. This is accomplished by virtue of the fact that the second Person of the Trinity takes up human flesh, but does not transubstantiate the human flesh of Jesus into something other than truly human flesh. See McCormack, *Critically Realistic*, pp. 327-28, 360-67; and Stephen H. Webb, *The Divine Voice* (Grand Rapids, 2004), pp. 191-97.

> Here is dissolved [*aufgehoben*] the terrible weight which infinity imposes upon what is finite. Dissolved also is that embarrassment which everything finite imposes upon infinity. … Dissolved is the impotence of life and the power of death, the mere humanity of men and the mere divinity of God. Dissolved[85] is the duality [*Doppeltheit*] of our life, by which at every moment we are pressed up against the narrow gate of critical negation. For it is this duality which gives us to fear, which makes us appalled by the ambiguity of our being and the riddle of our existence. The Spirit, which we have received and by which we have passed from death to life, brings this duality to an end [*die Aufhebung dieser Doppeltheit*].[86] Christ in us, the new man, stands in the singleness of His victory of life over death. By this One-ness the Gordian knot is severed, and men stand no longer over against God … Now they are Sons, hearing the voice of the Father, forgetting the 'otherness' of God but first forgetting their own 'otherness'—and from henceforth neither knowing or willing aught else but the glory and blessedness of God: God Himself, and God only! This Spirit of Sonship, this new man who I am not, is my unobservable, existential EGO. … "Such is the description of the Kingdom of Christ; such is the veritable work and the notable service of God; such is the operation of the Spirit in the believer" (Luther).[87]

The pneumatology reflected in this passage illustrates Barth's attempt to overcome the dangers of ontological dualism (i.e., distinction-in-separation) in favor of ontological union (i.e., distinction-in-conjunction, or distinction-in-union). Barth admitted that human "thought cannot escape from dualism." Nevertheless, he explained, "We know that we are unable to comprehend otherwise than by means of a dialectical dualism, in which one must become two in order that it may be veritably one. So it is when [God] manifests Himself to the men of this world as God."[88] In other words, ontic union between God and humanity, which Barth argued is the original created state between God and humans,[89] is broken down in noetic awareness of "Otherness" and degenerates into human awareness of what can only be described as a falsely perceived ontological dualism. This is not how it ought to be, and it is the work of the Spirit to dissolve the false noetic awareness

---

85 The original, *aufgehoben*, is emphasized.

86 The translation "brings to an end" is somewhat misleading because it is not as if the duality disappears per se. Though less smooth, the translation should probably read, "sublates the duality."

87 Barth, *Romans,* pp. 297-98.

88 Ibid., p. 358.

89 "How could I be led by the Spirit, … were it not that the chasm [*Kluft*] between 'Here' and 'There' was originally no chasm, were it not that originally I shared in the Truth and was originally God's Son? God and His creatures originally one stock and one family!" The last line is literally, "One stock with the Creator of humans!" [*Eines Geschlechts mit dem Schöpfer der Mensch!*] Ibid., p. 296.

of a false ontological dualism by bringing humans into real ontic union with God in Christ, but without destroying the real distinction that continues between the human and divine. According to Barth, this is what the Bible means when it speaks of the Spirit of Sonship.

This complex dialectical pneumatological concept is perhaps nowhere better illustrated than in Barth's discussion of the original state of Adam with God in the Garden. As Barth explained, "Originally, there was no separation. Men dwelt in the Garden of Eden, in which there were no absolute and relative, no 'Higher' and 'Lower,' no 'There' and 'Here': such distinctions marked the Fall." Thus he can insist, "Men ought not to be independently what they are in dependence upon God; they ought not, as creatures, to be some second thing side by side with the Creator. Men ought not to know that they are merely—men. God knows this, but in His mercy He has concealed it from them."[90] In short, ontic union with God in Christ by the Spirit means the dissolution of a noetic awareness of dualism between divine and human (i.e., as a return or recapitulation of the prelapsarian state in which human knowledge of distinction between God and man did not yet exist) while upholding and establishing the real created ontic distinction between divine and human (the eschatological redemption accomplished by the Spirit).

The Ontic Ground of the Spirit's Dialectical Work

Barth's dialectical pneumatology described above raises one more important question that needs to be answered: if the work of the Spirit is essentially to uphold a distinction-in-union and a union-in-distinction, what is the ontic ground upon which the Spirit is able to do this? In other words, is there evidence in *Romans* to suggest that Barth grounded the work of the Spirit in the economy of salvation by reference to that which he understood antecedently to be the case in the immanent Trinity? The short answer is "yes." However, it is also true that, at this point, Barth is decidedly not thinking explicitly in such technical and formal Trinitarian terminology. Nevertheless, he was already grasping at the ontic ground for the Spirit's work, and, as will be shown, his preliminary and sketchy answer to the question remained latent in his thinking and only resurfaced again in the latter parts of the *CD*.

The context in which Barth hinted at the ontic ground of the Spirit's work occurs in Barth's discussion of the love of the neighbor, as found in his comments on Romans 13 where he asked what it means to live in obedience to the command to love one's neighbor. Barth argues that all that can be said about this must presuppose that it is possible to love the neighbor only by the "outpouring of the Spirit in our hearts." Love of the neighbor is possible only as a "spiritual relationship" of "fellowship" presupposed by the fellowship of the Spirit in Christ. Barth asked, "Do we, in the unknowable neighbour, apprehend and love the Unknown God? Do we, in the complete Otherness of the other … hear the

[90] Ibid., p. 247.

voice of the One?"'[91] Here, again, there is evidence of Barth's desire to uphold, as an outworking of the pouring of the Spirit, both the "Otherness" of the neighbor and the union with the Other as One.

But how does the Spirit accomplish this spiritual fellowship between humans—the *communio sanctorum*—unless the Spirit also accomplishes this within God himself? Barth answered: "Love is the relation between men and their fellow men which is grounded—and therefore broken!—in the knowledge of God. In this relationship of love it is not men who confront men, but God who confronts God." Thus, he can assert, "Love beholds in every concrete neighbour only the parable of him who is to be loved; but nevertheless it does really see … in every temporal 'Thou' the eternal, contrasted 'Thou' apart from whom there is no 'I.'"[92]

Though Barth does not venture comment beyond this, it is our contention that his motif of "God confronting God," evident here only in muted tones in *Romans*, is nevertheless the root of his most mature application of the doctrine of the filioque. Though he does not explicitly specify it here, Barth will eventually identify this "confrontation in God" (or "problem in God" as he will call in it *CD* IV)[93] as a confrontation between the Father and the Son—a confrontation in which one or the other are in "danger" of overpowering or canceling the other, or in which the identity of one is in danger of being absorbed by the other. Yet this does not happen because it is the work of the Spirit within the Trinity simultaneously to hold them together without allowing one to overpower, cancel, or absorb the other. The Father and Son, upheld in their distinction, are also held together in a union of love by the Spirit—the *vinculum (*or *nexus) amoris,* the bond of love between Father and Son. But unlike the traditional Augustinian concept,[94] Barth's concept of the bond of union by the Spirit includes not only the idea of the Spirit as the divine "glue" which bonds Father and Son eternally together in love, but also the idea of a divine "boundary" or "barrier" which prevents the Father and Son from either cancellation or synthesis. In other words, it is the Spirit who overcomes the Kierkegaardian dialectic of antithesis, confrontation, and otherness between the Father and Son, as the one by which the Father and Son come together in union,

---

[91] Ibid., p. 494.

[92] Ibid., p. 495.

[93] See pp. 169-73 below.

[94] If indeed it is an Augustinian concept. According to Osborne, Augustine does not actually hold to a doctrine of the *vinculum amoris*; rather, it was incorrectly attributed to him by Aquinas. As Osborne argues, Aquinas noticed there were problems with speaking of about the Spirit as a "bond of love," and he thinks that Augustine teaches such a concept when in fact he did not. If Osborne is proven correct, this would have profound effects on the interpretation of Augustine's Trinitarian theology, particularly his view of the doctrine of the procession of the Spirit from the Father and Son. See Catherine Osborne, "The *Nexus Amoris* in Augustine's Trinity," in Elizabeth A. Livingstone (ed.), *Studia Patristica Vol. XXII: Proceedings of Tenth International Conference on Patristic Studies in Oxford 1987* (Leuven, 1989), pp. 309-14.

but it is also the Spirit who resists the Hegelian synthesis of Father and Son into a higher undifferentiated Oneness. For Barth, both the Kierkegaardian and Hegelian dialectic are upheld in a sense, but in mutual tension, and it is by the work of the Spirit that this is accomplished.

The pneumatology of *Romans* is one in which the Spirit is understood to be the one who upholds a distinction-in-union and union-in-distinction, not only in upholding the union of divinity and humanity in Jesus Christ (though in *Romans* Barth had relatively little to say about this relationship), but also between the Father and the Son. Therefore Barth felt that the identity and work of the Spirit is best understood when the Spirit is identified simultaneously as the Spirit of the Father and the Spirit of the Son. Consequently, it is not difficult to see how such a pneumatology would undergird and support Barth's later contention that the Spirit proceeds from the Father and the Son (filioque).

Of course, the question remains whether Barth's use of the filioque was ultimately the best way for him to develop this dialectical pneumatology, or even if the filioque was necessary for such development at all. But in whatever fashion that question is finally answered, it is important to keep in mind Barth's early dialectical pneumatology, formed in *Romans*, when one considers how he defended and applied the doctrine of the filioque in his *Church Dogmatics*. There Barth's dialecticism has not been abandoned, even if the expressionist and pastoral tones in which it was originally conceived have faded into the background.

The Göttingen Dogmatics: The Formal Emergence of the Filioque in Barth's Theology

Barth's Transition from Safenwil to Göttingen

A chain of events, beginning with the increased exposure following his famous Tambach lecture, led to an unexpected turn of events in Barth's life. In January 1921, in the midst of his exhausting work of revision on the *Romans* commentary, Barth received an invitation from Johann Adam Heilmann, pastor of the Reformed congregation at Göttingen, to become take up the newly planned post of chair of Reformed Theology at Göttingen.[95] The need for such a post was great, Heilmann explained, because "there [was] insufficient education of the ministers of the Reformed Church." Heilmann also made it clear that Barth was the man of the hour. He emphasized, "I do not want to recreate something old and past, nor even less conjure up any confessional narrowness, but what I would like is that the

[95] Barth himself was careful to clarify, "I owe my invitation to a chair at Göttingen … not to the famous second edition of *Romans*, but to the first, which afterwards faded into oblivion." Busch, *Karl Barth*, p. 123.

charismata that the Lord has given to the Reformed branch of the church should not remain unused, forgotten, and scorned."[96]

The move to Göttingen marked a significant point of transition in Barth's life, and raises the question of how this vocational shift affected his theological development. Migliore is right to assert that the movement from the pastorate in Safenwil to the professorate in Göttingen "involve[d] certain losses as well as gains."[97] As is commonly understood under the von Balthasarian schema, Barth's move to Göttingen marked the first step of transition away from his early dialectical style of theology to the foundations of his later dogmatic style.[98] In other words, it is assumed that Göttingen marked the end of Barth the dialectical preacher and the beginning of Barth the dogmatician. While certainly not wanting to underemphasize the obvious shifts evidenced in Barth's literary style, shifts in written style do not necessarily also imply a major alteration in his material pastoral concerns. Karl Barth the Safenwil preacher and Karl Barth the Göttingen dogmatician should not be divorced so quickly. After all, Barth's task was to educate ministers, and it is surely the case that his experience in Safenwil was at least partly responsible for his call to Göttingen. So it is not merely that the pastor became the theologian, but, as Migliore rightly notes, "[w]e see a Barth in the *Göttingen Dogmatics* who tenaciously does theology—indeed, defines theology—in relation to preaching and pastoral praxis."[99]

Barth himself supported this view when in his 1922 Schulpforta address, he asserted, "Understand clearly therefore that I speak to you today more as a minister to colleagues than as a professor. … If then I have not only a *view*point, but something also of a *stand*point, it is simply the familiar standpoint of the man in the pulpit."[100] In this sense, it may be helpful to understand Barth's material concern both in Safenwil and Göttingen to be that of a single standpoint—the

96 Letter to Karl Barth from Johann Adam Heilmann, 29 January 1921, Karl Barth Archives, Basel, Switzerland. As cited in Karl Barth, *The Theology of the Reformed Confessions,* ed. and trans. Darrell L. Guder and Judith J. Guder (Louisville, 2002), p. vii. A later letter, dated 16 August 1921, from Carl Heinrich Becker, a Prussian minister, instructed Barth that his first assignment at Göttingen was to teach "Introduction to the Reformed confession, Reformed doctrine and Reformed church life." As cited in Busch, *Karl Barth*, pp. 128-29.

97 Daniel I. Migliore, "Karl Barth's First Lectures in Dogmatics: Instruction in the Christian Religion," in Hannelotte Reiffen (ed.), *The Göttingen Dogmatics: Instruction in the Christian Religion*, trans. Geoffrey W. Bromiley (Grand Rapids, 1991), pp. xv-lxii at p. lxii.

98 Significantly, von Balthasar does not deal with the *Göttingen Dogmatics*, no doubt because they were not yet published when he completed his study. Instead, he moves from the second edition of the *Römerbrief* (1922) to the *Prolegomena zur Christlichen Dogmatik* (1928). One wonders how von Balthasar's periodization of Barth's theological development might have been different had he been able to examine the *Göttingen Dogmatics*!

99 Migliore, "Karl Barth's First Lectures," p. lxii.

100 Barth, *Word of God*, pp. 103-104. Emphasis in original.

preacher in the pulpit—though now from two distinct perspectives or viewpoints—in Safenwil as a minister and in Göttingen as a professor of dogmatics.

Another important factor to consider in the relationship between the Barth of Safenwil and the Barth of Göttingen is that Barth's appointment to the chair of Reformed theology forced upon him the need to think precisely about what it meant to do *Reformed* theology. This was, after all, a central part of his mandate at Göttingen: to teach the Reformed faith in the midst of a dominantly Lutheran faculty. The dawning realization of the weight of this task is appropriately illustrated in Barth's September 1923 Emden lecture addressed to the General Assembly of the German Reformed Church.[101] Reacting in part to the "practical unionizing tendencies of the old Reformed churchmen," Barth chastised those who sought fellowship "as untheologically as possible,"[102] arguing instead that the doctrinal identity of the Reformed church remained an essential matter. This was especially the case in light of the anticipated ecumenical clash with the Roman Catholic Church, which was still suspicious of Protestant ecumenical efforts.[103] As he put it, "[H]ow can we take issue with 'Rome' before we have genuinely taken issue with ourselves as to what we non-Roman Christians are, what we represent, and what we desire? Have we today any vigorous community of purpose in distinction to Catholicism?"[104] Barth therefore suggested that the Reformed churches should agree "upon a creed which should be Reformed but also plainly and explicitly *new*, speaking in *our own* language out of *our own* experiences to *our own* times."[105] Though he was clearly not ready to pronounce which Reformed creed should be the basis of future reflection,[106] he nevertheless saw the need for Reformed theology "to study toward a new conception of the 'scriptural principle,'" whereby the category of revelation would be redefined in such a way that the Bible could be reread from that viewpoint.[107] Indeed, Barth argued, "the problem of contingent revelation … is today more urgent than ever before. What pulpit is not concerned with it?" Consequently, he asserted, "We may, we must, address ourselves to [the doctrine of Revelation], and not in a haphazard, but in our specifically Reformed fashion; and some day, if the old discernment becomes new in us, we may re-establish for ourselves a theology of the second article, which today is sadly

101 Busch, *Karl Barth*, p. 149.

102 Barth, *Word of God*, p. 224.

103 In 1928 Pope Pius XI, in his encyclical, entitled *Mortalium Animos*, warned against certain Protestant movements that would seek unity of the Church without doctrinal agreement. See Pope Pius XI, *Mortalium Animos*, available from: http://www.vatican.va/holy_father/pius_xi/encyclicals/documents/hf_p-xi_enc_19280106_mortalium-animos_en.html (accessed 3 December 2008).

104 Barth, *Word of God*, p. 224.

105 Ibid., p. 249. Emphasis in original.

106 Though Barth himself appeared to have favored the *Catechismus Genevensis* (1545). Ibid.

107 Ibid., pp. 249-50.

lacking."[108] Beyond the recovery of a Chalcedonian anhypostatic/enhypostatic Christology with which Barth ultimately became associated, he was at this time also seeking to reformulate a "teaching of the Reformed doctrine of the Holy Spirit" that would "become for us a commanding task when in our way amidst our surroundings we witness to God's revelation as the fathers did in their way amidst their surroundings."[109]

The foregoing illustrates how vitally important it is to remember that, despite changes of location and vocation, Barth's substantial concerns were not so much changing as they were being sharpened and theologically focused from a different perspective afforded to him in the professorship at Göttingen. Whereas in Safenwil Barth was a minister—a self-admitted, uninformed Reformed preacher, to be sure[110]—in Göttingen he was now the theological representative "in an official capacity" of the Reformed minister and so sought to address what he deemed to be the central question facing him as such: the need and promise of Christian preaching.[111] If in *Romans* Barth wrote as a theologically concerned preacher, the *GD* furnishes evidence of Barth the pastorally concerned theologian. And whereas the form of the *GD* (in terms of style, genre, and structure) is substantially different from that of *Romans*, the material concern (*die Sache*) remained the same: how is the Word to be exposed in the words?[112] In other words, in Göttingen Barth set about to understand how one can preach with the confidence that one is not merely uttering a human speech, but is speaking the very Word of God, all without forgetting that one is still human, and not God. Barth's construction of his well-known doctrine of the threefold form of the Word of God was, at the very least, a comprehensive attempt to answer this question.

Finally, it should be noted that Barth's writing of the *GD* marks an important stage in the development of his pneumatology in general, and, of his theology

---

108 Ibid., pp. 260-61.

109 Ibid., p. 271.

110 In retrospect, Barth confessed that, upon arrival at Göttingen, "I didn't even have a copy of the Reformed confessions, and I certainly hadn't read them." As cited in Busch, *Karl Barth*, p. 129. Barth came into acquaintance with Heinrich Heppe's *Reformierte Dogmatik* in spring 1924 along with the parallel Lutheran sourcebook of H. Schmid. In light of the mandate to teach Reformed theology, Barth remarked in 1935, "I was equally quite clear that the right thing was, in particular, to link up again with the Reformed, as more than one designed to do at that time." And later, "[Heppe] has done me the service, which he can and will do for others, of bringing me to understand the special direction in which dogmatic science has proceeded in the early Reformed Church." See Karl Barth, "Karl Barth's Foreword," in Heinrich Heppe, *Reformed Dogmatics*, ed. Ernst Bizer (reprint edn, Grand Rapids, 1978), pp. v, vii. (Page citations are to the reprint edition.)

111 Barth, *Word of God*, p. 100.

112 Barth, *Romans*, p. 8. Cf. "[The] participation of human words in God's Word is the principial [*sic*] element in the scripture principle." Barth, *Göttingen Dogmatics*, p. 212. Earlier in the *GD* Barth expresses it more formally: "the principle behind every theological dogma is: *Deus Dixit* ["God speaks"]." Ibid., p. 10.

of the filioque more specifically. Unlike *Romans* where the filioque is not even mentioned (though, as was argued above, it was implicitly supported), in the *GD* Barth had apparently become aware of the filioque as a dogmatic problem. The lecture notes that Barth used to teach his students the theology of the Reformed confession offer evidence that one of his earliest (if not first) written reference to the filioque occurred somewhere in June or early July 1923.[113] Though Barth does not explore the problem to any great extent at this time, the *GD* is important in highlighting how he located the filioque primarily within the discussion of his doctrine of Revelation rather than as a speculative problem on the doctrine of the inner Trinitarian relations.

Barth's Discussion of the Filioque as a Dogmatic Problem

A great deal of scholarship remains to be done on the contribution of the *Göttingen Dogmatics* to Barth's theological development, and a full exposition of Barth's theology therein is clearly beyond the limits of this study.[114] Given the vast material covered in the *GD*, it will be necessary to focus first on Barth's explicit discussion of the filioque in the *GD*. Having accomplished this, we will then work back through the earlier sections to see how he came to conclude tentatively (though not yet tenaciously) in favor of the filioque.

Barth's discussion of the filioque appears in §5 of the *GD* entitled, "God: Father, Son and Holy Spirit" and more specifically (curiously enough) under section III entitled, "Jesus the Kyrios." It is in this section that Barth worked out the theological meaning of the primitive Christian confession, "*Iēsous Kyrios*" ["Jesus is Lord"].[115] An important aspect of this confession is how Christians were (and are) able to make such a confession. How, in other words, can people come to know and confess that Jesus is the divine Lord, that he is God's own revelation of himself, especially given the inaccessibility of such knowledge on the other side of the "gap" between the divine and the human? Barth's answer, which he saw as being clearly commensurate with the Apostle Paul, is by the Holy Spirit.[116] This means that to speak of the Holy Spirit, therefore, is "at all events acutely, existentially, and inescapably personal"[117] because it is by the Spirit that the Lordship of God is not only spoken, but is also spoken *to us*, revealed to us, as

[113] Barth, *Reformed Confessions*, p. 158. For a fuller review of the historical background to the *GD*, see McCormack, *Critically Realistic*, pp. 291-323.

[114] For a comprehensive critical review of the English translation of the *GD*, see George Hunsinger, "Karl Barth's *The Göttingen Dogmatics*," *Scottish Journal of Theology* 46/3 (1993): 371-82.

[115] Cf. Rom. 10:9; 1 Cor. 12:3. Barth, *Göttingen Dogmatics*, pp. 110-30.

[116] Ibid., p. 123. "Therefore I want you to understand that no one speaking by the Spirit of God ever says 'Let Jesus be cursed!' and no one can say 'Jesus is Lord' except by the Holy Spirit." 1 Cor. 12:3 (NRSV).

[117] Barth, *Göttingen Dogmatics*, p. 126.

it were, in contingency and freedom, but not by theological or logical necessity. Humans cannot possess the Spirit, or knowledge of revelation as a "given," but can only pray that the "Creator Spirit," by his "perpetual operation," would come.[118] We must never forget, Barth exhorts, that "even in his direct proximity as the Spirit of the Son, he is distant as the Spirit of the Father."[119] Evidently, Barth has not left his dialectic pneumatology, first evident in *Romans*, behind in the *GD*!

The Spirit's coming to humanity in revealing the Son of the Father, while contingent, is not arbitrary, nor merely the outworking of an accidental relation between God and humanity.[120] On the contrary, "God's relation [to humanity] … is necessarily contained and grounded in God's being. All that the Father does and the Son does, the Spirit does with them." Such a statement rests, Barth argues, "on the deep insight that God would not be God if the relation to us were not intrinsic to him from the very first."[121] Thus, Barth establishes in the *GD* a clear statement of his "rule" of revelation, namely, that God reveals himself economically in correspondence to his existence in eternity and in himself. Or in short, God reveals himself to us as God really is in himself.

Having made clear this theological principle, Barth thereby introduced the doctrine of the filioque to his students by informing them of the traditional language of pneumatology in which the Spirit's relation to the Father and the Son is spoken of in terms of *spiratio,* "the procession of God from himself."[122] Yet Barth admits that no one really can know the difference between the "procession" of the Spirit and the "generation" of the Son, and that theologians are hereby reminded that "our perspicacity really fails at some points."[123] Given the difficulty of the terminology, then, in introducing the filioque debate to his students, Barth admitted, "It is hard to discuss the matter. For us a certain obscurity lies over the conflict. I do not recall having heard or read anything very plausible about it."[124] Nevertheless, he acknowledged his awareness of at least two of the major attempts to bring resolution to the filioque controversy: the Council of Florence (1439) and the Old Catholic Conference in Bonn (1875). Barth noted that the Western Florentine theologians were ready to concede that the Spirit proceeded from the Father *through the Son* [*per filium*]. However, the Greeks wanted to insist that the Spirit proceeds from the Father alone. As he explains:

> In the West … this *per filium* was taken to mean that the Son has from the Father the power that means the Spirit proceeds from him as well as from the Father. They viewed the *spiratio* as the act of the Father and Son united as

[118] Ibid., p. 127.

[119] Ibid.

[120] Ibid., p. 128.

[121] Ibid.

[122] Ibid.

[123] Ibid., p. 129.

[124] Ibid.

> one *principium* in this instance. In contrast, the Easterners would agree only that the Son was a cause or instrument in the hand of the Father.[125]

At this point, Barth was clearly struggling to make sense of the debate, and one can justly be wary of Barth's own description of the positions. Nevertheless, Barth raised his own suspicions of the Eastern position. He asked:

> Do we have in the Greek view an unsubjugated remnant of sub-ordinationism, as though the Father were more and greater than the Son? Or is it a reflection of the very mystically oriented piety of the East which, bypassing the revelation of the Son, would relate man directly to the original Revealer, the *principium* or fount of deity, as though one could and should do this?[126]

On the one hand, it is not unjust to suggest that Barth had a weak understanding of the Eastern arguments against the filioque in particular or of Eastern Trinitarian thinking in general. He himself admitted that he did not fully understand the "motives of the Eastern Church clearly enough to reach any definitive conclusion."[127] Be that as it may, if anything, his reluctance to accept the Eastern objections to the filioque says more about his own prejudice against anything smacking of "mysticism"[128] than the theological reasons why he rejected a Greek account of the doctrine of the Trinity.

On the other hand, Barth's questions on the Eastern view disclose very clearly the priority of his own theological concern as a Reformed theologian, namely that of properly understanding the manner in which God reveals himself contingently to the human recipient. Thus, even in his questioning of the Eastern position, Barth assumed that the filioque question primarily concerns the manner of God's self-revelation rather than the manner of God's eternal self-subsisting. This is extremely significant: Barth transformed the filioque question—traditionally one about intra-Trinitarian "relations" and "origins"— first and foremost into a question about revelation, and only secondarily as a question about intra-Trinitarian relations. From the perspective of revelation, Barth was convinced that the Greek position needed to be rejected because it seemed to make it possible to conceive of God revealing himself independently of the Son. Such a conception was obviously highly suspect for Barth because it would result in two distinct revelations of the one God: one arising "directly" to the human from Father to Spirit, and another to the human from the Father *through* the Son. Consequently, Barth was at least

125 Ibid.

126 Ibid.

127 Ibid., p. 130.

128 In his defense, however, Barth had previously asserted that "Christianity knows itself more akin to ascetics and pietists, strange though their behaviour may be, than to 'healthy evangelical national piety'; more closely related to the 'Russian Man' than to his western brothers." Barth, *Romans*, p. 463.

tentatively convinced to hold on to the filioque, lest by its denial there would arise, in reading back to the immanent Trinity from the Trinity of revelation, "a threat to the unity of the concept of God."[129] Barth was not wrong to seek to protect the unity of God by seeking to protect the unity of revelation. Unfortunately, what Barth (and, until recently, many other theologians) did *not* understand was that the Eastern rejection of the filioque is itself also an attempt to maintain the unity of the Godhead, though through a different theological strategy: not by protecting the unity of revelation, but by protecting the monarchy of the Father as the sole origin of the Son and the Spirit and the locus of divine unity.

While admitting that some of the Reformed orthodox theologians of the seventeenth century[130] were convinced that the Greek teaching needed to be better understood, Barth remained steadfast: "We still have no reason to hold aloof from the Western form. It expresses much better the drift of the whole doctrine as we have thought we must understand it."[131] He went on to insist that the Spirit's procession from the Father and Son must be held because only "[God] is Lord not only *over* all things and *in* all things, but as we are special things among all other things, uniquely at the center of all things, God is *our* Lord, *mine* and *yours,* the God who stands related to us as I and Thou, as Thou and I, from eternity to eternity."[132] In other words, it is necessary to uphold the filioque on the basis of the possibility of a personal reception or apprehension of the revelation of the God who is both far (the Father) and near (the Son). For unless the Spirit is the Spirit of the Father and the Spirit of the Son, and proceeds from both, then temporal, contingent reception of the eternal is impossible. How can the Son be recognized as Lord, except by the Spirit? And how can the Spirit testify to this unless he is the Spirit sent by the Son? So, Barth's insistence on the contingent possibility of revelation is the main reason why he upheld the filioque. Beyond these barest of comments, however, Barth said nothing more explicitly on the filioque in the first volume of the *GD*.

The Problem of Dogmatics: Barth's First Attempt at a Dogmatic Prolegomenon

Of course, Barth's limited direct exploration of the filioque in the *GD* does not mean that nothing further can be said of the matter. On the contrary, the manner in which Barth located the filioque in the context of the question of revelation (rather than specifically with the context of theology proper) gives further clues as

129 Barth, *Göttingen Dogmatics*, p. 130.

130 The editors of the English translation of the *GD* have cited Heppe's *Reformed Dogmatics* as the probable source that Barth was using at this point. Examination of Heppe reveals that Barth follows closely the line of reasoning on the *per filium* and the explanation of what happened at the Council of Florence according to Riisen. See Heppe, *Reformed Dogmatics*, p. 131.

131 Barth, *Göttingen Dogmatics*, p. 130.

132 Ibid.

to why he felt he needed to hold on to the filioque. Consequently, it will be helpful to step back and locate Barth's discussion of revelation in the larger context of his wrestling with the problem of theological prolegomenon in the earlier sections of the *GD*.

The first section (§1) of the *GD* is Barth's first attempt to develop a prolegomenon for dogmatics. For Barth, dogmatics is a necessary burden—"a burden that we cannot and may not and will not avoid."[133] Unlike an Aquinas or a Calvin who could embark upon a work of dogmatics with little or no attention to matters of prolegomena, Barth pointed out that moderns could not enjoy such luxury. Before beginning the task of dogmatics, the modern theologian is compelled to address the question of what is going to be said concerning the God of which one speaks.[134]

It is this question of "what to say" about God that compelled Barth to embark upon a path largely distinct from that of the ancient, medieval, Reformed, and modern theologians before him. Although impressed by the "holy, lofty, beautiful and joyful work of art"[135] of dogmatics in Augustine, Aquinas or Calvin, Barth was unable to accept the definition of theology as "the science of God" because "it confuses dogmatics with a metaphysics that has become impossible since Kant" and because "it does not give faith its proper place in fixing the object."[136]

Furthermore, Barth is not convinced that the modern "Copernican reversal of the divine and human subjects"[137] can solve the problem of dogmatics. In his estimation, Schleiermacher may well have been the one responsible for this Copernican revolution in theology, but only as a "culmination of an older development" in which "theology in general and dogmatics in particular is the science of religion, the science of statements of pious experience such as is found in the Christian church."[138] Again, Barth was unable to accept dogmatics as the science of pious religion because "God's Word—and no one else, not even an angel—must establish articles of faith," and he added, "and if not an angel, then certainly not I, a man with my pious experience."[139]

If dogmatics is neither the descriptive science of God, nor the analytical science of divinely given dogma, nor even the reiterative science of pious experience of God, then what is it? Barth's answer lies in the attention he gives to the statement *Deus dixit* ("God speaks" or "God has spoken").[140] *Deus dixit*, Barth argued, is the absolute presupposition that the Christian is forced to take when approaching the Bible. The assumption that God speaks in the Bible is, as Burnett explains, a

133 Ibid., p. 4.

134 Ibid., p. 6.

135 Ibid., p. 4.

136 Ibid., p. 10.

137 Ibid., p. 11.

138 Ibid., p. 9.

139 Ibid., p. 10. Barth attributes his formulation here to Martin Luther.

140 For a fuller exposition of the significance of *Deus dixit*, see McCormack, *Critically Realistic,* pp. 337-46.

formal "biblicism … in which human thinking and speaking yields to the *Deus dixit* and hence recognizes the authority of the biblical canon and texts."[141] *Deus dixit*, in other words, acknowledges that "God is obviously the subject, not man. If God were not the speaking subject who creates faith by his Word, then what could he be but the object of a scholarly metaphysics?"[142] Thus, for Barth, dogmatics is not the science of God (as in Thomas or even Calvin) or the science of faith (as in Schleiermacher), but the science of dogmas which is really "reflection on God's Word"[143]—a Word which is nothing less than God's turning and address to humans, to which humans are called upon to answer in faith.[144]

Barth's conceptualization of the task of dogmatics *contra* his Thomistic and Schleiermacherian forebears means that attention to *Deus dixit* is extremely important to understanding even Barth's mature theology. At any rate, *Deus dixit*, becomes Barth's fundamental presupposition and guiding definition of revelation[145] in the *Göttingen Dogmatics* and the *Church Dogmatics* to follow. Without the assumption of revelation—that God has spoken—there is no possibility of dogmatics because dogmatics is necessarily a responsive, not a constructive or even strictly descriptive, discipline. When dogmatics is weak, Barth argued, it is precisely because "it believes so little in this *Deus dixit*."[146]

The Threefold Word of God and its Filioquist Structure Barth clearly presupposed the *Deus dixit,* but does this not beg the logically prior questions of how and where God speaks? Or, to be more direct, what *is* the Word of God for Barth? And where is it to be found? Barth's answer to the question of the identity of the Word of God unfolds in line with his understanding of *Deus dixit*: the Word of God is none other than God's own speech, not the speech of men seeking to approximate something akin to God's Word. *Deus dixit* means that, because God has spoken, God's Word is a real address to humans. However, a shift from his understanding of revelation in *Romans* (indeed, even from the earliest pages of the *GD*) can be perceived at

---

141 Burnett, *Barth's Exegesis*, p. 58.

142 Barth, *Göttingen Dogmatics*, p. 292. Burnett has helpfully distinguished between formal biblicism (which Barth accepts) and material biblicism (which Barth rejects). Formal, or relative, biblicism is "an attitude, a posture, a way of human thinking shaped by the Bible, in a way in which those cultivated by its 'rule of thought' learn to think its thoughts and hear its message again and again." In contrast, material biblicism "is a way which has nothing necessarily to do with hearing the Bible, but consists of applying (via proof-texting) what one thinks one has already heard from it simply by repeating its words." Burnett, *Barth's Exegesis*, p. 58.

143 Barth, *Göttingen Dogmatics*, p. 13.

144 Ibid., p. 12.

145 McCormack, *Critically Realistic*, p. 338.

146 Barth, *Göttingen Dogmatics*, p. 14. Cf. Calvin: "The highest proof of Scripture is uniformly derived from the person of God who speaks it." As cited in Heppe, *Reformed Dogmatics*, p. 16.

this point in his thinking. McCormack explains: "Whereas … Barth had said that Revelation, in itself, is an eternal event, he now made the contingent side of the event to be essential to it. … With this subtle but momentous shift of accent, '*Deus dixit*' comes to mean primarily 'God has spoken' in AD 1-30—and on this basis alone 'God continues to speak.'"[147]

In order to accommodate this "shift of accent," Barth realized that God's address cannot be understood as a merely punctiliar occurrence (this was closer to how he understood the "Event" or "Moment" character of revelation in *Romans*).[148] Rather, he began to speak of revelation more explicitly than ever, following what Dalferth calls a "unity-in-difference" model of revelation.[149] Barth posited that God's Word, while only one *unified* Word, comes in three *different* forms or addresses. In the first address "God himself and God alone is the speaker." In the second address, "it is the Word of a specific category of people (the prophets and apostles)." And the third address (and here the ongoing contingency of revelation is emphasized over against the punctiliar) it is one "in which the number of its human agents or proclaimers is theoretically unlimited." Nevertheless, "God's Word abides forever. It neither is nor can be different whether it has its first, its second, or its third form, and always when it is one of the three it is also in some sense the other two as well."[150]

In this regard, Barth referred to a "common formula"[151] to specify the three forms of the Word of God. The forms are:

---

147 McCormack, *Critically Realistic*, p. 340.

148 Burnett calls Barth's early understanding of revelation "actualistic in the sense that revelation always had the character of an event and was not bound to the Bible, to church doctrine, or to any normative conceptualization." Burnett, *Barth's Exegesis*, p. 222. Beyond the question of whether Barth speaks of God "acting" in revelation, which Barth continues to do through to the *CD*, it is nevertheless the case that revelation is "punctiliar" in that it occurs, but then, and only then, leaves an "impression" of revelation.

149 For an excellent comparison of the "neo-Protestant (Schleiermacherian) "difference-in-unity" model as compared to Barth's "unity-in-difference" model in reference to faith and reason, see Ingolf U. Dalferth, *Theology and Philosophy* (Oxford, 1988), pp. 99-126.

150 Barth, *Göttingen Dogmatics*, p. 14. Barth's use of "address" and "form" is somewhat confusing and inconsistent here. However, it appears that Barth thought of the *Deus dixit* in terms of a single *address* coming in three *forms*.

151 Barth does not identify the source from which he is drawing this "common formula." Richardson suggests that the origin of Barth's threefold form of God's Word is the Second Helvitic Confession, §I.2A. Kurt Anders Richardson, *Reading Karl Barth* (Grand Rapids, 2004), p. 178; Bromiley suggests that the threefold form of the Word (which found its way into the *CD* without major alteration from the *GD*) is based on "divisions already suggested and partly developed in reformation theology, for example, in Bullinger's *Decades*. His originality here lies in the way in which he works out the concept and not in the concept itself." Geoffrey W. Bromiley, *An Introduction to the Theology of Karl Barth* (Grand Rapids, 1979), p. 6. Whatever the case, this adoption of the formula marks a significant shift for Barth, who, in his preparation for his lectures on the Reformed confessions (dated

> … one in three and three in one: revelation, scripture, and preaching—the Word of God as revelation, the Word of God as scripture, and the Word of God as preaching, neither to be confused nor separated. One Word of God, one authority, one power, and yet not one but three addresses. Three addresses of God in revelation, scripture, and preaching, yet not three Words of God, three authorities, truths or powers, but one.[152]

It is clearly no accident that the form of Barth's language here reflects the form of the Athanasian Creed[153] that attributes a quality to each of the three divine persons in turn, and then clarifies by saying that there are not three Gods, Lords, Almighties, etc., but one God, Lord, Almighty, etc. Even more significant than Barth's formulation, which distinguishes the Word of God from Scripture,[154] is how he related the three forms together in what is clearly a filioquist Trinitarian form:

> Scripture is not revelation, but from revelation. Preaching is not revelation or scripture, but from both. But the Word of God is scripture no less than it is revelation, and it is preaching no less than it is scripture. Revelation is from God alone, scripture is from revelation alone, and preaching is from revelation and scripture. Yet there is no first or last, no greater or less. The first, the second, and the third are all God's Word in the same glory, unity in trinity and trinity in unity.[155]

Diagrammatically, Barth's formulation could be represented as follows:

---

15 May 1923), readily affirmed the "Reformed scripture principle" whereby "the Church recognizes the rule of its proclamation solely in the Word of God and finds the Word of God solely in Holy Scripture." Barth, *Reformed Confessions*, p. 41.

152 Barth, *Göttingen Dogmatics*, pp. 14-15. Cf. the Augustinian parallel: "Therefore the Father is light, the Son is light, and the Holy Spirit is light; but together not three lights, but one light. And so the Father is wisdom, the Son is wisdom, and the Holy Spirit is wisdom, and together not three wisdoms, but one wisdom." Augustine, *On the Holy Trinity,* in *Nicene and Post-Nicene Fathers*, first series, vol. 3, ed. Philip Schaff (Peabody, 1994), p. 109.

153 See Philip Schaff (ed.), *Creeds of Christendom. Vol. 2: The Greek and Latin Creeds* (3 vols, repr. edn, Grand Rapids, 1993), p. 66ff.

154 Heppe, for example, argues that "the older Reformed theology distinguished between the 'Word of God" and "Holy Scripture" most definitely. … It was therefore taught by CALVIN and his immediate successors in Church teaching … that the "Word of God," i.e., the manifold revelations or words in which God had spoken to men, were transmitted orally at the start and that it was only later that they were recorded." Heppe, *Reformed Dogmatics*, p. 15.

155 Barth, *Göttingen Dogmatics*, p. 15.

(God)
↓
Revelation ⟶ Scripture
↓ ↓
Preaching

Barth further elucidated his formulation by relating the three forms' distinct relationships to human history. In light of the dogmatic presupposition of *Deus dixit*, the "Word of God is God's speaking. It is ongoing as Christian preaching." This is in contrast to revelation which "is not ongoing in the strict sense." Indeed, for Barth, revelation "never took place as such. The statement 'God revealed himself' means something different from the statement 'revelation took place.' Revelation is what it is in time, but as the frontier of time, remote from us as heaven is from earth."[156] Furthermore, neither is Scripture God's ongoing Word, but "it is in time as such. It took place as the witness given to revelation. But in itself it is a self-enclosed part of history which is as far from us as everything historical and past."[157] Thus, the three forms of God's Word and their relationship to time can be summarized as follows. First, revelation is God's eternal Word as it intersects with time (cf. *Krisis*); or, to put it another way, revelation is eternally in time while remaining completely distinct from time. Second, Scripture is God's Word located in time, but not as something currently "present" but only as a self-enclosed part of time which is historical and therefore distant from the present. The Church's possession of Scripture is not a presupposition of Scripture's contemporaneousness with the Church. Third, preaching is God's Word in the "here and now" [*hic et nunc*], in the daily contingencies of human history. Even when *Deus dixit* is understood as a "here and now," the situation of the preacher is such that "*Deus dixit* is our confidence, not experience. We can only believe."[158] Consequently, the "knowledge, courage, and authority of the Christian preacher" is made possible only in "reference to the Holy Spirit, that is, to God himself in the present, in the church … that God himself bears witness to himself."[159]

The threefold form of the Word of God in its filioquist form is crucial to Barth. He identifies the three forms of the Word of God as reflecting a structural analogy to the relationships that God has in himself, both as one who relates to human history (i.e., the economic Trinity)—as one who stands above, through, and contemporaneous with created time—and as one who in his inner triune relationships is Father, Son and Holy Spirit (i.e., the immanent Trinity). Though in the *GD* the language of "economic" and "immanent" Trinity is not yet typical in Barth's vocabulary, the emerging correlation between the two is clearly evident. Thus, "revelation … is remote from us as heaven is from earth"; Scripture is "in

156 Ibid. Cf. the "qualitative infinite distinction" of *Romans*.

157 Ibid.

158 Ibid., p. 67.

159 Ibid., p. 68.

time as such … as the witness given to revelation" but as a witness of the past.[160] "But as Christian preaching"—here Barth made the bold connection—"which proceeds from revelation and scripture (as the Holy Spirit proceeds from the Father and the Son), the Word of God is ongoing. It is present."[161] The correlation to the doctrine of the Trinity, Barth argued, cannot be ignored: As God (the Father) is infinitely and qualitatively distinct from us, so too is revelation beyond human grasping; as the Incarnate Son is "in time as such" as the manifestation of God's revelation, so too is Scripture the witness given in time to a revelation occurring in a distinct time in history, but now past; and as the Holy Spirit is the one who binds together the eternal Father and the eternal Son in an eternal procession, so too preaching proceeds from revelation and Scripture in history into the contingency of the present world of men who hear God's Word.

The Filioque in the Göttingen Dogmatics: Implications and Assessment

It is manifestly clear that by 1924 Barth had become aware of the filioque controversy and had taken a preliminary, even if tentative, stance on the issue. But, in a very real sense, Barth had only barely begun to work through its material dogmatic significance. In this regard there is little evidence that Barth's preliminary acceptance of the filioque was the result of extensive study or interaction with the primary sources of any of the classical Western proponents, whether Augustine, Anselm, or Aquinas, even though their indirect influence is evident. Rather, his focus at the time of writing the *GD* was on becoming acquainted with the Reformed tradition itself—a task imposed on him by the nature of his post at Göttingen. While it is clear he consulted the classical sources via his Lutheran or Reformed source books (i.e., Schmid and Heppe, respectively), the actual material contribution of Barth's reflections on the filioque problem in the *GD* is minimal. It is no overstatement to say that he had a long way to go before making any kind of lasting contribution to the filioque debate proper.

However, Barth's lack of material contribution to the filioque debate should not obscure the fact that it was in the *GD* Barth took a major methodological step forward toward what would eventually become a thoroughly filioquist stance, with revelation, rather than metaphysics, being his dogmatic starting-point. Understanding this point is much more significant than discerning what Barth had to say about the filioque problem itself. Beyond that, it is important to recall that the driving impetus for Barth in coming to Göttingen was to teach Reformed theology to those training for ministry in Reformed churches and that he had just left the pastorate himself. Consequently, he was unusually located between pulpit and podium such that his initial forays into dogmatics were significantly shaped by his own perceptions of the demands placed on the preacher. And the primary

160 Ibid.

161 Ibid., p. 16.

situation for the preacher,[162] as Barth discovered in his study on *Romans* and as he began his post at Göttingen, was not "How does one preach?" (i.e., the homiletical question) but "How *can* one preach?" (i.e., the theological question).[163] Having rejected the pneumatology of his liberal teachers (i.e., of Schleiermacher), Barth was left searching for a theology that could adequately address his fear on the one hand of mistaking man's spirit for God's Spirit and his fear on the other hand of oversimplistically identifying the Bible with God's Word. Was there not a way of mediating between the two, such that God's Spirit was actively and contemporaneously present and such that God's Word could be apprehended by human listeners, even while protecting God's Word from becoming a permanent possession in human hands? Barth's development of his doctrine of the threefold Word of God was his initial attempt to solve that problem. Consequently, the doctrine of the filioque, though only formally present in his account of the internal structure of the threefold form of the Word of God, arose for Barth as that which he had read off of revelation, and not as a theological axiom or presupposition from a metaphysics of the ontology of God.

This was an important strength of Barth's dealings with the filioque in the *GD.* The sparseness of his comment on the controversy itself indicates that Barth was rightly concerned that statements about intra-Trinitarian relations could only be made once he had sought to understand the structure of God's self-revelation (i.e., by seeking to speak properly of the economic Trinity). In this way, Barth wanted rightly to order theological discussion by giving priority to analysis of revelation in advance of speculation on the structure of the immanent Trinity. To reverse this order would have been to engage in a speculative metaphysics of God; the *GD* therefore reflects Barth's first attempt to resist traditional metaphysical modes of doing dogmatics. Thus, Barth can be commended, at the very least, for resisting hard and fast conclusions on the filioque controversy, if for no other reason than because he was still seeking to understand the structure of God's revelation before venturing to say anything further on the debate.

Nevertheless, some significant difficulties were inadvertently introduced into Barth's theological program, and these are illustrated by his handling of the filioque problem. One can certainly marvel at Barth's theological ingenuity in constructing a set of relations between the three forms of the Word of God that he saw as being analogous both to God's internal Trinitarian relations and in seeking to understand God's relationship to time and history. However, there are two problems with this strategy. First, Barth never provided a clear rationale for why the threefold Word of God must in fact be analogous to the intra-Trinitarian relations. Indeed, he appeared to accept this as a given. One is thus left wondering if Barth ultimately accepted the analogy to the Trinity because of its rhetorical, aesthetic, or pedagogical appeal over against any internally coherent dogmatic or exegetical rationale. Indeed, it will be shown in the next chapter that, when

162 Ibid., pp. 63-68.

163 Barth, *Word of God*, p. 103.

Barth pushed the Trinitarian analogy even further to incorporate the concept of perichoresis, it is pushed to its breaking-point.

Second, by pressing the analogy from the threefold Word of God back to the intra-Trinitarian relations, Barth ended up setting up a schedule of relations that restricted his pneumatology primarily to what is traditionally called the doctrine of "illumination" to the denigration of the pneumatological aspects of "inspiration" and "incarnation." This needs some brief explanation.

The way in which Barth set up the relationship between the three forms of the Word of God meant that each form corresponded analogously to one of the three Persons of the Trinity. Thus, in Barth's model, revelation corresponds to the Father, Scripture to the Son, and preaching to the Holy Spirit. However, by making the Holy Spirit correspond to the third form, Barth restricts the operation of the Spirit to the noetic work of illuminating the identity of the Son as the Son of the Father. In so doing, Barth may have inadvertently made it difficult to say how the Spirit is related to the production of Scripture or to speak of his ontic role in bringing about the incarnation of Jesus as the revelation of the Father. When he comes to the first volume of the *Church Dogmatics*, Barth refused to acknowledge that the procession of the Spirit has anything to do with the appearance of the Son in his humanity.[164] This indicates how far the effects of the move made by Barth in the *GD* extended. To his credit, Barth was more critically aware of the problem of the relationship of the Spirit to the Son by the time he wrote *CD* I/1, as demonstrated in his reformulation of the schedule of divine relations in a more perichoretic and less geometric fashion.[165] But, at any rate, his formulation in the *GD* of the relations of the three forms of the Word of God, read back analogously to the intra-Trinitarian relations, formally isolated Barth's pneumatology from his doctrine of the Incarnation and in his doctrine of Scripture. This is a problem that Barth apparently struggles to overcome, and more will need to be said about this in Chapter Three.

---

[164] *CD* I/1, p. 485.

[165] *CD* I/1, p. 121.

Chapter Three
The Defense of the Filioque in *Church Dogmatics* I/1

The foregoing sketch of the genesis and development of the filioque antecedent to the *Church Dogmatics* demonstrates, at the very least, that the theology of the filioque that appears there is not a theological *novum.* Barth's first direct (albeit brief) discussion of the filioque appears in the *Göttingen Dogmatics,* though it was also demonstrated that the emerging dialectical and Christocentric pneumatology of *Romans* undergirded what would eventually become Barth's filioquist outlook. It was shown that when Barth finally dealt with the filioque in the *GD*, the doctrine arose as an appropriate theological analogy to his developing doctrine of the threefold Word of God—a doctrine developed in light of the pressures he had earlier felt to clarify the ground and possibility of preaching. Thus, for Barth, the filioque represented, *a posteriori*, an encapsulation of the pattern of revelation that confronted him both as a preacher and a theologian.

This chapter will have three overarching purposes. First, after providing a brief overview of the historical context in which the writing of the *Church Dogmatics* took place, attention will be given to Barth's restatement of the doctrine of the Word of God in its threefold form, especially noting how he sought to clarify and modify the analogy to the Triune relations in reference to the doctrine of perichoresis. In this regard it will be important to compare Barth's statement to his earlier conceptualization in the *Göttingen Dogmatics*, noting especially the relation of the doctrine to Barth's support of the filioque. Second, Barth's defense of the procession of the Spirit from the Father and Son as represented in *CD* I/1, will be analyzed and evaluated, especially through the lens of his rule of identity between the economic and immanent Trinity. Finally, the chapter will compare Barth and T. F. Torrance on the doctrine of the Spirit's procession not only to show some of their essential similarities, but also to help clarify the grounds upon which Barth continued to defend the filioque. This will serve to provide a clearer picture of the systematic function of the filioque in Barth's thinking up to *CD* I/1 and will pave the way for closer attention in Chapter Four to Barth's material applications of the filioque in the remainder of the *CD.*

Theologia Viatorum: The Road to Basel and the *Church Dogmatics*

In summer 1930 Barth took up the chair of systematic theology at the University of Bonn, replacing Otto Ritschl (son of Albrecht).[1] During his first semester at Bonn, Barth, along with the philosopher Heinrich Scholz of Münster, held a seminar on Anselm's *Cur Deus Homo?* On the basis of his seminar preparations, Barth published his well-known book on Anselm in the summer of 1931.[2] In retrospect, Barth viewed the book as having been written "with more loving care than any other of my books,"[3] and he identified the book as a signpost of his turn away from the last remnants of a philosophical search for grounds upon which the Church can establish her faith in God on a source outside of herself. It was this search for an anthropological justification for dogmatics which had so plagued the liberal agenda and which Barth sought now to leave behind.[4] Thus, in Barth's view, it was his adoption of Anselm's method in theology, *fides quaerens intellectum*, which convinced him that he needed to abandon working on his *Die christliche Dogmatik* in favor of a genuinely new *Church* dogmatics—a dogmatics arising in and for the *fides* rather than a dogmatics of *apologia* before the world. In the Anselm book, Barth concluded that theology "is a question of the proof of faith by faith which was already established in itself without proof."[5] It is in light of this newly discovered understanding of theology that he asked, "What option did

---

1 Eberhard Busch, *Karl Barth: His Life from Letters and Autobiographical Texts*, trans. John Bowden (Grand Rapids, 1976), pp. 198-99.

2 Karl Barth, *Anselm: Fides Quaerens Intellectum* (Pittsburgh, 1975), p. 7.

3 Karl Barth, *How I Changed My Mind*, ed. John D. Godsey (Richmond, 1966), p. 43. In the preface to the second edition of the Anselm book, Barth informed readers that his interest in Anselm was "never a side-issue" and he laments that so few commentators on his work, von Balthasar being the noted exception, "realized how much it has influenced me or been absorbed into my own line of thinking." Barth then goes on to insist that "in this book on Anselm I am working with a vital key, if not the key, to an understanding of that whole process of thought that has impressed me more and more in my Church Dogmatics as the only one proper to theology." Barth, *Anselm*, p. 11.

4 Barth's concluding paragraph of the Anselm book reveals much of Barth's attitude toward the claims of modern theological epistemology beginning with Descartes: "That Anselm's Proof of the Existence of God has repeatedly been called the 'Ontological' Proof of God, that commentators have refused to see that it is in a different book altogether from the well-known teaching of Descartes and Leibniz, that anyone could seriously think that it is even remotely affected by what Kant put forward against these doctrines—all that is so much nonsense on which no more words ought to be wasted." Barth, *Anselm*, p. 171.

5 Ibid., p. 170. Von Balthasar is convinced that Barth was able "energetically" to "overcome the existential and anthropological starting point of the Prolegomena [to the Münster Dogmatics] to offer a purely theological doctrine of the Word of God, that is, one firmly rooted in the Word of God itself." Hans Urs von Balthasar, *The Theology of Karl Barth: Exposition and Interpretation*, trans. Edward T. Oakes (San Francisco, 1992), p. 108.

I have but to begin again from the beginning, saying the same thing, but in a very different way?"[6]

It is noteworthy that, in setting the context for the *Church Dogmatics,* scholars have tended to place more emphasize on the latter part of Barth's statement (i.e., "in a very different way") than on the former (i.e., "saying the same thing.").[7] However, as McCormack has argued, such a view has allowed Barth's own perception on the matter to obscure the extent to which Barth was methodologically consistent—even after his book on Anselm—to the theological program he had already embarked upon at Safenwil and Göttingen.[8] Moreover, Terry Cross has observed that if the newly discovered *analogia fidei* expressed in the Anselm book was the source of paradigmatic change, then it is not at all evident why Barth himself does not mention this "discovery" more clearly in the prolegomenal volumes of the *CD*.[9]

Though Barth eventually depicted his *Die christliche Dogmatik* (the so-called "Münster Dogmatics") as a dogmatic false start that required dropping of all philosophical baggage,[10] the beginning of *Die Kirchliche Dogmatik* was more likely the result of Barth's own desire to make a clean break with some of his current colleagues, including Gogarten and Bultmann. When the German authorities eventually suspended (and subsequently expelled) Barth from his post for refusing to give an unqualified oath of loyalty to the *Führer*, his move to distance himself as clearly as possible from his time in Münster and Bonn became increasingly clear.[11] As McCormack has noted, it was not unusual for Barth to

---

[6] As cited by Busch, *Karl Barth*, pp. 209-10.

[7] In this regard, von Balthasar's interpretation has continued to exercise an important influence. He identifies the production of the Anselm book one of two critical turning-points in Barth's career (the former being Barth's *Romans*). Von Balthasar, *Theology of Karl Barth*, pp. 79-80. Accordingly, von Balthasar highlights Barth's years at Bonn and early years at Basel as a "transitional stage between Romans and Church Dogmatics." Ibid., p. 90.

[8] See Bruce L. McCormack, *Karl Barth's Critically Realistic Dialectic Theology: Its Genesis and Development, 1909-1936* (Oxford, 1995), pp. 421-23.

[9] Terry L. Cross, *Dialectic in Karl Barth's Doctrine of God* (New York, 2001), pp. 135-36.

[10] Joseph McLelland has labeled Barth's desire to explicate revelation as giving, independently of external philosophical categories, an analytic *a posteriori* approach. Joseph C. McLelland, "Philosophy and Theology--A Family Affair (Karl and Heinrich Barth)," in H. Martin Rumscheidt (ed.), *Footnotes to a Theology: The Karl Barth Colloquium of 1972* (Waterloo, 1974), p. 38.

[11] As McCormack has shown, the most compelling reason to take Barth's own testimony of the inadequacy of his earlier work with a grain of salt is that, in the 1932 preface to *CD* I/1, he calls the first volume of D*ie christliche Dogmatik* a "first edition." It was only after his break with Gogarten and his Zwischen den Zeiten colleagues in 1933—after *CD* I/1 was already completed—that Barth began to speak of the deficiencies of *Die christliche Dogmatik*. McCormack, *Critically Realistic*, p. 447.

make sharp, public breaks with those with whom he disagreed or from whom he wanted to be dissociated.[12] These factors all led Barth to "overemphasize the newness of *Church Dogmatics* I/1."[13]

Following the tumultuous years at Bonn, Barth was offered a post at Basel, his home city, a post he took up on 6 July 1935.[14] Though the first half-volume of the *CD* was already completed in 1932 at Bonn, it was not until the summer of 1937 that Barth completed, in Basel, the massive second half of his prolegomenon that extended an astonishing 1011 pages in the original.[15]

Barth's exposition in the *CD* mushroomed in size on nearly every topic, including the number of trademark "small-print" exegetical and historical soundings that are so characteristic of the work. This material expansion can also be observed in his discussion of the filioque, as a comparison with his previous work clearly demonstrates. In the *Göttingen Dogmatics* Barth's explicit discussion of the question extends barely to one page of text;[16] in the so-called Münster dogmatics it has grown modestly to just over four pages, though close to half of the material is direct historical citation to Latin and Greek sources.[17] By the time he comes to deal with the filioque in the *Church Dogmatics*, the discussion has expanded to 14 pages.[18] But before moving on directly to consider this particularly important section of the *CD,* it will be helpful to return once again to Barth's discussion of the doctrine of the Word of God in its threefold form, which is at the heart of the first chapter of Barth's *magnum opus.*

The Threefold Form of the Word of God Revisited

One of the most important carry-overs from the *GD* into the *CD* is Barth's continued description of the Word of God in its threefold form as revelation, Scripture, and preaching. However, despite the obvious continuity, there is a significant shift in how he sought to relate the three forms to one another. Careful attention to this shift provides important clues in assessing the internal coherence of Barth's actual defense of the filioque as carried out in *CD* I/1.

After a relatively brief introduction to the "task of dogmatics" (§1) and the "task of prolegomena to dogmatics" (§2), Barth moved into Chapter 1 entitled,

---

12 Ibid., pp. 446-47, 442.

13 Ibid., p. 443.

14 Ibid., p. 449.

15 Even Barth quipped that the size of the book made "a real mockery of its title 'half-volume.'" Letter to K. L. Schmidt, 7 August 1937, as cited by Busch, *Karl Barth*, p. 282.

16 Barth, *The Göttingen Dogmatics*, ed. Hannelotte Reiffen, trans. Geoffrey W. Bromiley (Grand Rapids, 1991), pp. 129-30.

17 Karl Barth, *Die christliche Dogmatik im Entwurf: Die Lehre vom Worte Gottes. Erster Band*, ed. Gerhard Sauter (Zürich, 1982), pp. 284-89.

18 *CD* I/1, pp. 473-87.

"The Word of God as the Criterion of Dogmatics." According to Barth, any talk about God in the Church, any proclamation, has as its presupposition the reality of the Word of God itself. Though Church proclamation always remains a human word, it nevertheless speaks in expectation and faith that God may freely use this proclamation in the event of God's self-revelation. In this scheme, then, knowledge of God is grounded in God's own self-revealing Word concerning himself, but access to that Word is made possible through the preaching of the Church, the testimony found in creeds, sermons, hymns, and confessions throughout the ages.[19] However, such proclamation is not grounded merely in human thoughts and ideas about God, but is simultaneously an ecclesial "recollection," to use Barth's terminology, of the original witness of Scripture to revelation and a collective "anticipation" in the Church of the possibility of future revelation. The preaching of the Church is what it is because it both points back to the original witness of revelation and yet eagerly looks forward and expects that revelation will occur yet again. As Barth put it, "Proclamation must ever and again become proclamation."[20]

Barth explored the nature of Church proclamation more fully in section §4, entitled "The Word of God in its Threefold Form."[21] As the four subsections of the paragraph indicate, Barth's doctrine of the Word of God is structured to correspond with the noetic structure of the Word of God that comes to humans—namely, preaching, Scripture, and revelation, all of which are forms of a single unified Word of God. In this regard, to characterize Barth, as some carelessly have, as beginning with the Oneness of God (unity) and only then moving to the Threeness of divine

[19] Barth's understanding of preaching in the *CD* narrowed relative to his ideas of preaching reflected in the *GD*. In the *GD*, Barth can insist: "[W]e are not restricting the term 'Christian preaching' to sermons from the pulpit, or to the work of pastors, but including in it whatever we all 'preach' to ourselves in the quiet of our own rooms. The only point is that outwardly or inwardly this must be a speaking, a mediated addressing and hearing of the Word of God from revelation and scripture." Barth, *Göttingen Dogmatics*, p. 16. However, in the *CD*, Barth's concept of preaching is more ecclesially restricted. There preaching is "the attempt by someone called thereto in the Church, in the form of an exposition of some portion of the biblical witness to revelation, to express in his own words and to make intelligible to men of his own generation the promise of the revelation, reconciliation and vocation of God as they are to be expected here and now." *CD* I/1, p. 56.

[20] *CD* I/1, p. 88.

[21] The four subsections of this paragraph in *CD* I/1 include: 1. The Word of God Preached; 2 The Word of God Written; and 3. The Word of God Revealed; 4. The Unity of the Word of God. It should be noted that Barth generally, though not exclusively, resists speaking of three "forms" of the Word of God in favor of the threefold "form" of the Word of God. For Barth there is an evident tension between speaking of the threefold form, as singular, and the three forms, as plural, of the Word of God. As he explained, "We have been speaking of three different forms of the Word of God and not of three different Words of God. In this threefold form and not otherwise—but also as the one Word only in this threefold form—the Word of God is given to us and we must try to understand it conceptually." *CD* I/1, p. 120.

revelation is simply misleading and runs roughshod over the overt structure of *CD* I/1.[22] On the contrary, the outworking of Barth's prolegomena moved from the threefold form of revelation (in his doctrine of the Word of God) but then moved in reverse in paragraph §9 ("The Triunity of God") back to "Unity in Trinity." He then reversed the direction yet again and addresses "Trinity in Unity," only to conclude that God is best understood as a "Triunity" [*Dreieinigkeit*]. This movement from unity to trinity to triunity is itself, Barth argued, "[a] trinitarian dialectic,"[23] a "rational wrestling with the mystery" of the Triune God.[24] Lest anyone think that

---

[22] The usual point of focus in this regard is Barth's choice of the term *Seinsweisen* ("modes of being") in place of the traditional term "Person" to refer to the "three" in God. Moltmann, for example, felt that Barth's "trinitarian monarchianism" results in "the subjectivity of acting and receiving" being transferred "from the three divine Persons to the one divine subject." Consequently, "viewed theologically this is a late triumph for the Sabellian modalism which the early church condemned" even if "these are certainly only dangers if these ideas are taken to their ultimate conclusion." Jürgen Moltmann, *The Trinity and the Kingdom*, trans, Margaret Kohl (Minneapolis, 1983), p. 139. Catherine LaCugna also concluded that Barth's concept of *Seinsweisen* leads him into a form of modalism, though she carefully qualifies, "whether this modalism is Sabellian could be debated." Catherine Mowry LaCugna, *God for Us: The Trinity & Christian Life* (San Francisco, 1991), p. 252. Gunton sees a Cappodocian influence in Barth's use of the *Seinsweisen*, but also feels there is an "Augustinian weakness" repeated in Barth. Colin E. Gunton, "The Truine [*sic*] God and the Freedom of the Creature," in S. W. Skyes (ed.), *Karl Barth: Centenary Essays* (Cambridge, 1989), pp. 46-68 at p. 60.

Barth's adoption of "mode of being" (*Seinseweise*) was indeed adopted from Cappadocian influence and should be understood as the equivalent of the Greek term *tropos hyparxeos*. See Paul M. Collins, *Trinitarian Theology West and East: Karl Barth, the Cappadocian Fathers, and John Zizioulas* (Oxford, 2001), p. 146. For other assessments of Barth's use of *Seinsweisen*, see also Thomas F. Torrance, "Karl Barth and Patristic Theology," in John Thompson (ed.), *Theology Beyond Christendom* (Allison Park, 1986), pp. 215-39 at p. 225; Alan J. Torrance, *Persons in Communion: Trinitarian Description and Human Participation* (Edinburgh, 1996), pp. 239-62; Eberhard Jüngel, *God's Being is in Becoming* (Grand Rapids, 2001), pp. 37-42; Iain Taylor, "In Defence of Karl Barth's Doctrine of the Trinity," *International Journal of Systematic Theology* 5/1 (March 2003): 33-46.

In the end, we are apt to agree with Webster who argues that many critiques of Barth's use of *Seinsweisen*, especially in English-language theology, "have sometimes forced Barth onto the Procrustean bed of a certain monistic reading of Augustine and the Western trinitarian tradition, and so have been less alert to Barth's frequently expressed commitment to the differentiation of the divine persons." John Webster, "Translator's Introduction," in Jüngel, *God's Being*, pp. ix-xxiii at pp. xviii-xix.

[23] Barth chose to speak of the *Dreieinigkeit* of God rather than *Dreifaltigkeit* or *Gedritt* because the term "gives expression to both the decisive numerals, and its stress on the unity indicates that we are concerned here, not just about unity, but about the unity of a being one which is always also a becoming one." *CD* I/1, p. 369.

[24] *CD* I/1, p. 368.

he was more interested in emphasizing the Oneness of God over the Threeness of God, Barth cited Gregory Nazianzus' well known formula as stating very well what he called "this dialectic in the knowledge of the triune God": "I cannot think of the One without immediately being illumined by the Three. I cannot distinguish the Three without immediately being led to the One."[25] Thus, for Barth, Oneness and Threeness in God can never be spoken of in isolation; indeed, "[i]n practice the concept of triunity is the movement [*Bewegung*] of these two thoughts."[26] The concept of a "triune" God, therefore, is itself to be understood as something which is itself in continual and dynamic movement precisely because of the continual dynamic movement that takes place in God's own being between the three and the one, the one and the three.[27]

In addition to his identification of the triune form of God's Word, Barth addressed the means by which this Word comes to humanity. For Barth, the Word of God is first of all encountered through the preaching of the Church. Not only is preaching in some way *related* to the Word of God, but Barth boldly asserted that true preaching *is* the Word of God when God's Word is its theme: "[T]he Word of God is the theme which must be given to proclamation as such if it is to be real proclamation."[28] But Barth was also cautious in saying this. For though the Word of God comes in the first instance through Church proclamation, such proclamation is not to be confused with the Word itself, but is to be properly and consistently understood as a witness to the Word. Such witness becomes Word only by the free act of God. That is, preaching only *is* (and simultaneously, *becomes*) the Word of God when "God Himself gives Himself to it as its theme."[29] In this sense, Barth sought to maintain that true preaching is simultaneously no less the Word of God and no less the word of man. It does not cease to be a word of man, but it is also a Word of God when God himself freely enlivens it and graciously adopts it for his own purposes in revelation.

However else preaching may be described, Barth continued to insist on the essential nature of preaching as a witness to the Word. Necessarily, then, even true preaching *as* the Word of God, points away from itself toward something else, even while it continues to share its status as one of the forms of the Word of God itself. In this regard, preaching, though an integral form of the Word of God, "must be ventured in recollection of past revelation and in expectation of

---

25 "οὐ φθάνω τὸ ἕν νοῆσαι καὶ τοῖς τρισὶ περιλάμπωμαι· οὐ φθάνω τὰ τρία διελεῖν καὶ εἰς τὸ ἕν ἀναφέρομαὶ." *CD* I/1, p. 369.

26 *CD* I/1, p. 369.

27 Or as one Orthodox theologian explained, "Our thought must be in continuous motion, pursuing now the one, now the three, and returning again to the unity; it must swing ceaselessly between the two poles of the antinomy." Vladimir Lossky, *The Mystical Theology of the Eastern Church* (London, 1957), p. 46.

28 *CD* I/1, p. 91.

29 *CD* I/1, p. 95.

coming revelation."[30] So what is this "past" and "coming" revelation? In the first instance, "past revelation" is identified by Barth as the second form of the Word of God—the Word of God written, the Scriptures. It is on the ground of the scriptural canon—the historical witness to revelation—that the present proclamation of the Word of God through preaching makes possible future revelation. For Barth, then, the relationship of present-day proclamation and the Scripture ought to be understood as "two entities … set initially under a single genus, Scripture as the commencement and present-day preaching as the continuation of one and the same event, Jeremiah and Paul at the beginning and the modern preacher of the Gospel at the end of one and the same series."[31] In making this point, Barth appealed to Luther who said, "We let John the Baptist's finger point and his voice sound: 'Behold, the Lamb of God that taketh away the sin of the world'; we deliver John Baptist's sermon, point to Christ and say: This is the one true Saviour whom you should worship and to whom you should cleave."[32]

The commonality between preaching and Scripture, however, has less to do with the fact that both are, in some sense, forms of proclamation separated in history (though this is true so far as it goes), but more with the fact that both likewise point away from themselves to God's self-revelation. Neither preaching nor Scripture are regarded by Barth as revelation in-and-of-themselves, as it were, but both attest to revelation and thereby share in revelation in a primary (and not merely secondary) way. In this regard, "the Bible is God's Word as it really bears witness to revelation, and proclamation is God's Word as it really promises revelation. The promise in proclamation, however, rests on the attestation in the Bible."[33]

Since the first two forms of the Word of God—proclamation and Scripture—are in the form of witness, they necessarily testify to a third form—namely, the revelation of God in Jesus Christ. According to Barth, "in revelation our concern is with the coming Jesus Christ and finally, when the time was fulfilled, the Jesus Christ who has come. Literally, and this time really directly, we are thus concerned with God's own Word spoken by God Himself. … On the one hand *Deus dixit*, on the other *Paulus dixit*."[34] Or ,as Barth later encapsulated it, "This fulfilled time which is identical with Jesus Christ, this absolute event in relation to which every other event is not yet event or has ceased to be so, this 'It is finished,' this *Deus dixit* for which there are no analogies, is the revelation attested in the Bible."[35]

---

30 *CD* I/1, p. 99.

31 *CD* I/1, p. 102.

32 *CD* I/1, p. 102. It is well known that Barth kept a reproduction of a panel of the Isenheim Altarpiece by Matthais Grünewald in which John the Baptist is depicted as pointing to Christ on the cross. For Barth's reflections on the depiction, see *CD* I/2, p. 125.

33 *CD* I/1, p. 111.

34 *CD* I/1, p. 113.

35 *CD* I/1, p. 116.

Therefore, "revelation is originally and directly what the Bible and Church proclamation are derivatively and indirectly, i.e., God's Word."[36]

As in the *GD,* Barth is careful to qualify that the three forms of the Word of God are not to be confused with the concept of three different "Words" or "addresses" of God. Rather, all three forms, though distinct, are fully unified:

> There is no distinction of degree or value between the three forms. For to the extent that proclamation really rests on recollection of the revelation attested in the Bible and is thus obedient repetition of the biblical witness, it is no less the Word of God than the Bible. And to the extent that the Bible really attests revelation it is no less the Word of God than revelation itself. As the Bible and proclamation become God's Word in virtue of the actuality of revelation they are God's Word: the one Word of God within which there can be neither a more nor a less. Nor should we ever try to understand the three forms of God's Word in isolation. The first, revelation, is the form that underlies the other two. But it is the very one that never meets us anywhere in abstract form. The direct Word of God meets us only in this twofold mediacy. But Scripture too, to become God's Word for us, must be proclaimed in the Church.[37]

It is important to note how Barth emphasized that no single form of the Word of God can be spoken of in isolation or in abstraction from the other two. Each derives its status as God's Word in virtue of its relationship to the other two, though primacy is given to revelation (God in Jesus Christ) as the form that "underlies the other two." Likewise, Barth insisted that there is no direct unmediated Word of God per se to humans, but only, paradoxically, a *direct mediated* Word: direct inasmuch as it is *God's* Word, yet mediated inasmuch as human apprehension of Jesus Christ comes in and through Spirit-filled preaching of Scripture. Thus, sure knowledge of God comes only in and through the unified threefold form of the Word of God and never in one form isolated from the other two.

In order to clarify the complex relationships between the three forms of the Word of God, Barth advanced what he called a "schedule of mutual relations":

> The revealed Word of God we know only from the Scripture adopted by Church proclamation or through proclamation of the Church based on Scripture.
>
> The written word of God we know only through the revelation which fulfils proclamation or through the proclamation fulfilled by revelation.
>
> The preached Word of God we know only through the revelation attested in Scripture or the Scripture which attests revelation.[38]

---

36 *CD* I/1, p. 117.

37 *CD* I/1, pp. 120-21.

38 *CD* I/1, p. 121.

An analysis of Barth's schedule of mutual relations is especially illuminating when compared with a similar schedule outlined some years earlier in the *GD*. It will be recalled that while in Göttingen Barth wrote: "Revelation is from God alone, scripture is from revelation alone, and preaching is from revelation and scripture."[39] On the one hand, there is a degree of affinity between the two "schedules," especially in how Barth continued to speak generally of the primacy of revelation over Scripture and preaching. On the other hand, Barth was evidently dissatisfied with the geometric linearity of the relations highlighted in the *GD* and so sought more carefully to qualify those relations in the *CD*. Consequently, whereas the statement in the *GD* yields an immediate analogy to the filioque (in that preaching is said to "proceed" from revelation and Scripture), the schedule of relations in the *CD* is structured in such a way that the analogy to the filioque is no longer obvious. Rather, the three forms of the Word of God are said to be related in a more interdependent or *perichoretic* manner such that each form of the Word in some way co-inheres with the other two.[40] Even the primacy given to "revelation" in the *GD,* while still present in the *CD* (i.e., "The first, revelation, is the form that underlies the other two"[41]), is qualified in favor of a description of the mutuality of relations among all three forms in the *CD.* Consequently, Barth adopted a schedule of relations in which each form of the Word is inextricable from the other two. Thus: 1) the *revealed* Word is known from Scripture adopted by proclamation or proclamation based on Scripture; 2) the *written* Word is known from revelation fulfilling proclamation, or proclamation fulfilled by revelation; and 3) the *preached* Word is known through revelation attested by Scripture or Scripture attesting revelation.

As in the *GD*, Barth goes on to remind his readers that the nature of the relations between the three forms of the Word of God cannot be understood by reference to any earthly analogy. On the contrary, he argued, there is but one analogy to the doctrine of the Word of God: "the doctrine of the triunity [*Dreieinigkeit*] of God."[42] Indeed, in Barth's estimation the analogy between the doctrine of the Word of God and the doctrine of the Trinity corresponds so closely that he can insist, "[W]e can substitute for revelation, Scripture and proclamation the names of the divine persons Father, Son and Holy Spirit and *vice versa,* that in the one

---

[39] Karl Barth, *Göttingen Dogmatics*, p. 15.

[40] We are using the terminology of "perichoresis" or "co-inherence" in the sense used by pseudo-Cyril and John of Damascus (albeit in reference to Christology rather than to the doctrine of the Trinity), for whom the word meant "coterminous and co-extensive." See G. L. Prestige, *God in Patristic Thought* (2nd edn, Guildford and London, 1952), p. 299. For an account of the ancient usage of the terminology of perichoresis, see especially Leonard Prestige, "ΠΕΡΙΧΩΡΕΩ and ΠΕΡΙΧΩΡΗΣΙΣ in the Fathers," *Journal of Theological Studies*, XXIX [Old Series] (1928): 242-52; and Prestige, *God in Patristic Thought*, pp. 291-301.

[41] *CD* I/1, p. 120.

[42] *CD* I/1, p. 121. On Barth's choice of the term *Dreieinigkeit*, see n. 22 above.

case as in the other we shall encounter the same basic determinations and mutual relationships."[43]

An important degree of continuity exists between the *GD* and the *CD* in terms of Barth's insistence that revelation, Scripture, and proclamation can stand in respectively for the three divine persons of Father, Son, and Holy Spirit. However, if there was reason for Barth to discern a filioquist analogy in the *GD* to the threefold Word of God, it became problematic to discern that same analogy from the threefold Word of God as outlined in the *CD*. Two issues need to be noted in this regard.

First, not only did Barth fail to give a clear rationale for why there is an obvious interchangeability of terms, but he went on to identify "revelation" here with the Father instead of the Son. As Clark rightly remarks, "[A]side from the highly imaginative origin of the analogy, it breaks the previous identification of revelation with the Son."[44] This alone is problematic.

Second, and more important, in restructuring and restating the "schedule of mutual relations" of the threefold Word of God, Barth altered—apparently without realizing—the way one must also speak of the intra-Trinitarian relations. In other words, though Barth continued to insist that the mutual relationships within the Trinity are the same as those outlined in the schedule of relations between the threefold form of the Word of God, one is left with a significantly different portrait of the Trinitarian relations in the *CD* than in the *GD*. Whereas in the *GD* Barth insisted that the relations speak concerning the origin of the three forms of the Word, he was hesitant to speak along the lines of "origin" in the *CD*, preferring to speak in terms of a "co-inherence" of the forms. Indeed, Barth contended in the *CD* that a *spirituque* is to be rejected on the grounds that perichoresis must not be confused with speaking of "origin" in God.[45]

This leads to a problem either way. If the perichoretic schedule of relations of the three forms of the Word of God in the *CD* rules out reaching conclusions about the divine origins of the divine persons corresponding to each form, then the evidence from which to discern the filioque from the threefold Word of God has disappeared. On the other hand, if the perichoretic schedule of relations of the three forms of the Word of God does give insight into the origins of the divine persons, then Barth is in conflict with himself when he later insists that the doctrine of perichoresis does not provide information about intra-Trinitarian relations, but is only another way of speaking about the *homoousia* of the Father, Son, and the Holy Spirit.[46]

Despite the appearance of this theological dilemma, one ought to exercise a degree of critical restraint here and insist that Barth not be pushed too far. He does not explicitly clarify what the modification of the schedule of relations in

---

43 *CD* I/1, p. 121.

44 Gordon H. Clark, *Karl Barth's Theological Method* (Philadelphia, 1963), p. 176.

45 *CD* I/1, p. 485.

46 *CD* I/1, p. 485.

the *CD* means for what can be said about the Trinity, and his construal of the interrelationship of the three forms of the Word of God in perichoretic form in the *CD* introduces a theological factor which was not present in the *GD*. In the end, we judge this new construction in the *CD* to be an important improvement over the more problematic construction evident in the *GD*. However, it is also the case that Barth did not appear to have perceived, when writing *CD* I/1, that the revelatory grounds for holding to the filioque on the basis of the structure of the threefold Word of God had been essentially removed when he introduced the three forms as being fully co-inherent. Even if it is granted that by the time he began the *CD* Barth was realizing the limitations of pushing the Trinitarian analogy to the threefold Word of God, he nevertheless continued to hold to the filioque in the *CD*, though, as will be demonstrated later in this chapter, his rationale for defending it was on new theological grounds.

One final issue to be addressed is to identify what factors may have been involved in leading Barth to reconfigure the schedule of relations along more perichoretic lines in the *CD*. Barth never supplied an explicit rationale for this development, but arguably he was seeking to provide a better theological account of the unity of the Word of God in its threefold form.[47] In order to bring this implicit rationale to light, one more comparison of the *GD* and the *CD* may be instructive.

It will be recalled that in the *GD* Barth spoke of the Word of God as "one in three and three in one" in which "there is no first or last, no greater or less."[48] Nevertheless, he could emphasize the priority of revelation as coming "from God alone," unlike Scripture and preaching which are both derived from revelation.[49] Since revelation alone comes from God, but is also wholly inseparable from Scripture and preaching, Barth's position in the *GD* is more closely aligned with the insistence of the fathers—especially those in the East—on the monarchy of the Father as the locus of the unity of the Trinity.[50] It is in the Father (corresponding, somewhat confusingly, to "revelation" in the threefold form of the Word of God)[51]

---

47 Indeed, Barth's schedule of relations falls exactly within the subsection called "The Unity of the Word of God." *CD* I/1, pp. 120ff.

48 Barth, *Göttingen Dogmatics*, pp. 14, 15.

49 Ibid., p. 15.

50 Lossky represented the Eastern position well: "The Trinity is therefore not the result of a process, but a primordial given. It has Its [sic] principle only in this, not above it: nothing is superior to It. Ἀρχη, the monarchy manifests itself only in, by and for the Trinity, in the relationship of the three, in a relation always ternary, to the exclusion of all opposition, of every dyad." Vladimir Lossky, *Orthodox Theology: An Introduction*, trans. Ian and Ihita Kesarcodi-Wilson (Crestwood, 1989), p. 47.

51 A more charitable reading, however, is possible. It is possible that it is here that Barth actually opened the door to speaking of the filioque as a procession of the Spirit from the "common source" of the shared essence of the Father and the Son—a particular construction which will be dealt with later in this chapter.

that the unity of the three is located. But in the *CD* Barth's emphasis, also ancient in pedigree, is more on the interdependence or interpenetration (*perichoresis*) of the three modes/forms as the locus of the unity of the Trinity/revelation. This becomes especially evident in how Barth thrice recounted the three forms of the Word relative to the other two. In this way, he sought to uphold the unity of the three forms in terms of their co-inherence to one another rather than in terms of a unity founded on a common primary "source" from which the other two are derived. The question is, however, can a perichoretic defense of the unity of the Word of God be allowed to stand in, without remainder, want or conflict, where previously Barth had sought to defend the unity on a common relation to the first or primary form of the Word—revelation? Barth appeared to think so, though, as will be shortly argued, such a move seems to undermine the very ground on which he sought to defend the filioque in the first place.

This is not to say that Barth was permanently bound by the analogy of relations originally posited in the *GD*. From a charitable perspective, it might be possible to consider Barth's movement toward a perichoretic account of the unity of the threefold Word in the *CD* as a theological complement to his earlier account of the more geometric relations identified in the *GD*. Thus, one might view the schedules of relations represented in the *GD* and the *CD* together as constituting a "Trinitarian dialectic" in which Barth's view of the triunity of the Word of God seeks, on the one hand, to uphold the "priority" (or monarchy) of revelation relative to the other two (i.e., the emphasis of the *GD*), and, on the other hand, to uphold the "co-inherence" of the three forms relative to one another (i.e., the emphasis of the *CD*). If the priority of revelation (Father) over Scripture (Christ) and preaching (Spirit) is highlighted in the *GD*, it is the perichoresis of the three that is highlighted in the *CD*, without setting aside the filioquist feature of the analogy.

However, it is also entirely possible to view Barth's shift to the perichoretic form of the unity of the Word as a genuine correction of his earlier position and that the two schedules of relations should not be reconciled. This seems more likely for two reasons.

First, though Barth continued to speak of the threefold form of the Word of God beyond *CD* I/1,[52] he ceased to appeal to it as an analogy to the triune relations after *CD* I/1. He continued to insist that in speaking of the Word of God, one speaks of "God Himself, with Jesus Christ through the Holy Ghost,"[53] and that to speak of the Word is to speak of the Trinity. But beyond continually identifying God as Triune, Barth ceased to insist that the structural relationship among the three forms of the Word is analogous to the Trinitarian relations. Thus, by the time Barth carefully distinguished between perichoresis and divine origins at the end of *CD* I/1,[54] he may also have realized the limits to which he could push the Trinitarian analogy of

---

[52] E.g., *CD* I/2, pp. 699, 743ff, 802.

[53] *CD* I/2, p. 744.

[54] As Barth put it, "the perichoresis, though it is complete and mutual, is not one of origins as such, but a perichoresis of the modes of being as modes of being of the one God."

the threefold Word of God. This indicates that the Trinitarian analogy—so clear to Barth in the geometric relations outlined in the *GD*—is eventually muted in favor of an emphasis on the co-inherence of the forms, but without speaking of the intra-Trinitarian relations per se.

Second, Barth's move toward the perichoretic view of the threefold Word of God may have been an attempt to address the methodological problem noted in Chapter Two—namely, how Barth's developing pneumatology can be called in to address the doctrines of Incarnation and Inspiration. The perichoretic schedule of relations outlined in the *CD* provides, in a way that the geometric form of relations in the *GD* could not, a more consistent method of upholding the principle of *opera Trinitatis ad extra sunt indivisa.* However, though this is an important strengthening of Barth's doctrine of the Word of God over against that which he laid out in the *GD*, by recasting the threefold Word of God in perichoretic form had Barth also shifted dramatically away from what he could say about the immanent Trinity in the *GD*? One has to ask whether, in leaving behind the geometric schedule of relations outlined in the *GD*, Barth was actually leaving behind the Trinitarian analogy itself, and therefore the very grounds upon which, originally at least, he sought to uphold the filioque. Thus, an important question is whether Barth identified any other ground or grounds upon which to defend the filioque—a question which will need to be dealt with before the end of this chapter.

Barth's Formal Defense of the Doctrine of the Filioque

At this point, it is necessary to examine closely Barth's exposition and defense of the doctrine of the filioque as it is found in *CD* I/1. This will be accomplished in four steps. First, it will be necessary to set Barth's doctrine of the filioque into its immediate context within *CD* I/1. Second, Barth's view of the theological meaning and significance of "procession" and the concept of "origin" in God will be examined. Third, an outline of Barth's Trinitarian rule of identity will provide the framework for, fourth, an analytical exposition and evaluation of Barth's material defense of the filioque.

The Context of the Doctrine of the Filioque in CD *I/1*

Barth's examination and defense of the filioque appears in §12, "God the Holy Spirit," in Chapter 2, "The Revelation of God." This is clearly in line with the pattern established in the *GD* where the filioque is dealt with as a category of "revelation" rather than being subsumed under the doctrine of God proper. In fact, Barth had virtually nothing to say about the filioque once he actually started to write his doctrine of God in *CD* II. This suggests that, for Barth, the filioque

Indeed, he adds, "It is a further description of the homoousia of Father, Son, and Spirit, but has nothing to do with begetting and breathing as such." *CD* I/1, p. 485.

continues to reflect something of the very structure of God's own self-revelation as he himself had perceived it.

The whole of §12 is built upon Barth's analysis of the New Testament witness of the primal Christian confession, "Jesus is Lord." In analyzing this confession, "we are confronted by the question: How do [Christians] come to say this?"[55] Though, indeed, Jesus is said to reveal the Father, the question remains as to how it is possible for humans to assert with such confidence Jesus' lordship in a world "in which everything is problematical."[56] How is such knowledge made manifest? This special problem, Barth explains, is solved by God's third repetition of himself, the Holy Spirit—the means by which "absolutely unproblematical knowledge of God in Christ" is accomplished. As Barth put it:

> Becoming manifest [*gegebensein*] has to be something specific, a special act of the Father or the Son or both, that is added to the givenness of the revelation of the Father in the Son … This special element in revelation is undoubtedly identical with what the New Testament usually calls the Holy Spirit as the subjective side in the event of revelation.[57]

In God's "being-present" to the creature by the Spirit's creative work, Barth continued to be wary of what he perceived as the Schleiermacherian mistake of allowing the Holy Spirit to become identical with, or confused with, the spirit of the creature. But neither is the Spirit to be confused with Jesus Christ, the Son of God incarnate.[58] On the contrary, a distinguishing characteristic of the Holy Spirit vis-à-vis the Son is the utterly eschatological nature of the Spirit. He is "The Eternal Spirit"[59] who, though received by humans, remains beyond any human standpoint and experience as "the eternal reality of the divine fulfilment and consummation."[60] This is why, for Barth, the Spirit of God, really and properly, as the Spirit of the Father and the Spirit of the Son, is spoken of as the Redeemer, "as the Lord who sets us free."[61] Moreover, it is the Spirit who completes and consummates the work of God by bringing humans into communion with the Son who reveals the Father in time and history. Such communion between God and humans is possible only because the Holy Spirit is antecedently the eternal communion of the Father and the Son. Or, in Barth's words, the Holy Spirit is "the act in which the Father is the Father of the Son or the Speaker of the Word and the Son is the Son of the Father or

---

55 *CD* I/1, p. 448.

56 *CD* I/1, p. 448.

57 *CD* I/1, p. 449.

58 *CD* I/1, pp. 451-52.

59 This is the subtitle in §12 under which Barth dealt with the filioque. CD I/1, pp. 466-89.

60 *CD* I/1, p. 464.

61 *CD* I/1, p. 448.

the Word of the Speaker."[62] Thus Barth consistently spoke of the Holy Spirit in §12 (and beyond) as "the common factor in the mode of being of God the Father and that of God the Son." Indeed, it is on the presupposition that the Spirit is common to Father and Son that Barth was willing to say (and here he is best heard on his own terms), that:

> … even if the Father and the Son might be called "person" (in the modern sense of the term), the Holy Spirit could not possibly be regarded as the third "person." In a particularly clear way the Holy Spirit is what the Father and the Son also are. He is not a third spiritual Subject, a third I, a third Lord side by side with two others. He is a third mode of being of the one divine Subject or Lord. … He is the common element, or, better, the fellowship, the act of communion, of the Father and the Son.[63]

It is in is this context—in which Barth consistently upholds the Spirit as "common" to the Father and Son—that the procession of the Spirit must be understood. As Barth argued, the Eastern view "is not meant to lead to that on which everything seems to us to depend, namely, to the thought of the full consubstantial fellowship between Father and Son as the essence of the Spirit, corresponding as a prototype to the fellowship between God as Father and man as His child, the creation of which is the work of the Holy Spirit in revelation."[64] Most importantly,

---

62 *CD* I/1, p. 470.

63 *CD* I/1, pp. 469-70. As Barth had cautiously put it earlier (evidently being careful not to rely solely on the Hegelian terminology), the biblical witness to revelation has three elements, variously known as "unveiling, veiling, and impartation, or form, freedom and historicity [cf. Hegel], or Easter, Good Friday and Pentecost, or Son, Father and Spirit." *CD* I/1, p. 332.

A close examination of the relationship of Barth's Trinitarian thinking with that of Hegel is beyond the scope of this study, though the parallels between the two have often been observed and critiqued. Most significantly, Barth's firm stance upon the single Subjectivity of God within the stream of German Idealism cannot be ignored. However, Barth was clearly not unaware of some of the dangers of the Hegelian notion of God as absolute *Geist*. In this regard, see Barth's veiled criticism of Hegel (and perhaps Luther?) in *CD* II/1, p. 265. For Barth's assessment of Hegel, see Karl Barth, *Protestant Theology in the Nineteenth Century*, trans. Brian Cozens and John Bowden (London, 2001), pp. 370-407.

In a superb study of German Idealist influence in the trinitarian theology of both Karl Barth and Wolfhart Pannenberg, Bradshaw argues that both exploit "elements of profoundest truth and insight" of Hegel's vision of theology, but that both, in their distinctive ways, seek "to overcome its difficulty, to hear the protest of Kierkegaard, [and] to maintain a proper distinction of the creature over against the triune God." See Timothy Bradshaw, *Trinity and Ontology: A Comparative Study of the Theologies of Karl Barth and Wolfhart Pannenberg* (Edinburgh, 1988), p. 363. For a lucid account of Hegel's doctrine of the Trinity, see Samuel M. Powell, *The Trinity in German Thought* (Cambridge, 2001), pp. 104-41.

64 *CD* I/1, p. 482.

Barth insisted that the filioque is grounded upon the eternal fellowship that exists between Father and Son:

> [T]he *Filioque* expresses recognition of the communion between the Father and the Son. The Holy Spirit is the love which is the essence of the relation between these two modes of being of God. And recognition of this communion is no other than recognition of the basis and confirmation of the communion between God and man as a divine, eternal truth, creation in revelation by the Holy Spirit. The intra-divine two-sided fellowship of the Spirit, which proceeds from the Father and the Son, is the basis of the fact that there is in revelation a fellowship in which not only is God there for man but in very truth—this is the *donum Spiritus sancti*—man is also there for God.[65]

Thus, it must be emphasized yet again that Barth was convinced that the filioque is confessed *a posteriori* to the revelation of the Father's union with the Son in the Spirit: that is, for Barth, the filioque is properly understood to be a *recognition* of the communion of the Father and the Son—a communion that Barth insists he has read off of the economy—and not a theological *a priori* that is pressed into service against revelation. The difficult question that eventually needs to be answered, of course, is whether Barth has indeed *rightly* read the economy.

The Theological Meaning and Significance of "Procession"

Barth's defense of the filioque is prefaced by a discussion of what has been a vital corollary to the debate, namely the question of what it means to speak of "procession" in the Godhead. Historically, the biblical and patristic terminology of *procession* had a clear parallel in Neoplatonic philosophy. The term is also frequently used by various Christian thinkers, most likely because of its original Johannine usage (e.g., John 15:26).[66] However, when used to refer to the procession of the Holy Spirit, the term also takes up a distinctively Trinitarian flavor in Christian discourse.[67] So the question is: how does Barth understand what it means to assert specifically that the Spirit "proceeds" from the Father and the Son?

It should be noted at the outset that Barth pointedly refuses to define the exact nature of the "procession" (*processio*) or "breathing" (*spiratio*) of the Spirit, just as he refuses to define the "generation" (*generatio*) of the Son.[68] This refusal stems

65 *CD* I/1, p. 480.

66 The Greek term in John 15:26 is ἐκπορεύεται. For an excellent study of the meaning and usage of "procession" in a neo-platonic context, see Jean Pépin, "Theories of Procession in Plotinus and the Gnostics," in Richard T. Wallis and Jay Bregman (eds), *Neoplatonism and Gnosticism* (Albany, 1992), pp. 297-335.

67 See Prestige, *God in Patristic Thought*, pp. 249ff.

68 *CD* I/1, pp. 475-79. For a fuller discussion of Barth's interpretation of the phrase "begotten, not made," see *CD* I/1, pp. 430-37.

from his conviction that a "successful definition" of the relationship between Father, Son and Holy Spirit would also succeed in overthrowing the Father, Son and Spirit *as* God. That is, any attempt to come to a positive definition of the theological content of these terms would itself overturn the fundamental presupposition that guided Barth ever since *Romans* that "God is God." At best, an understanding of what it means that the Spirit "proceeds" can be no more than a "description of the fact that God Himself is there in His revelation."[69] Consequently, Barth suggested that the term "procession," like "generation," can at best only "denote" something of the Spirit, but neither generation nor procession can be used to "comprehend" the Son or the Spirit respectively.[70] Nevertheless, this does not mean that the terms themselves are arbitrarily chosen or able to be replaced with carefully chosen linguistic alternatives. Rather, the terms fulfill a definite theological function appropriate to revelation. How, then, does Barth view the function of the term "procession" in reference to the Holy Spirit? For Barth, the Christian usage of the term "procession" fulfills three particular functions.

First, Barth identified the confession of the procession of the Holy Spirit in the third article of the Creed as corresponding in function to the phrase "*genitum non factum*" ("begotten, not made") at the beginning of the second article. Just as the core of the second article consists of a contrast between "begotten" and "being made," so, too, the term "procession" in the first instance leads implicitly to a negation: the Holy Spirit is not to be regarded in any way as a creature. Barth explained, "[N]o creature can be said to have proceeded from God," and "the creation of the world and man is not a procession or emanation from God."[71] Since the Spirit is said to proceed from the Father, and because that which proceeds from God the Father can only be God himself and not any created thing, the Church is thus led to confess that the Holy Spirit is of the same essence—consubstantial or *homoousia*—with God the Father. "What proceeds from God can only be God once again." Or, to put it yet another way, Barth argued that the procession of the Spirit from God guarantees that "[his] reality is of a kind that marks it out as being of divine essence with the Father and the Son."[72] Procession thus serves in the first instance to differentiate, as clearly as possible, God the Spirit from all created reality, including human spiritual reality. In Barth's words, "statements about the

[69] *CD* I/1, p. 477.

[70] *CD* I/1, p. 476.

[71] *CD* I/1, p. 473. Cf. Barth's earlier discussion of what it means for the Son to be begotten: "[T]he negative part [of the phrase 'begotten, not made'] … tells us that as a mode of being in God Jesus Christ is certainly from God, yet He is not from God in the way that creatures from the highest angel to the smallest particle of sun-dust are from God, namely by creation." *CD* I/1, p. 430. Torrance argues that it was Athanasius who most clearly made the distinction between God's existence and creation: "According to Athanasius, if that sharp distinction is not drawn, then there is finally no distinction between theology and cosmology." Thomas F. Torrance, *Theology in Reconciliation* (London, 1975), p. 221.

[72] *CD* I/1, p. 474.

operations of the Holy Spirit are statements whose subject is God and not man, and in no circumstances can they be transformed into statements about man."[73] Thus, even in the first volume of the *CD*, Barth is still vigilantly guarding against what he deemed to be the Schleiermacherian confusion or identification of the spirit of man with the Spirit of God.

Second, Barth argued that the term "procession" not only differentiates between God and created reality, but also serves to differentiate God from God. Whereas the Son is said to be begotten of God (John 3:16), Scripture also speaks of the Spirit's procession from the Father (John 15:26). Thus, procession indicates "the work of the Holy Spirit in revelation is different from that of the Son." The procession of the Spirit, then, in contrast to the "generation" of the Son, makes it clear that "there are not … two Sons or Words of God."[74]

In regard to this second function of procession, it should also be noted that Barth viewed the terminology of procession being related primarily to the *work* of the Spirit in revelation (i.e., economically) and not as a direct speculative assertion on the eternal relationship of the Spirit to the Father (and Son). If anything can be concluded about an immanent or eternal relationship among Father, Son and Spirit—which Barth undoubtedly affirmed as a possibility—it is first arrived at analogically from observation of the *work* of the Spirit (and Son) and only then moves back to "the reality of what the Son and Spirit are antecedently in Themselves."[75]

Before moving to the third function of procession, an important question needs to be put to Barth: if the procession of the Spirit is to be understood as a statement arising from observation of the economy, what event in the history of salvation—in the economy—does he identify as corresponding to the eternal procession of the Spirit? Though Barth does not directly answer this question in the terms supplied, there is good evidence that he identifies the pneumatological event of the economy as the event known in Scripture as the outpouring (or "descent") of the Holy Spirit. According to Barth, it is in the outpouring of the Spirit, most clearly identified in the book of Acts, that it becomes clear that the Holy Spirit is not identical to the Son. As Barth has explained:

> In the context of the New Testament witness the non-identity between Christ and the Holy Spirit seems to be as necessarily grounded as possible. Thus we find the Holy Spirit only after the death and resurrection of Jesus Christ or in the form of knowledge of the crucified and risen Lord, i.e., on the assumption that objective revelation has been concluded and completed.[76]

[73] *CD* I/1, p. 462.

[74] *CD* I/1, p. 474.

[75] *CD* I/1, p. 474. This differentiation is wholly consistent with Barth's earlier insistence that "The Holy Spirit is not identical with Jesus Christ, with the Son or Word of God." *CD* I/1, p. 451.

[76] *CD* I/1, p. 451.

The preceding statement might be used (and sometimes has been used) to suggest that Barth has carelessly ignored the work of the Spirit that is clearly attested to prior to the day of Pentecost. For example, critics sometimes argue that Barth does not address well the work of the Spirit in the conception of Christ in the Virgin or in the descent of the Spirit on Jesus in his baptism.[77] However, it seems improbable that one could accuse Barth of committing an error of such obvious oversight. Though more will need to be said about this, suffice it to say at this point that, for Barth, these events in the Gospel narrative are to be understood as pre-Pentecostal attestations of what he deems to be the "economic" outpouring of the Spirit. Thus, for Barth, the outpouring of the Spirit is not to be understood as restricted solely to the Pentecostal event testified to specifically in Acts 2, but can be identified with any act of God in his Lordship by which he adds "to the completed *kerygma* of the life, death, and resurrection of Jesus by Him of whom this *kerygma* speaks." Consequently, the outpouring of the Spirit is "an event which chronologically was not restricted either forwards or backwards to Pentecost."[78] Such an outpouring of the Spirit, Barth contended, is evident both in the form of Jesus' promise to send the Spirit (e.g., John 7:38ff; 14:26; 15:26; 16:7) and in the fulfillment of that promise in the actual giving of the Spirit (e.g., John 20:22; Acts 2:2; 10:44; 11:15). In this way, Barth sought to ground the procession of the Spirit in the economic actions of the Spirit testified to in Scripture, whether in passages where the Spirit is spoken of as coming in an explicit manner such as at Pentecost (Acts 2) or in passages where the working of the Spirit is anticipated but remains implicit, such as in the account of the Transfiguration (Mark 9:2ff. and par.).[79] Consequently, Barth views Pentecost not as an independent event in salvation history that goes beyond the cross, resurrection, and ascension of Jesus, but as an event that testifies to the ongoing presence of Jesus in the Church by the Holy Spirit.[80]

The third function of the terminology of procession for Barth, insofar as it stands alongside the generation of the Son, is that it speaks similarly to the fact of the Spirit's origin in the Father, but not to how the Spirit's origin can be said to be different in nature from the generation of the Son. There is no implicit meaning to the terms "procession" and "generation" that would indicate how it is that the Spirit and the Son originate uniquely from the Father, and such knowledge is beyond human comprehension. Even though the terms themselves might imply

---

77 E.g., Thomas A. Smail, "The Doctrine of the Holy Spirit," in John Thompson (ed.), *Theology Beyond Christendom* (Allison Park, 1986), pp. 87-11o at pp. 96ff.

78 *CD* I/1, p. 452.

79 *CD* I/1, p. 452.

80 Or as O'Donovan has explained, "Pentecost is not added to the sequence, Christmas, Easter, Ascension, as a further and additional moment of divine revelation, but rather stands apart from them, casting light back on them and interpreting them." Oliver O'Donovan, *On the Thirty Nine Articles: A Conversation with Tudor Christianity* (Exeter, 1986), pp. 45-46.

that the Spirit and Son both have their origin in the Father, neither term is to be understood independently or in isolation from one another; nor should procession or generation be understood to stand logically or chronologically prior to the other. Rather, the generation of the Son and the procession of the Spirit are dialectically related in such a way that one relies eternally and continually on the other in order to differentiate itself from the other. Here, Barth needs to be cited at length:

> [W]hat does the term "procession," ἐκπορεύσις, mean here? It is neither chance nor carelessness that this term is one which in itself might well be applied to the origin of the Son from the Father, so that it does not specifically denote the distinctiveness of the origin of the Holy Spirit, but strictly and properly only that alongside the begetting of the Son or speaking of the Word the Holy Spirit has His own and "in some way" different "procession" in God. The peculiarity of this procession as compared with the first one might be denoted by the term "breathing," *spiratio*, though in the strict sense it could only be "denoted" thereby. For what is the difference between breathing and begetting if in the same unconditional way both are meant to denote the eternal genesis of an eternal mode of being of God? Would not any conceivable or expressible distinction entail a denial once again either of the deity or the autonomy of the divine mode of being [*Seinsweise*] of the Holy Spirit? The difficulty which confronts us here is in fact insurmountable [*unüberwindlich*].[81]

At least three things need to be observed here. First, Barth's argument resonates with the Orthodox idea that the terms "generation" and "procession" are not to be understood as the defining basis or content of the divine "modes of being" [*Seinsweisen*], but, in the words of Lossky, "serve only to *express* the hypostatic diversity of the three."[82] Similarly, Barth insisted, in line with Athanasius, that "[w]e cannot establish the How of the divine processions and therefore of the divine modes of being. We cannot define the Father, the Son, and the Holy Ghost, i.e., we cannot delimit them the one from the other." Rather, "[w]e can state the fact of the divine processions and modes of being. But all our attempts to state the How of this delimitation will prove to be impossible."[83] Beyond the fact of these limits, Barth further argued that to assume that either procession or generation

---

81 *CD* I/1, p. 474-75. Cf. Karl Barth, *Die Kirchliche Dogmatik* (Zurich, 1932-70) I/1, p. 498. Hereafter *KD.*

82 Lossky, *Image and Likeness*, p. 79.

83 *CD* I/1, p. 476. Torrance explains Athanasius' position as follows: "[F]or Athanasius the proceeding of the Spirit from the Father is inextricably bound up with the generation of the Son from the Father which exceeds and transcends the thoughts of men. Since it would not be reverent to ask how the Spirit proceeds from God, Athanasius did not and would not entertain the question, for that would have implied an ungodly attempt to intrude into the holy mystery of God's Being." Thomas F. Torrance, *The Christian Doctrine of God, One Being Three Persons* (Edinburgh, 1996), p. 188.

defines the Spirit or the Son is to deny the autonomy of both Spirit and Son to define themselves. For Barth, the only difference denoted between generation and procession, from the perspective of the human onlooker, is *that* they are different; but humans are in no way able to pinpoint how it is that procession defines the Spirit any more than how generation defines the Son. Rather, the Spirit is who the Spirit is because of his eternally free self-differentiation from the Son, and the Son is who the Son is because of his eternally free self-differentiation from the Spirit.

Second, it is important to note Barth's concerted effort to maintain the unity of revelation in his discussion of the meaning of procession. Though procession and generation alike denote a differentiation in God—*per appropriationem*—between the Spirit and the Son respectively, the terms themselves are not to be understood as speaking of two revelations of God, but as a double element of one revelation—as two sides of one coin. "There is no special and second revelation of the Spirit alongside that of the Son."[84] Rather, in the unity of revelation there is mutual interdependence between the Son and the Spirit such that, by one act of revelation, God gives of himself to man in the Son and simultaneously allows himself to be known in the Son by man in the Spirit. Put in terms appropriate to the discussion, the generation of the Son is the theological complement to the procession of the Spirit in revelation. Neither generation nor procession denotes the particularity of how the Son and Spirit have their origin in God, but the terms do denote the fact that, mutually and in complementary fashion, they serve to reveal the one God from whom Son and Spirit derive their identity in unique ways. As Barth put it, the terminology of generation and procession together seeks to unify and ultimately, "[to] interrelate the objective element of the Word in revelation and the subjective element of the Spirit."[85]

Finally, Barth's language also indicates that he did not merely view the failure to identify the difference between generation and procession as a particularly thorny problem that theologians might eventually be able to solve, given enough time and intellectual resources; rather, the problem was *in fact* unable to be overcome (*unüberwindlich*) precisely because each term ceaselessly points to the other in order to maintain its distinction from the other. Though one might continue to wrestle with the terms as given, it would always be a rational wrestling with revelation as a mystery.[86] In this regard, "procession" and "generation" are terms which must be uttered in response to the "fact" of revelation, but which cannot be used to get behind God's own revelation of himself. The terms themselves cannot be defined, transcended, synthesized, or explained.[87] Rather, they must be upheld as pointing to an eternal dialectic—an unceasing, eternal interplay, a *Realdialektik*—within God himself.

---

84 *CD* I/1, p. 474.

85 *CD* I/1, p. 474.

86 *CD* I/1, p. 477.

87 *CD* I/1, pp. 476-77.

To summarize, Barth was aware that Scripture attests to two distinct "processions" in God—begetting and proceeding—but drew little positive content from the terminology other than that they are *distinct*. Thus, it is the *peculiarity* [*die Eigenart*] of procession vis-à-vis generation that he sought to emphasize, not the manner in which that peculiarity is enacted. In setting it up this way, Barth implicitly called into question the appropriateness of ever speaking of procession and generation in non-dialectical or linear fashion—a non-dialectical linearity that is often implicit when the begetting and procession are said to speak of the Son and the Spirit's distinct "origin" in God. Rather, as he put it, both the *spiratio Spiritus* and the *generatio Filii* are "an attempt to express what man cannot essentially express, what his language is unable to achieve." Consequently, for Barth, questions such as, "How is the Son of God begotten?" or "How does the Spirit proceed?" cannot, on the basis of revelation, be answered at all.[88] Even if an answer were ventured, it would be forthcoming only by recourse to an abstract principle (i.e., "origin") over and above the concrete revelation of the fact of the *Seinsweisen* themselves. Indeed, to define that the Son's eternal origin is one of begetting and the Spirit's eternal origin is that of proceeding is to smuggle in, at the outset, the assumption that begetting and procession primarily denote something about the hypostatic mode of origination. It presumes to know at least part of the content of the generation and procession before it is encountered, namely that generation and procession can both be subsumed under a single conceptual category called "origin." For Barth, this would be to transgress the boundary between the *That* and the *How*. As he argued, "our knowledge can only be an acknowledgement of …fact",[89] namely that "what is there in God's revelation is the Father, the Son and the Spirit."[90] Theologians seeking witness to the revelation given can say "no more and no less than that we cannot establish the How of the divine processions and therefore of the divine modes of being. … We can only state that in revelation three who delimit themselves from one another are present … But all our attempts to state the How of this delimitation will prove to be impossible."[91] Barth concluded, "Therefore, for the sake of what the doctrine of the Trinity must state, namely, that the Father, the Son, and the Spirit are God, no more must be said at this point and

---

88 Barth's reasoning bears striking resemblance to that of Gregory of Nazianzus: "How was he begotten? Again with displeasure I will say this same thing. Let the generation of God be honored by silence. Learning that he was begotten is a great thing for you. But we will not acquiesce that you discern it. Do you wish that I suggest how it was? The Father who begot knows how it was, and the Son who was begotten. Beyond these things, it is hidden by a cloud, escaping your dim sightedness." Gregory of Nazianzus, "Third Theological Oration" in William G. Rusch (ed.), *The Trinitarian Controversy* (Philadelphia, 1980), p. 136.

89 *CD* I/1, p. 475.

90 *CD* I/1, p. 477.

91 *CD* I/1, p. 476.

no definition must result here. This is the general significance of the *qui procedit* in trinitarian theology."[92]

Barth's Trinitarian Rule of Identity and the Filioque

It is possible that much of Barth's specific reasoning on the theological significance of the procession of the Spirit as delineated above could be accepted, with perhaps only minor modification, by those in the Orthodox camp. Vladimir Lossky, for example, has argued that "[t]erms such as … procession and origin [are] but inappropriate expressions for a reality alien to all becoming, all process, all beginning."[93] In a similar vein, Barth readily conceded that the terms themselves can never claim to be the exclusively correct terms to speak of the Holy Spirit and the Son because "[c]orrectness belongs exclusively to that about which we have thought and spoken, not to what we have thought and spoken."[94] What is vital for Barth is that an attempt has been made in response to God's self-revelation, even if the attempt itself cannot finally and utterly express that which ought to be expressed. Lossky and Barth here, it must be admitted, are in essential agreement.

Despite the apparent affinity, however, the significant difference between Barth and Lossky (and all Eastern doctrines of the Trinity) must be noted. As Reid's study has highlighted so well, Eastern and Western Trinitarian theologies construe the relationship between the economic and immanent Trinity in fundamentally different ways, even while sharing some common concerns.[95] Following the logic of the characteristic Byzantine (and Palamite) distinction between the divine essence (*ousia*) and the divine energies *(energeiai)*,[96] Lossky, for example, has applied the concepts of "procession" and "generation" to the divine energies only—roughly equivalent to the Western concept of the economic Trinity. Barth, on the other hand, was prepared to say that procession and generation speak not only of the work of Spirit and Son, but also of their eternal identity as eternal Son and eternal Spirit—an identity antecedent to their work, but known only *a posteriori* through their work.[97] Thus, Barth (along with a long line of other

---

92 *CD* I/1, p. 477.

93 As cited by Robert Jenson, *Systematic Theology* (2 vols, New York and Oxford, 1997), vol. 1, p. 152.

94 *CD* I/1, p. 432.

95 See pp. 38-39 above.

96 Torrance argues that Athanasius consistently resisted this distinction and instead posited the unity of God's act and being as an Act in Being and a Being in Act—ἐνόυσιος ἐνέργεια. Torrance, *Theology in Reconciliation*, p. 236.

97 It is noteworthy that in §10 "God the Father," §11 "God the Son," and §12 "God the Holy Spirit" Barth structured his discussion in each section by beginning with a discussion of the distinctive work (i.e., God as Creator, God as Reconciler, God as Redeemer) and only then discusses each in reference to their eternal nature, i.e., The Eternal Father, The Eternal Son, The Eternal Spirit. See *CD* I/1, pp. 384-489.

Western Trinitarian theologians) stuck resolutely to what Reid calls the "principle of identity" between the economic and immanent Trinity.[98]

Barth's affirmation of this principle can be found at various places in the *CD*, and in various forms: "the reality of God which encounters us in His revelation is His reality in all the depths of eternity,"[99] or "What [the Holy Spirit] is in revelation He is antecedently in Himself. And what He is antecedently in Himself He is in revelation."[100] He even went so far—which is admittedly rare—as to call this a "rule" for his theology: "we have consistently followed the rule [*Regel*], which we regard as basic [*grundlegend*], that statements about the divine modes of being antecedently in themselves cannot be different in content from those that are to be made about their reality in revelation."[101] Specifically, this means that the Holy Spirit "is the Spirit of both the Father and the Son not just in His work *ad extra* and upon us, but that to all eternity—no limit or reservation is possible here—He is none other than the Spirit of both the Father and the Son."[102] Put more boldly, then, to be fair to Barth, one cannot suggest that the filioque functions as an axiomatic *a priori* for him as much as one can suggest that the filioque is the necessary conclusion arrived at on the basis of a consistent following of the rule of identity between the economic and immanent Trinity.

Given Barth's commitment to the "rule of identity" between economic and immanent Trinity, it becomes even more clear why he cannot accept Eastern monopatrism. To his credit, Barth did not fall prey to an oversimplistic position that the filioque can be defended against the East simply because the Scripture speaks of the Spirit as both the Spirit of the Father and the Spirit of the Son, as if Orthodox theology has overlooked this obvious scriptural fact.[103] Indeed, East and West can stand in full agreement that the Spirit given in Pentecost is a gift sent by the risen Christ from the Father and is therefore spoken of in Scripture as both the Spirit of God and the Spirit of Christ.[104] However, the failure of Eastern theology, Barth argued, is that it "does not read off from revelation its statements about the being of God 'antecedently in Himself.' It does not stand by the order of the divine

[98] Duncan Reid, *Energies of the Spirit: Trinitarian Models in Eastern Orthodox and Western Theology* (Atlanta, 1997), p. 125.

[99] *CD* I/1, p. 479.

[100] *CD* I/1, p. 466.

[101] *CD* I/1, p. 479.

[102] *CD* I/1, pp. 479-80.

[103] It is a fundamental misunderstanding of basic Orthodox theology when some Western theologians naively argue for the filioque solely upon the basis that the Spirit is the Spirit of the Father and of the Son, as if this were denied by Eastern Orthodoxy. For a fuller discussion of this criticism, see David Guretzki, "The *Filioque*: Assessing Evangelical Approaches to a Knotty Problem," in Stanley E. Porter and Anthony R. Cross (eds), *Semper Reformandum: Studies in Honour of Clark H. Pinnock* (Carlisle, 2003), pp. 183-207 at pp. 189ff.

[104] O'Donovan, *Thirty Nine Articles*, p. 45.

modes of being which by its own admission is valid in the sphere of revelation." On the contrary—and here Barth went on the offensive—"[Eastern theology] goes beyond revelation to achieve a very different picture of God 'antecedently in Himself.'"[105] Barth's logic is that if both East and West can accept that the Spirit is understood in the economy to have been given by Christ from the Father, it is difficult to see why it should not also be said that the Spirit is given by the Son from the Father in all of eternity. Consequently, he contests the use of scriptural texts such as John 15:26 by proponents of monopatrism as scriptural proof that the Spirit proceeds only from the Father. To use scriptural texts in such a manner, Barth argued, is to "isolate them from the many other [texts] which equally plainly call Him the Spirit of the Son." Thus, in Barth's estimation, the Eastern rejection of the filioque that appeals to John 15:26 is "already suspect from the formal standpoint because it is patently a speculation which interprets verses of the Bible in isolation, [and] because it bears no relation to the reality of God in revelation and for faith."[106]

It is difficult to fault Barth in his own internal logic. One can justifiably understand his reluctance to accept, on a matter of principle, Eastern argumentation that suggests that the filioque is true in the economy, but not in the immanent Trinity.[107] By putting it this way, Barth feared that a revelation of God that is distinct in form and content from God as he is in eternity is to posit a hidden God behind the God of revelation—making sure, saving knowledge of God suspect, if not theoretically impossible. Barth's fears, of course, hinge upon the assumption that a distinction between the economic and immanent Trinity is necessary. And, beyond a shadow of a doubt, Barth argued, such a distinction *is* theologically necessary:

> [I]t is not just good sense but absolutely essential that along with all older theology we make a deliberate and sharp distinction between the Trinity of God as we may know it in the Word of God revealed, written and proclaimed, and God's immanent Trinity, i.e., between "God in Himself" and "God for us," between the "eternal history of God" and His temporal acts.[108]

It is important not to reject out of hand Barth's insistence on a distinction between the economic and immanent Trinity,[109] but to consider whether in fact

---

[105] *CD* I/1, p. 480.

[106] *CD* I/1, p. 480.

[107] *CD* I/1, p. 479.

[108] *CD* I/1, p. 172.

[109] In this regard, Molnar is right to uphold Barth's doctrine of the immanent Trinity as being "clear and distinct" from that of the economic Trinity, though we have cause to wonder whether Molnar has critically applied that same criterion to Barth's own work. See Paul D. Molnar, "Toward a Contemporary Doctrine of the Immanent Trinity: Karl Barth and the Present Discussion," *Scottish Journal of Theology* 49/3 (1996): 311-57; and Paul

the filioque is a necessary conclusion arising out of that assumed distinction. In other words, given the increasing agreement that Eastern and Western theologies can be viewed as complementary dogmatic perspectives on the doctrine of the Trinity,[110] the question is whether, within his Western Trinitarian logic, Barth has given sufficient grounds to continue to hold to the filioque. Though the answer to this question will be addressed in Chapter Four below, it will remain central to the exposition of Barth's defense of the filioque in what follows.

Barth's Material Defense of the Filioque

In light of Barth's Trinitarian rule of identity, it now becomes possible to pay closer attention to his material defense of the doctrine of the filioque in *CD* I/1 and to note how he sought to apply the rule. Barth's defense of the filioque, as will be seen, is multifaceted, and he sought to address historical, ecumenical, exegetical, and systematic matters. Though it is not necessary to recount every detail of Barth's argument, it is important, at least in outline form, to understand some of the reasons why he continued to defend the doctrine.

Historical and Ecumenical Issues

Barth is well aware that "from the Son" [ἐκ τοῦ υἱοῦ] was not in the original text of either the 325 or 381 versions of the third article of the Creed. However, he noted that there is literary evidence that neither the Greeks nor Latins would have been explicitly opposed to the material addition of "from the Son." He cited Epiphanius,[111] Ephraem[112] and Cyril of Alexandria[113] as providing concrete evidence of writers who spoke in terms appropriate to what would later coincide with the doctrine of the filioque.

Barth readily admitted that the later interpolation and dogmatization of the filioque in the Latin version of the Creed was "not in fact a shining testimonial to the Roman Catholic theory of the certainty of the Church's teaching authority

D. Molnar, *Divine Freedom and the Doctrine of the Immanent Trinity* (London and New York, 2002).

[110] Mary Ann Fatula, "The Holy Spirit in East and West: Two Irreducible Traditions," *One in Christ* 19/4 (1983): 379-86.

[111] "πατὴρ ἦν ἀεὶ, καὶ τὸ πνεῦμα ἐκ πατρὸς καὶ υἱοῦ πνέει" (Ancoratus, 75). *CD* I/1, p. 477.

[112] "The Father is the Begetter, the Son the Begotten from the bosom of the Father, the Holy Ghost he that proceedeth from the Father and the Son" (*Hymnus de defunctis et trinitate*, 11). *CD* I/1, p. 477.

[113] "τὸ πνεῦμα τὸ ἅγιον …ποόεισι δὲ καὶ ἐκ πατρὸς καὶ υἱοῦ" (*Thes. de trin.*, 34). *CD* I/1, p. 477.

as concentrated in the hands of the pope."[114] Nevertheless, he rightly insisted that the history of the formation of the Creed, including a reconstruction of the theological intentions of the original authors, can in no way be used as "proof" that the dogmatic truth of the filioque is to be rejected. He rightly countered what amounts to an argument from silence—whether for or against the filioque—that could be constructed upon the brute fact of the filioque's absence from the original Creed. As Barth rightly concluded, "there was no necessary reason—the factual reason adduced is not a necessary one—why the filioque should not have been in the original creed."[115]

By the time Barth came to speak of the filioque in the *CD*, he has clearly gained a better historical and ecumenical understanding of the problem than he had in his original discussion in the *GD*, including a clearer understanding of the Orthodox literature. In reference to Orthodoxy, Barth noted, on one end of the spectrum, the position of L. P. Karsavin—"even if he is not to be taken too seriously"—that the filioque is responsible for the doctrine of the Immaculate Conception, papal infallibility, Kantianism, the belief in progress, and other evils of Western culture.[116] At the other end, he cites Archimandrite Sylvester of Kiev who was prepared to accept, for the purposes of seeking union between Orthodox and Old Catholics, that the filioque is a faithful expression of God's work *ad extra*, but not in regard to the inner Trinitarian life. Not surprisingly, Barth rejected both ends of the spectrum as untenable. However, he was noticeably more attentive to the "incomparably saner" view of V. Bolotow[117] who argued that the Augustinian filioque was to be accepted as a private opinion that had wrongly taken on the status of official Church dogma. It was Bolotow's position that Barth discerned as the "prevailing view in Eastern Orthodoxy to-day."[118]

---

114 *CD* I/1, p. 478.

115 *CD* I/1, pp. 477-78. Though Barth should hardly be regarded as an historical authority on the development of the Creed, it is sufficient to note that scholars have been increasingly cautious against making inflated claims for or against the filioque on the basis of a historical reconstruction of the original intentions of the Nicene doctors.

116 Barth was not alone in his suspicions that so much can be pinned to the filioque. Even from an Eastern perspective, Orthodox theologian Theodore Stylianopoulous has argued, "In view of the complexities and divergent phenomena of history the charges that the filioque doctrine has led to ecclesiasticism, authoritarianism, clericalism, and even the dogma of the Pope are wholly unconvincing. … [I]t does not at all follow that the specific doctrine of the filioque itself has caused such developments in the West." Theodore Stylianopoulos, "The Filioque: Dogma, Theologoumenon or Error?," *Greek Orthodox Theological Review* 31/3-4 (1986): 255-88 at 284. More pointedly, Catholic theologian Yves Congar can say, "In the final analysis, then, the quarrel about the ecclesiological consequences of the Filioque is of doubtful value." Yves Congar, *I Believe in the Holy Spirit*, trans. David Smith (3 vols, New York, 2001), vol. 2, p. 211.

117 Or, more commonly, Bolotov.

118 *CD* I/1, p. 479. If Barth was optimistic that Bolotow represented the majority opinion among Orthodox theologians in the 1930s, it is certainly the case that Bolotow's

Exegetical Issues

Whether or not the East-West schism should have taken place—Barth ultimately took this to be a moot point—the substantive question remains whether the filioque should be retained on dogmatic grounds. Thus, Barth took considerably more time to examine the exegetical evidence that might be used to counter the truth of the filioque.

In this regard Barth admitted that the most significant exegetical argument leveled against the filioque is that various biblical texts speak of how the Spirit is plainly presented as acting upon the Son in one manner or another. How does one explain, for example, that Scripture presents the Spirit as bringing about the conception of Jesus in the Virgin Mary (Luke 1:35), as alighting upon Jesus in his baptism (Mark 1:9 and par.), or as the one by whom Jesus was declared to be Son of God by being raised from the dead (Romans 1:3)?[119] Do these texts not compel one, to use Barth's own phraseology, to accept that "material dogmatic statements about the immanent Trinity can and must be taken from definitions of the modes of being of God in revelation"?[120]

Barth responded to this line of exegetical reasoning by distinguishing between Christ's divine and human origins. Whereas Christ's eternal identity as the Son—the second *Seinsweise*—is based on his being begotten of the Father in contradistinction from the procession of the Spirit, his human constitution comes about by and through the working of the Holy Spirit. "[T]he work of the Holy Spirit in relation to the Son in revelation … is not of such a kind that it can be described as commensurable with the eternal begetting of the Son by the Father or the eternal breathing of the Spirit by the Father and the Son, so that another eternal relation of origin can and should be read off from it."[121] On the contrary, "what the Son 'owes' to the Spirit in revelation is His being as man, the possibility

position is becoming more and more prevalent among Orthodox and Catholic theologians alike. For example, Stylianopoulos is ready to accept the filioque as a theologoumenon, but also insists that the filioque ought to be regarded neither as a blatant theological error, nor as an official dogma. On the contrary, he suggests that the difference dividing East and West is a difference of interpretation of a dogma, not a difference of dogma itself. He even goes so far as to argue that "the theological use of the filioque in the West against Arian subordinationism is fully valid according to the theological criteria of the Eastern tradition." Stylianopoulos, "The Filioque," p. 287. Roman Catholic theologian Ralph Del Colle has also argued that Eastern and Western conceptions may be viewed as complementary understandings of the mystery of the Holy Trinity. See Ralph Del Colle, "Reflections on the Filioque," *Journal of Ecumenical Studies* 34/2 (Spring 1997): 202-17.

119 For two examples of this type of exegetical reasoning, see Smail, "Holy Spirit," pp. 163-64; and Clark H. Pinnock, *Flame of Love: A Theology of the Holy Spirit* (Downers Grove, 1996), pp. 85-91.

120 *CD* I/1, p. 485.

121 *CD* I/1, p. 485.

of the flesh existing for Him, so that He, the Word, can become flesh."[122] Thus, Barth argued that the Spirit's action upon the Son in the birth, baptism, and resurrection "is always a bringing forth from some other essence whose existence is presupposed."[123] True, it is the eternal Son of God, the second mode of being, who becomes flesh by the power of the Spirit, but the Spirit does not bring the Son qua Son into existence per se. In that regard, the Son is the eternal Son by virtue of being eternally generated by the Father. As for the resurrection, the Spirit enables "the exaltation and revelation of Him who was crucified and who died to the glory of the Son of God."[124] In so doing, the Spirit does not bring forth the Son of God *as* the Son of God; the Son does not *become* the Son in the resurrection. Rather, in the resurrection by the Spirit Jesus is publicly attested to be the eternal Son of God.

Barth recapitulated the distinction between Christ's divine and human origins even more clearly in *CD* I/2 when commenting on the significance of the conception of Jesus by the Holy Spirit [*conceptus de Spiritu sancto*]:

> The man Jesus of Nazareth is not the true Son of God because He was conceived by the Holy Spirit and born of the Virgin Mary. On the contrary, because He is the true Son of God and because this is an inconceivable mystery intended to be acknowledged as such, therefore He is conceived by the Holy Spirit and born of the Virgin Mary. And because He is thus conceived and born, He has to be recognised and acknowledged as the One He is and in the mystery in which He is the One He is.[125]

Barth similarly applied this reasoning to the work of the Spirit upon humans in being "born again" (John 3:5ff). As he explained, "Birth of the Spirit is a new birth, a regeneration, and the man to be born of the Spirit as a child of God is already there when this happens. … But one obviously cannot say that the child of

---

[122] *CD* I/1, p. 486.

[123] *CD* I/1, p. 485.

[124] *CD* I/1, p. 486.

[125] *CD* I/2, p. 202. Barth would return to the question of the relationship of the person of Jesus to the Spirit at length in *CD* III/2, pp. 332-40. There he described what he saw as the view of the New Testament authors: "The relationship of this man to the Holy Spirit is so close and special that He owes no more and no less than His existence itself and as such to the Holy Spirit." *CD* III/2, p. 333.

In continuity with this sentiment, Barth would much later argue, "The particular existence of the Son of God as man, and again the particular existence of this man as the Son of God, the existence of Jesus Christ as the Lord who becomes a servant and the servant who becomes Lord, His existence as the Guarantor of truth is itself ultimately grounded in the being and work of the Holy Spirit. He is *conceptus de Spiritu sancto*." *CD* IV/1, p. 148. For a more extensive examination of the relationship between the Spirit and incarnation, see John Thompson, *The Holy Spirit in the Theology of Karl Barth* (Allison Park, 1991), pp. 41-52.

God this man becomes is created or begotten by the Spirit."[126] Or to put it another way, "not directly but indirectly, *per adoptionem*, in faith in Christ, we become that which we are not by nature, namely, children of God."[127]

In all this, Barth argued that the biblical passages that speak of the Holy Spirit's action upon Jesus (i.e., birth, baptism, resurrection), in no instance, have anything to do whatsoever with "origin" in God. Rather, each instance is a "confirmation" that "the Holy Spirit in revelation unites God and man, Creator and creature, the Holy One and sinner, so that they become Father and child, in the same way He is in himself the communion, the love, which unites the Father to the Son and the Son to the Father."[128]

What should be said of Barth's exegetical reasoning here? Positively, two things should be noted. First, Barth rightly sought to resist any form of theological adoptionism that might result in interpreting the significance of the action of the Spirit upon Jesus as attested to in the biblical accounts. Given Barth's lifelong dialogue with his liberal theological counterparts whom he discerned as reducing Christology to an account of the divine influence on the historical Jesus of Nazareth, it is reasonable to assume that he was likely seeking to be responsive to such viewpoints. That is, Jesus' significance is that he comes in human flesh as the one who antecedently already is the eternal Son of God. Barth rightly identified the work of the Spirit in the conception, baptism and resurrection as acts of the Spirit in which the Son is attested to be one who is identified with, and comes from, God the Father and not simply as one human among many upon whom God confers a special mark of his blessing or grace.[129] In other words, it is helpful to continue to be reminded that the concerns of the Barth of the Safenwil and Göttingen period—particularly the concern to speak clearly the confession that "God is God"—are still real concerns for the Barth writing the *CD*.

Second, Barth's interpretation of the significance of the Spirit's action upon the Son implicitly upholds the *novum* of the incarnation in the divine economy. The eternal Son's conception in the Virgin by the Holy Spirit indicates a genuinely new action of God whereby the eternal Son takes up human flesh, and is the one who, in that same human form, is baptized and resurrected from the dead. Barth affirmed this new action of God in Christ while simultaneously maintaining the continuity of Jesus of Nazareth with the eternal Son of God. In this regard, his way of putting

---

126 *CD* I/1, p. 485.

127 *CD* I/1, p. 486.

128 *CD* I/1, p. 486.

129 In *CD* I/2, Barth upheld this explanation by distinguishing between the act of the Spirit as a "sign" or "confirmation" of Christ's Sonship rather than as an act in which Jesus Christ was constituted as the Son of God. "This [baptism] story naturally does not assert that because God the Spirit descended upon Jesus like a dove He became the Son of God, but it states (cf. Jn 1:32f) that He upon whom the Spirit descended, as the sign of the dove bore witness, actually is the beloved Son of God." *CD* I/2, p. 199. For further comments on the baptism of Jesus, see *CD* IV/1, p. 164.

it insures that both the Son and the Spirit are said to be engaged in genuinely new actions in that the eternal Son takes up flesh through the Holy Spirit, who uniquely makes it possible.

Despite these strengths, however, Barth's way of dealing with these important biblical texts raises some problems. First, by arguing that the Spirit's work upon the Son, as attested to in the Gospel accounts, has only to do with Jesus' humanity, Barth is in danger of isolating Jesus' humanity from his divinity. This tendency of Barth, while not properly a full-blown Nestorianism, is nevertheless in danger of setting the humanity received by the Son in the Spirit into a secondary and separate position in the function of revelation. While Barth properly resisted making Jesus' humanity constitutive of his identity as the eternal Son of God, in *CD* I at least, it is unclear how he can maintain the full unity of humanity and divinity in Jesus Christ without allowing the work of the Spirit in bringing about Jesus' humanity in some way to speak of the relationship of the Spirit to the Son in the immanent Trinity.

Second, despite the clarity by which he can speak of a "rule" by which observation of the economic Trinity leads to conclusions about the immanent Trinity, it is unclear how Barth believed this rule was to be applied. How is he able to identify the Spirit's work in the conception, the baptism, and the resurrection of Jesus as having primarily to do only with Jesus' humanity and nothing at all to do with the intra-Trinitarian relations that are ontologically antecedent to them? If these events are revelatory at all, then, in accordance with Barth's own rule, one should expect that they should be theologically informative about how the Spirit relates to the Son eternally and not simply about how the Spirit relates to the temporal humanity of Jesus. This should especially be the case if in fact it is by the Spirit poured out at Pentecost that the theological significance of the humanity of Jesus is perceived.

Furthermore, Barth does not acknowledge the converse truth that comes with affirming that it is Jesus (the man) who is clearly presented in the Gospels as the one who sends the Spirit from the Father (e.g., John 15:26; 20:22-23). If Barth is able to appeal to this action of the *human* Jesus as being constitutive of the Spirit's identity as one who antecedently and eternally proceeds from the Father and the Son, it is not clear why he disallows the converse action of the Spirit upon the human Son as being legitimately read back into the immanent Trinity. In this regard, O'Donovan astutely wonders whether the biblical accounts of the baptism of Jesus might in fact be a better guide than Pentecost in standing at the centre of God's self-revelation in all its fullness. As O'Donovan has explained:

> Indeed, Pentecost, we might claim, is the *wrong* starting point, because the Spirit is there concerned inescapably with the formation of the church; and we must therefore presuppose a prior moment, a relation of the Spirit to the Father and the Son in which the believing church is not yet present, except implicitly in the person of the Son.[130]

[130] O'Donovan, *Thirty Nine Articles*, p. 47.

The foregoing criticism of Barth's potential separation of Jesus' humanity from his divinity in revelation in the early volumes of the *CD*, of course, is clearly not new in the literature[131] and is ventured here only in recognition of Barth's tendency to be ever open to theological correction. In other words, it would be imprudent to suggest that Barth is *finally* to be judged to be Nestorian in his Christology.[132] More importantly, Barth continued to hold to the rule of the correspondence between the economic and immanent Trinity, but assumed Pentecost to be the primary pneumatological event by which all other aspects of the Christ-event must be judged when considering the relationship of the Spirit to the Son. Not surprisingly, therefore, for Barth the filioque continued to be a necessary recognition that the Spirit goes out from the Father and the Son. But while it is certainly important to consider Pentecost as being significant in the economy, it is not necessarily self-evident that Pentecost is inherently a better revelatory starting-point than reflection upon, say, the birth or baptism of Jesus.

Excursus: Karl Barth and T. F. Torrance on the Filioque

It was noted in Chapter One that T. F. Torrance was one theologian who, despite his significant reflections upon the filioque problem, provided little by way of direct critique of Barth's position. However, Torrance did make it clear that Western adoption of the filioque, while properly understood as an appropriate response to Arianism, would have been unnecessary if the Church had more closely followed the lead of Athanasius over the Cappadocians. Instead of providing a direct critique of Barth per se, Torrance sought to explain how the filioque debate could have been avoided altogether. In this regard Torrance's position on the matter cannot be neatly categorized either as Eastern monopatrist or Western filioquist, and he

131 Baillie, for example, argued that in Barth the doctrine of the divine incognito of the nature of revelation in Christ reaches an extreme. "Barth seems to hold that there was nothing very distinctive or impressive, nothing very God-revealing, in either the teaching or the personality of this man Jesus. His human life was not a revelation, but a concealment, of God." D. M. Baillie, *God Was in Christ* (New York, 1948), p. 17. More recently, Hart has sought to defend Barth from the Nestorianist charge brought against him by scholars such as Baillie through a broader consideration of Barth's work from the *Römerbrief* through to the latter volumes of the *CD* as well as through a closer consideration of Barth's anhypostatic-enhypostatic Christology. See Trevor Hart, *Regarding Barth* (Downers Grove, 1999), pp. 1-27.

132 There were signs in the mid-1950s that Barth appeared to have become increasingly aware of the potential of separating Christ's humanity from its function in revelation in this way of speaking about the humanity of Christ. This was especially evidenced in how he could speak of a *Retraktation* or "revision" that better recognized God's humanity. As he put it, "It would be the false deity of a false God if in His deity His humanity did not also immediately encounter us. … In [Jesus Christ] the fact is once for all established that God does not exist without man." Karl Barth, *The Humanity of God* (Richmond, 1960), p. 50.

clearly took his primary theological cues from Athanasius. There is a degree of Athanasian affinity between the core of Barth's and Torrance's interpretation of the meaning of the procession of the Spirit that has been all too easily overlooked and which also makes Barth's position—including his explicit defense of the filioque—somewhat less Western than it may appear. Thus, the remainder of this chapter will bring Torrance and Barth into a closer dialogue not only to note their similarities, but also to discern why Barth deemed it necessary to maintain the filioque while Torrance did not. The benefit of this comparative exercise is that it offers an initial clarification of how the filioque doctrine functions systematically in Barth's thought.

A first point of comparison between Barth and Torrance is on their view of the significance of the doctrine of the Spirit's procession. Torrance is largely convinced that the general problem of the doctrine of the procession comes down to "the fact that we do not know at all what 'proceeding (ἐκπόρευσις) from the Father' really means."[133] He goes on to say, "This problem is particularly acute when we think of the Spirit as going forth (ἐκπόρευόμενον) from the Father in a way that is different from the begetting of the Son by the Father and have to find a way of expressing that difference."[134] Here he explicitly agrees with his teacher: "As Karl Barth pointed out, we can no more offer an account of the 'how' of these divine relations and actions that [*sic*] we can define the Father, the Son and the Holy Spirit and delimit them from one another."[135]

Second, and more important than the agreement on the indescribability on the meaning of the concept of procession, both theologians agree that the procession of the Spirit is decidedly *not* properly described, as it has been traditionally done, as a "double-procession," though each approaches this problem from a different direction. This assertion will require considerable unpacking.

Almost without exception, historical discussion of the procession of the Spirit has tended to treat the word "filioque" as if it entailed a commitment to the "double procession" of the Spirit. The standard English translation of *ex patre filioque* as "from the Father and the Son" has undoubtedly contributed to an understanding of a "double procession." Even Torrance has characterized the Western position as one in which "the Spirit proceeds from the Son as well as the Father."[136] How else might one speak of the Spirit proceeding from the Son, "as well as" the Father, without immediately adducing that the procession must be "double"?

Those who assume that the procession of the Spirit in the Western tradition is a "double procession" can hardly be faulted for doing so, if for no other reason than because Western theologians, for the most part, have accepted this designation. However, it is important to note how an innocent conceptual translation brings

---

[133] Torrance, *Christian Doctrine of God*, p. 192.

[134] Ibid.

[135] Ibid., p. 193.

[136] Thomas F. Torrance, *Trinitarian Perspectives: Toward Doctrinal Agreement* (Edinburgh, 1994), p. 113.

with it a significant theological assumption, namely that the procession of the Spirit, whether from the Father alone (as in Eastern thinking),[137] or from Father and Son, though principally (*principaliter*) from the Father[138] (as in Western thinking), concerns the *hypostatic origin* of the Spirit. Despite the deep divisions that have arisen between Eastern and Western theology, the procession of the Spirit has been deployed by both traditions to designate the origin of the third divine *hypostasis* as one which is said to proceed from another *hypostasis* or *hypostases*. Thus, in Eastern theology it is commonly held that the second and third hypostases, the Son and the Holy Spirit, are generated and proceed from the *hypostasis* of the Father, thereby safeguarding the monarchy of the Father.[139] Similarly, the West continues to hold that the third Person of the Trinity proceeds from the Father and the Son in a "double procession"—i.e., as a procession from both divine Persons. Either way, East and West have tended to agree that the procession, whether single or double, is from the Father either singularly or principally.[140] However, both Barth and Torrance resist this assumption (Torrance more explicitly). Barth rejects the notion of a "double" procession by interpreting the meaning of filioque in a certain way, while Torrance seeks to go behind the filioque by reinterpreting the

---

137 Orthodox theologian Boris Bobrinskoy's statement is representative: "The Holy Spirit proceeds hypostatically from the Father alone, in a complete simultaneity of origin with the Son." Boris Bobrinskoy, *The Mystery of the Trinity: Trinitarian Experience and Vision in the Biblical and Patristic Tradition*, trans. Anthony P. Gythiel (Crestwood, 1999), p. 296.

138 "And the Son is born of the Father; and the Holy Spirit proceeds from the Father principally, the Father giving the procession without any interval of time, yet in common from both [Father and Son]." Augustine, *De Trinitate*, 15.26.47; ET: Augustine, *On the Holy Trinity*, in *Nicene and Post-Nicene Fathers* (Grand Rapids, 1994), vol. 3, p. 225.

139 As Zizioulas puts it, "Among the Greek Fathers the unity of God, the one God, and the ontological 'principle' or 'cause' of the being and life of God does not consist in the one substance of God but in the hypostasis, that is, the person of the Father. The one God is not the one substance but the Father, who is the 'cause' both of the generation of the Son and of the procession of the Spirit. Consequently, the ontological 'principle' of God is traced back, once again, to the person." John D. Zizioulas, Being As Communion (Crestwood, 1985), pp. 40-1.

140 This agreement is well summarized by the so-called "Roman Clarification on the Filioque": "The Greek Fathers and the whole Christian Orient speak, in this regard, of the "Father's Monarchy," and the Western tradition, following St Augustine, also confesses that the Holy Spirit takes his origin from the Father ***principaliter***, that is, as principle (*De Trinitate XV, 25, 47, PL 42, 1094-1095*). In this sense, therefore, the two traditions recognise that the "monarchy of the Father" implies that the Father is the sole Trinitarian Cause (Aitia) or Principle (Principium) of the Son and of the Holy Spirit." See "The Greek and Latin Traditions about the procession of the Holy Spirit" in L'Osservatore Romano, 38 (September 20, 1995): 3. Emphasis and italics original.

traditional doctrine of the monarchy of the Father in conjunction with the concept of perichoresis. Each will need to be dealt with in order.

The evidence that Barth resisted the double procession is twofold. First, there is not, as far as has been ascertained, a single instance in the *CD* where Barth succumbs to the terminology of "double procession" or where he implied such a concept when speaking of the procession of the Spirit. He had already expressly denied such a view in the opening half-volume of the *CD*: "[T]he *ex patre Filioque* denotes, not a twofold [*doppelten*], but rather a common origin [*gemeinsamen Ursprung*] of the Spirit from the Father and the Son."[141] Second, Barth preferred to speak of the procession of the Spirit not as from the Father and the Son as from individual *Seinsweisen*, but as proceeding from the one being of God [*Gottsein*] shared by the modes of being of the Father and the Son. He explained:

> The fact that the Father is the Father and the Son the Son, that the former begets and the latter is begotten, is not common to them; in this respect they are different modes of being. But the fact that between them and from them, as God's third mode of being, is the Spirit, love—this they have in common. This third mode of being cannot result from the former alone, or the latter alone, or the co-operation of the two, but only from their one being as God the Father and God the Son, who are not two "persons" either in themselves or in co-operation, but two modes of being of the one being of God. Thus the one Godness [*Gottsein*] of the Father and Son is, or the Father and the Son in their one Godness [*Gottsein*] are, the origin of the Spirit.[142]

Two major observations from this passage are in order. First, Barth correctly understood that a "double procession" of the Spirit, when taken to its logical end, would infer that in some very real sense there must be two points from which the procession arises—i.e., two "origins." Barth, in general consonance with the East, rejected this possibility: one cannot speak of a "double procession" or a "two-fold procession" of the Spirit without inferring that there are two "origins" in God, two first principles. Consequently, he preferred to speak of a "common origin" of the Spirit (i.e., denoting at the very least a singularity of origin) in the modes of being of the Father and the Son.

Second, Barth also insisted that the procession of the Spirit is not from the two persons or modes of being of Father and Son qua modes of being (i.e., *hypostases*). That is, the Spirit does not have as its origin either the Father (as *hypostasis*) alone, or the Son (as *hypostasis*) alone, or even from the Father and Son as two

---

141 " …das ex Patre Filioque bezeichnet nicht einen doppelten, sondern es bezeichnet einen gemeinsamen Ursprung des Geistes vom Vater und vom Sohne." *CD* I/1, p. 486; *KD* I/1, 510. Emphasis in original.

142 *CD* I/1, pp. 486-87. The German of the last sentence reads: "Also: das eine Gottsein des Vaters und des Sohnes oder: der Vater und der Sohn in ihrem einen Gottsein sind der Ursprung des Geistes." *KD* I/1, p. 511.

hypostases working cooperatively together. Thus, Barth refused to allow that the Spirit's procession is a procession from the individuated *hypostases*, whether from the Father, from the Son, or from the conjunction of Father and Son. To speak of them in this way is to abstract them from the unity of their shared divine Being [*Gottsein*]. Or to put it yet another way, to speak of the Father or the Son in their "mode of being" in abstraction from the shared divine Being is to fail to speak of God in the depths of his reality as a Triunity [*Dreieinigkeit*] of one-being in three-modes-of-being. This is a significant point that nearly every scholar commenting on Barth's doctrine of the filioque has missed,[143] including Torrance himself.

Does this mean that Barth has shifted the focus of his attention in defending the filioque to the divine being of God, and has made the procession of the Spirit a procession from the divine *ousia?* While this might seem to be the only solution available (i.e., if the procession is not from the *hypostases*, then it must be from the *ousia*), this is not the path that he takes. This is because a procession from the divine *ousia*, without reference to the concrete *hypostases*, would once again be an unreal abstraction. It would mean that the Spirit proceeds from a hidden essence behind, above, or beneath the actual *hypostases* of the Father and the Son. In this regard, Barth was evidently no more ready to adopt the position that the procession is from the *ousia* than the position that the procession is from the *hypostases.*

Returning once again to the citation above, it is evident that Barth's solution to the problem is not to be forced into choosing between a procession from the *hypostases* and a procession from the *ousia.* The solution is not framed as an either/or, but as a both/and. Though worded in an unusually reserved economy of language for Barth, his answer is that the Spirit's procession is not from the *hypostases* alone, nor from the *ousia* alone (since neither exist independently as such), but from the common *ousia* shared by the *hypostases* of the Father and Son. In other words, the procession of the Spirit *ex patre filioque* denotes that the Spirit has his "common origin"[144] in the shared being of the two modes of being of Father and Son, not merely from their status as "modes of being" alone, nor merely from the divine essence abstracted from the hypostases. In a manner analogous to Barth's Christology—Barth always insisted it is necessary to speak in two words of Jesus Christ—the doctrine of the procession of the Spirit cannot be spoken of in a single word, but only in a compound word. To put it in as concise a theological paraphrase as possible, Barth's position is that *the Spirit proceeds from the common-being-of-Father-and-Son's-modes-of-being.* Such a compounding is

---

[143] The only exception uncovered in my research was John McIntyre, who noted that Barth took "an unusual step in refusing to characterise the procession of the Spirit as from the Father and the Son, as a double procession from the Father and from the Son in the form of two single processions." John McIntyre, *The Shape of Pneumatology* (Edinburgh, 1997), pp. 153-4. Unfortunately, McIntyre does not go on to explore the theological significance of this move for Barth, even though he appears to grasp its importance.

[144] Barth's use of the terminology of "common origin" or "common source" is consistent throughout the *CD*. Cf. *CD* III/1, pp. 45, 49, 59; *CD* IV/1, pp. 209, 308.

necessary to maintain the delicate dialectical unity that Barth appeared to want to maintain between the *Sein* and the *Seinsweisen* as the "common origin" of the Spirit. Furthermore, as will be shown shortly, it appears that Torrance follows Barth's lead, except that he takes the dogmatic reasoning one step further and argues that the Spirit's procession is a procession from the full monarchy of the Trinity—a monarchy understood as *the-common-being-of-the-Father-and-the-Son-and-the-Holy-Spirit*.

It is important to recall, as noted above, that, unlike Barth, Torrance is less concerned with defending the filioque and more concerned about reinterpreting the very meaning of the concept of the procession itself. Torrance's argument hinges upon his understanding, similar to Barth's, that the procession of the Spirit is a "procession from the one Being of God the Father which is common to the Son and the Spirit."[145] He further insists, citing Athanasius as his authority, that "the procession of the Spirit is from the *Being* of the Father, and not from the *Person* (ὑπόστασις) of the Father, in distinction from his *Being*."[146] Furthermore, Torrance notes, Epiphanius, in line with Athanasius, also taught that the Holy Spirit has his "personal subsistence not only 'out of the Father through the Son,' but 'out of the same Being,' 'out of the same Godhead' as the Father and the Son, for the Holy Spirit is ontologically (οὐσιωδῶς) inseparable from the Father and the Son."[147] On the contrary, Torrance argues, the Cappadocians became sidetracked by focusing too narrowly upon the Father alone as the locus of the divine monarchy.

Thus, Torrance argues, the Church would have done better to follow the lead of Athanasius, who insisted on the full consubstantiality of the Holy Spirit along with the Father and the Son. It was Athanasius who taught that "the three divine Persons … share completely and equally in the one homogeneous (ὁμογενής / ὁμοφυής) Nature and Being of God. The whole Godhead (ὁλόκληρος Θεότης) belongs to each divine Person as it belongs to all of them, and it belongs to all of them as it belongs to each of them."[148] Consequently, Torrance rejects a distinctively Eastern view of the monarchy of God that is identified with the Father only. Athanasius, he says, "declined to advance a view of the Monarchy in which the oneness of God was defined by reference to the Father alone or to the Person of the Father."[149] Instead, he "held that since the whole Godhead is in the Son and in the Spirit, they must be included with the Father in the one originless Source or Ἀρχή of the Holy Trinity."[150] While Torrance is grateful to the Cappadocians for expounding the doctrine of one *ousia* and three *hypostases* in helping the Church "to have a richer and fuller understanding of the Three Persons of the Trinity in their distinctive

---

145 Torrance, *Christian Doctrine of God*, p. 186. The parallel to Barth is immediately evident here.

146 Ibid., p. 188.

147 Ibid.

148 Ibid., p. 190.

149 Ibid., p. 183.

150 Ibid., p. 181.

modes of existence," it was also the case that "this was done at the expense of cutting out the real meaning of *ousia* as *being in its eternal relations*, and of robbing *ousia* of its profound *personal* sense that was so prominent at Nicaea, and had been reinforced by Athanasius and Epiphanius."[151]

More central to the present concern, however, Torrance argues that a reinterpretation of the monarchy, taken together with the concept of perichoresis, would make it possible "to think through and restate the doctrine of the procession of the Holy Spirit from the Father in a way that cuts behind and sets aside the problems that divided the Church over the *filioque.*"[152] On the basis that all three persons "perichoretically penetrate and contain one another," he argues that the proper way to speak of the Spirit's procession must acknowledge this fact. As an alternative to either monopatrism or the filioque, he proposes, "the Holy Spirit proceeds from the One Being which belongs to the Son and to the Spirit as well as to the Father, and which belongs to all of them together as well as to each of them. … Strictly speaking, then, it must be said that the Holy Spirit proceeds from the one monarchy of the Triune God."[153] In short, Torrance is convinced that the Holy Spirit proceeds from the one Triune God.

Admittedly, both Barth's and Torrance's attempts to speak consistently of the procession of the Spirit strains the limits of intelligibility. Yet both appear to agree with the Athanasian strategy of extending *homoousion* fully to the Holy Spirit, and that such a move is closely related to the concept of perichoresis. In Barth's words, "the *perichoresis,* though it is complete and mutual, is not one of origins as such, but a *perichoresis* of the modes of being as modes of being of the one God. It is a further description of the *homoousia* of Father, Son and Spirit."[154] Furthermore, Barth has insisted that the eternal reality of the Holy Spirit "is of a kind that marks it out as being of divine essence with the Father and the Son."[155] In this regard, Torrance would most certainly uphold Barth's pneumatological description.

However, Torrance also took a theological/dogmatic step that Barth did not. Whereas Torrance is ready to speak of a procession of the Spirit from "the whole Being of God to whom the Father and the Son with the Spirit belong,"[156] Barth restricted himself to speaking of the Spirit as the essence—"no mere relation"[157]—of love between the Father and the Son, the Spirit whose common origin is in the Being of the modes of being of the Father and the Son. In this respect, Torrance insists that Barth could have maintained "the inner Trinitarian communion of the Eternal Spirit with the Son and the Father" without having to uphold the filioque. For Torrance, an affirmation of the Athanasian formula "from the Father,

151 Ibid. Emphasis in original.

152 Ibid., p. 190.

153 Ibid.

154 *CD* I/1, p. 485.

155 *CD* I/1, p. 474. Emphasis added.

156 Torrance, *Christian Doctrine of God*, p. 191.

157 *CD* I/1, p. 487.

through the Son and in the Spirit" would have been sufficient to uphold Barth's concerns.[158]

Given the remarkable extent of general and specific agreement between Torrance and Barth, one question still remains: why did Barth continue to insist on the filioque when Torrance did not? Though Torrance's position deserves more attention than can be given here, even a preliminary answer helps to clarify the grounds upon which Barth continued to hold to the filioque. Barth holds on to the filioque for at least two important reasons. First, the filioque functions as a means of safeguarding the distinctive unity attested to in Scripture between the Father and Son—a communion of love in the Spirit who is "an independent divine mode of being over against them."[159] Indeed, Barth could not have been more explicit than when he argued that the filioque is necessary because it "expresses recognition of the communion between the Father and the Son."[160] In contradistinction to Torrance, Barth upholds the filioque because of his desire to uphold not only a perichoretic unity of the monarchy of the Trinity based on a shared divine essence, but also the unique reciprocal unity of relationship that exists between the Father and the Son in the Spirit. Second, the filioque is necessary as a guarantee of the communion between God and humanity. Barth continued to insist that a failure to uphold the filioque—not only in the economic, but also in the immanent, Trinity–-would mean that "the fellowship of the Spirit between God and man is without objective ground or content." Consequently, the procession of the Spirit would become "a purely temporal truth with no eternal basis, so to speak, in itself." So, Barth insists, if the Spirit does not proceed from the Father and the Son both eternally and temporally, then whatever one might say about "the communion between God and man … does not have in this case a guarantee in the communion between God the Father and God the Son as the eternal content of its temporal reality."[161]

Barth shares with Torrance the concern to safeguard the unity of the monarchy by reference to the shared divine being of the Father, Son and Holy Spirit as a triunity of *Seinsweisen.* However, he is additionally concerned, in a way that Torrance is not, to safeguard the unique relational dialectic that exists between the Father and the Son in the Holy Spirit—a dialectic of identity and differentiation he had originally identified in his *Römerbrief* period.[162] In this regard, Barth's continued adherence to the filioque is his attempt to recognize the unique relationship that exists between the Father and Son as testified to especially in the Johannine literature[163]—a relationship not spoken of in the same regard in reference to the Spirit. For example, Scripture does not speak of the Father's love for the Spirit

158 Torrance, "Barth and Patristic Theology," p. 234.

159 *CD* I/1, p. 487.

160 *CD* I/1, p. 480.

161 *CD* I/1, p. 481.

162 Cf. p. ??? above.

163 E.g., John 10:30, 38; 14:10-11; 17:11, 21.

in the way that it speaks of his love for the Son, or vice versa. Consequently, for Barth, the relationship of Father to Son is a unique and dialectically structured relationship which does not exclude the Holy Spirit, but is utterly dependent on the Holy Spirit for its reality. The Father and the Son are in a relationship "whose reciprocity is not a being against, but a being to and from and with one another."[164] It is a relationship that depends uniquely on the Spirit as the one who relates and distinguishes the Father and the Son as Other, and Other by means of the Holy Spirit who is also Other (*alius, alius, alius*).

While Barth and Torrance share many similar concerns to push back behind the historical filioque debate, there are hints that Barth would not have been ready to accept the dogmatic conclusion of Torrance's line of thinking that the Spirit's procession from the Father means a procession equally from all three hypostases. This is evidenced by the fact that Barth is unwilling to accept that the Holy Spirit is a "person" in the same way that the Father and the Son are "persons" but, rather, is a third mode of being that is "neutral" to Father and Son—neutral in the sense of being both "distinct" from the reciprocity which exists between Father and Son and yet "related" to both Father and Son as that which makes possible that very reciprocity.[165] Whereas Torrance emphasizes the perichoretic nature of the three hypostases to affirm their shared essence and thereby the full monarchy of the Trinity, Barth emphasized the unity and distinction between the Father and Son in their shared Being (*Sein*) as distinct modes of Being *(Seinsweisen)*—shared yet distinct in the third *Seinsweise* which is common to Father and Son alike. Consequently, it is difficult to see how Torrance and Barth would have been able to see eye-to-eye on this point.

Barth, quite unlike Torrance, continued to perceive in God a *Realdialektik* between the Father and Son as "Other" within the One God. In a rather important passage near the end of the section on the filioque, Barth shifted from providing a critical defense of the filioque to providing what he viewed as "the positive meaning of the Western version of the [filioque]."[166] Most significantly, he allowed himself once again to reach deep into the storehouse of his dialectical vocabulary to speak about God—though now with far less of a sense of the rhetorical urgency characteristic of his *Römberbrief* period. If only for two pages, Barth speaks of the relationship between Father and Son in the familiar dialectical terms of "negation" and "otherness." Starting with the relationship of the Father to the Son, Barth painted the following theological portrait:

> As He is the Father who begets the Son He brings forth the Spirit of love, for as He begets the Son, God already negates in Himself, from eternity, in His absolute simplicity, all loneliness, self-containment, or self-isolation. Also and precisely in Himself, from eternity, in His absolute simplicity, God is orientated

164 *CD* I/1, p. 469.
165 *CD* I/1, p. 469.
166 *CD* I/1, p. 483.

> to the Other, does not will to be without the Other, will have Himself only as He has Himself with the Other and indeed in the Other. He is the Father of the Son in such a way that with the Son He brings forth the Spirit, love, and is in Himself the Spirit, love.[167]

Though the Father brings forth the Son in such a way that he is not alone, it is from Father and Son together that the Spirit overflows. As Barth explained, "in the Son of his love … [the Father] then brings forth in the *opus ad extra* too, in creation, the creaturely reality which is distinct from Himself, and in revelation the reconciliation and peace of the creature that has fallen away from Him."[168] Together, it is the Father and the Son who send forth the Spirit to hover over the waters of creation—*Veni Spiritus*—to seek and to find fellowship with the Other—the human creature—who is the creative fruit of the overflow of the Father's love for the Son in the Spirit. In putting it this way, Barth insisted, the *qui procedit ex Patre* is given "explanation and proof."[169]

Lest the relationship of Father to Son in the Spirit be inappropriately construed as a unidirectional vector rather than as a dialectical movement, Barth reversed the emphasis to speak of the relationship of the Son to the Father. Once again, a second word is in order to speak after, and in response to, the *Realdialektik* in God:

> [A]s God is the Son who comes forth from the Father, He brings forth the Spirit, He brings forth love. In this mode of being, too, He negates loneliness in His absolute simplicity; He is orientated to the Other; He does not will to be without the Other out of whom He is. How else could He be the Son but as the Son of the Father? How could He be less the origin of love in being the Son than in being the Father?[170]

In light of this dialectical explication of Father to Son in the Spirit and of the Son to the Father in the Spirit, Barth insists that:

> … distinct as Father and Son, God is one in the fact that His distinction is that of the Father and the Son, so that it is not the kind of distinction which might also arise in a supreme principle of separateness and fellowship, a loveless distinction, but the distinction which affirms *fellowship in separateness* and *separateness in fellowship*.[171]

It is this latter phrase—"fellowship in separateness and separateness in fellowship"—that most succinctly, at this point in Barth's work, expresses why

---

167 *CD* I/1, p. 483.

168 *CD* I/1, p. 483.

169 *CD* I/1, p. 484.

170 *CD* I/1, p. 484.

171 *CD* I/1, p. 484. Emphasis added.

he continued to hold to the filioque. Because Father and Son and Son and Father exist by way of negation of loneliness and absolute simplicity, it is in the Spirit that proceeds commonly from both that Father and Son are both oriented and sustained in fellowship to the Other by resisting, on the one hand, One to be sublated or overcome by the Other, and holding together and preventing the falling away into isolation or division of One from the Other. It is only as the Father of the Son and as the Son of the Father that both are *spirator Spiritus.* "This is," Barth insisted, "how we explain and prove the *qui procedit ex Patre Filioque.*"[172] In summary, then, Barth held firmly to the filioque as an appropriate theological recognition of the unique relationship of the Father and the Son as testified to in Scripture while upholding—and perhaps even heightening—the crucial role of the Spirit in being the third eternal divine *Seinsweise* who maintains and protects that relationship in his commonality to both.

Summary and Conclusions

Two important lines of thought in this chapter can now be summarized. First, from the perspective of the genesis and development of the doctrine of the filioque in Barth's thinking, this chapter has demonstrated that a significant shift took place between the *GD* and the *CD* in reference to the ground of support for the filioque put forth by Barth. Whereas in the *GD* Barth implied that the filioque was supported by the structure of the threefold Word of God read back into the eternal Trinitarian relations, in the *CD* he modified the schedule of relations in perichoretic terms such that the original grounds for his support of the filioque was cut out from under him. If the analogy from the threefold Word of God "worked" in the *GD* (even if there is reason to doubt that it did work in the first place), the analogy is rendered even more problematic by Barth's reconstrual of the relationship of the three forms of the Word along perichoretic lines in the *CD.* Nevertheless, such a move—whether Barth intended it as a self-corrective measure or not, we cannot be sure—also led to new and better theological grounds on which to handle the problem of the filioque itself. In addition, it was because of Barth's work that Torrance, following his teacher's lead, was able to come to the conclusions he did in reconstructing the doctrine of the monarchy along perichoretic lines, even if in the end Barth and Torrance disagree on the necessity of the filioque itself.

Furthermore, it is noteworthy that the exposition of Barth's position illustrates that, early in the *CD*, he is still dealing with the filioque in the terms he inherited from centuries of Western dogmatic debate, of which he is not yet sufficiently critical. Yet, by the end of the first half-volume of the *CD*, Barth has already made two significant systematic moves. First, he continues to discuss the filioque (as he had already in the *GD*) as a topic subsumed under the doctrine of revelation rather than as a topic, as had been traditionally done, under theology proper. Second, he

[172] *CD* I/1, p. 484.

refused to discuss the filioque under the terms of a presupposition that it implies a "double procession" of divine origin of the Spirit from another divine *hypostasis* (or hypostases), preferring to think instead of the procession of the Spirit as a common origin of the Spirit from the shared being of the distinct modes of being of Father and Son.

Arguably, this "breakthrough" of Barth has yet to be sufficiently understood or worked out in the larger ecumenical debates over the filioque. This is because it is generally only in recent years that Barth interpreters have become attuned to his consistent dialecticism. Without perceiving this element of Barth's thinking, it is difficult to see that Barth's breakthrough comes when he addresses the problem of the filioque in dialectical terms—something which even he appeared largely to resist throughout the first half-volume! It is only when Barth allows himself to provide a positive dogmatic statement of the significance of the filioque[173] that Barth the "critically realistic dialectical theologian" (McCormack) once again begins to show through. Fortunately, this dialectical reasoning foreshadows how Barth, in the remaining volumes of the *CD*, will move toward treating the doctrine of the filioque in increasingly dialectical terms. It will be the task of the next chapter to show how this was accomplished.

A second important line of thought has to do with reference to the systematic function of the filioque for Barth. It has been demonstrated that, by the end of the first half-volume of the *CD*, the filioque had taken on a twofold function for Barth. On the one hand, the filioque is a theological safeguard to the unique Father-Son relationship—a relationship guaranteed and protected by the Holy Spirit common to, and proceeding from, the common being of the two modes of being, Father and Son, Son and Father. On the other hand, the filioque, which is true both for the economic and immanent Trinity, is the guarantee of the communion between God and humanity. The question is, however, whether Barth's adherence to the filioque is the *only* way to safeguard the unique Father-Son relationship and the communion between God and humanity. While Torrance's work might be promising in this regard, it is not yet clear whether it can suffice. Though Torrance's view of the Spirit's procession from the monarchy of the Trinity might be dogmatically deduced, it is not clear that it is intelligible or coherent (i.e., what might it possibly mean for one divine hypostasis to proceed from all three hypostases, including itself?), nor whether Torrance's account faithfully reflects how the Gospel of John, for example, can affirm the Oneness of the Father and the Son in a way that it does not affirm a congruous Oneness between the Father, Son, and Spirit. In this regard, Barth's dialectical view of the filioque, while certainly not without its own problems, might be a more satisfying way of responding to the Johannine witness in such a way that the Spirit is brought to bear upon the unique Father-Son relationship.

[173] *CD* I/1, pp. 483-84.

Chapter Four
The Function of the Filioque in the *Church Dogmatics*

Beyond his analysis in *CD* I/1, Barth never returned to the filioque as a dogmatic problem in need of further defense or clarification. However, he did occasionally appeal to the filioque at various points throughout the *CD*. An analysis of these occasions, therefore, will serve to clarify the systematic function that the filioque played in his thought. Thus, this chapter will identify, analyze, and evaluate those instances in the *CD* where Barth made explicit material application of the filioque beyond the initial defense found in the first half-volume. As will be demonstrated, Barth does appeal to the filioque in a traditional Western manner, but it is also true that he applied it in novel ways, especially when he allowed himself to speak in a more explicitly dialectical mode—a mode which is often muted in the earlier volumes of the *CD*. Indeed, Barth's late use of the filioque can best be understood as an attempt to speak dialectically in response to the revealed eternal dialectic that exists antecedently in God between Father and Son in the Holy Spirit (*Realdialektik*).

Filioquist Grammar in the *Church Dogmatics*

Sweeping generalizations about the systematic influence of the filioque in Barth's theology are too often made without consideration of those occasions when Barth actually made use of it in his reasoning. It is important, therefore, to examine how Barth actually appealed to the filioque in his theological argumentation. Before doing so, however, it must be acknowledged that there are many places in the *CD* where an implicit "filioquist grammar" is evident. That is, Barth would often relate Father, Son and Holy Spirit in such a way that his commitment to the filioque clearly shines through, even if he did not explicitly mention the doctrine per se.

Such a filioquist grammar is especially evident when Barth spoke at length of the work of any one of the three divine Persons. For example, after a discussion in reference to the Father as Lord and Creator of humanity, Barth asserted: "[I]n eternity God is the Father of his own eternal Son and with Him the source [*Ursprung*] of the Holy Spirit."[1] Or, "As the Father, God procreates Himself from eternity in His Son, and with His Son He is also from eternity the origin

[1] *CD* II/1, p. 48.

[*Ursprung*] of Himself in the Holy Spirit."[2] Similarly, when speaking of the Son, Barth can say: "Jesus Christ is Himself God as the Son of God the Father and with God the Father the source of the Holy Spirit, united in one essence with the Father by the Holy Spirit."[3] In reference to the Holy Spirit he says: "God is Himself eternally the Holy Spirit, proceeding from the Father and the Son, and of one essence with them both"[4] or "The Holy Spirit … is the Spirit of God, God Himself, as he eternally proceeds from the Father and the Son, as He unites the Father and the Son in eternal love."[5] All of these statements reflect Barth's acceptance of the dogmatic truth of the filioque. The question is: what is the theological purpose of such filioquist grammar?

First, Barth's Trinitarian language, generally considered, consistently specifies the interrelated unity of all three divine modes of being while simultaneously seeking to maintain their distinctiveness. There can be no way to speak of a "mode of Being" [*Seinsweise*] in abstraction from the "Being" [*Sein*] to which it is related. The distinctiveness of one mode of being consists not as something independent, but only as a complex set of unique relations to the other modes of being. To speak of the Father, the Son or the Holy Spirit apart from their triune relationships would be to violate their identity as persons sharing in the divine essence. Nevertheless, for Barth the triune relationships themselves cannot simply be "equalized," but, as noted at the end of Chapter Three, they must be spoken of in light of the unique relationship existing between the Father and the Son in the commonality of the Spirit. Thus, in Barth's way of speaking of the triune relationships, since it is revealed that the Father alone is related to the Son as Father (and vice versa), the Spirit can only be spoken of in reference to the unique eternal relationship of Father and Son. The procession of the Spirit from the Father and Son (*ex patre filioque*) insures the distinctiveness of the Spirit from both Father and Son. It guarantees that the Spirit is said to be related not only to the Father (as is the tendency in Eastern thought), but also simultaneously to the Son. In this regard Barth can be understood as standing well within the Thomist tradition that defends the filioque on the basis of relations of opposition within the Trinity,[6] and his filioquist grammar is consistent with the definition of divine triunity laid out in the

---

2 *CD* III/1, p. 49.

3 *CD* IV/1, p. 129. Cf. "[T]he Holy Spirit of God is the self-communication of His fatherhood as well as His lordship as Creator, so that without Him God could not partake of the name of Father and Creator." *CD* III/1, p. 49.

4 *CD* II/1, p. 48.

5 *CD* IV/1, p. 646.

6 Ngien points out that the doctrine of "relations of opposition" is clearly important for Aquinas, but finds its roots in Augustine, mediated by Anselm. For expositions of Thomas Aquinas's view of relations of opposition, see Dennis Ngien, *Apologetic for Filioque in Medieval Theology* (Milton Keynes, 2005), pp. 88-94; and Jaroslav Pelikan, "The Doctrine of the Filioque in Thomas Aquinas and Its Patristic Antecedents," in Etienne Gilson (ed.), *St. Thomas Aquinas, 1274-197 : Commemorative Studies* (Toronto, 1974), pp. 315-36.

thesis of §9: "The God who reveals Himself according to Scripture is One in three distinctive modes of being [*Seinsweisen*] subsisting in their mutual relations."[7] That is, a triune mode of being subsists not in and of itself, but only relative to the other two.

It is also possible to view Barth's manner of speaking about the inner triune relationships as reflecting his ongoing concern to uphold the full divinity of all three Persons of the Trinity; to speak of one is to speak of the other two in the fullness of their shared divinity. Eberhard Busch has argued that Barth's pneumatology must be generally understood as being centered on an insistence on the full divinity of the Holy Spirit. As Busch explains, "Barth's Christologically formulated theology includes within itself a certain doctrine of the Holy Spirit *and* ... he clearly was endeavoring to rediscover the knowledge of the deity of the Holy Spirit that had been lost in the pneumatology of Neo-Protestantism."[8] This "certain doctrine" of the Spirit is one in which the divinity of the Spirit is wholly related to the full consubstantiality and hypostatic diversity of Father and Son—a consubstantiality and diversity enabled in and by the Spirit himself only because he fully shares in the divine essence. Thus, Barth's Trinitarian statements are structured in light of the filioque, and their systematic purpose is to insure that the hypostatic diversity and full deity of each person is consistently upheld at every dogmatic turn. The Father and Son are divine in virtue of their reciprocal relationship shared in the Holy Spirit who is divine, not in and of himself, but divine in commonality to the Father and the Son. This is the proper way to speak of God, not because of an *a priori* commitment to abstract principles of diversity or unity in the Godhead, but because *a posteriori* this is how God reveals himself to be.

It is beyond the scope of this work to identify every occasion in the *CD* where Barth's implicit filioquist grammar comes to the foreground and the summary above must suffice. Rather, in order to discern the systematic function of the filioque in Barth's thought, attention will be focused in the remainder of the chapter on those instances where Barth explicitly appeals to the doctrine of the filioque. To preserve a sense of the diachronic development, the occurrences will be dealt with in the order of their appearance in the *CD* beyond the first half-volume.

Church Dogmatics I/2: The Filioque as Recognition of the Unity of Word and Spirit

Barth's first explicit appeal to the filioque beyond the first half-volume's analysis comes in *CD* I/2.[9] Though the reference itself appears roughly one-quarter of the

[7] *CD* I/1, p. 348.

[8] Eberhard Busch, *The Great Passion: An Introduction to Karl Barth's Theology* (Grand Rapids, 2004), p. 222.

[9] Incidentally, this is the only reference to the filioque listed outside of *CD* I/1 in the *Index* volume. This fact alone may help explain why it is often assumed that Barth's stance

way through the massive volume, Barth arguably already had the doctrine in mind somewhat earlier. In his sections on "The Holy Spirit the Subjective Reality of Revelation" and "The Holy Spirit the Subjective Possibility of Revelation,"[10] Barth was particularly dedicated to guarding against a "concealed or open sectarianism" in which Christians might appeal to "immediate spiritual inspiration" as a means of being convinced of an objective fact of revelation. In such cases, Barth warned, "we are not convinced by God himself" (and by God Barth here meant the "Father"); such an appeal to direct spiritual inspiration "forgets that the Holy Spirit is not only the Spirit of the Father but also the Spirit of the Word. It forgets that the Holy Spirit certainly comes to us, not by an independent road which bypasses the Word and its testimonies, but by the Word and its testimonies."[11]

Barth suspected that the subjective element of revelation (i.e., the Holy Spirit) becomes confused with the spirit of the human recipient when the objective element (i.e., Jesus Christ) is bypassed in favor of "an intensifying of interest in the depths of the believing subject, his sin, his pardon, his sanctification, and the perceptions, moods and feelings accompanying those processes."[12] This is evidenced by increasing fascination with "religious poetry,"[13] and the "complementary opposites" of "mysticism and morality."[14] In Barth's estimation, the "heresy of the third article" could nowhere be better illustrated than in the hymn books of his day. There "the Holy Spirit has ceased to be the Spirit of Jesus Christ. … To all appearances He is still a spirit of God, even a Christian spirit. In fact, however, He is the spirit of human inwardness and seriousness, the spirit of mysticism and morals." Where this confusion takes place, Barth insisted, "we do

---

on the filioque is restricted to his exposition in *CD* I/1!

10 Barth's ordering of these two sections was quite deliberate, even if counterintuitive. As he explained, "[O]ur first question is this: How does this freedom in man become real? It is not: How does it become possible? The latter question will also have to be raised and answered, but *secundum ordinem,* and therefore not first. Only when raised second is it the genuine question of our attitude to God's revelation. If raised first it again leads to lack of objectivity. It means that we are first trying to lay down the conditions upon which we can regard the way from God to man as traversible [*sic*]. … The former is the question of fact, the latter the question of our attitude to it." *CD* I/2, p. 205. Barth's actualistic ordering of the question was further reflected in his doctrine of God when he stated, "Where the actuality exists there is also the corresponding possibility. The question cannot be posed *in abstracto* but only *in concreto;* not *a priori* but only *a posteriori.*" *CD* II/1, p. 5.

11 *CD* I/2, p. 236. Barth's insistence that the Spirit is the Spirit of the Father and the Spirit of the Son is scattered liberally throughout the *CD*. E.g., *CD* I/1, p. 479; *CD* I/2, pp. 199, 247-48; *CD* II/1, p. 101; *CD* II/2, p. 308; *CD* III/1, p. 56; *CD* III/4, p. 94; *CD* IV/1, pp. 129, 646; *CD* IV/2, pp. 323-33, 345; *CD* IV/3.2, p. 759; *CD* IV/4, pp. 99-100.

12 *CD* I/2, p. 253.

13 *CD* I/2, p. 254.

14 *CD* I/2, p. 255.

not yet enjoy, or enjoy no longer, the communion with God which is realised in the revelation of God."[15]

However, is it not possible that the Spirit could in some way provide some direct knowledge of God? Could there not be an experience of God, of God's Spirit, apart from a direct knowledge of the person of Jesus Christ? In response to these questions, Barth was understandably skeptical. This is because any appeal to the Holy Spirit, whether for guidance, illumination or inspiration *is* an appeal to God himself, who is none other than the Father of the Son. "As He is in the essence of God Himself the Spirit of the Father and of the Son, the Holy Spirit does not come independently, or for Himself, as immediate truth to man, but through the Son and as the Spirit of the Son."[16] This is the clear evidence of the New Testament, Barth retorted. "Where in the New Testament can the Holy Spirit of Pentecost be anything other than the light of Christmas, the light of Good Friday and of Easter morning?"[17] Barth's emphasis here reflected his wariness, already evident in *GD* and *CD* I/1, of the possibility of direct knowledge of God the Father apart from knowledge of the Son.[18]

In binding together the Spirit with the Son in revelation, as he does here, Barth was unflinchingly consistent. For him, "one of the most self-evident themes" of the Bible is that "the Holy Spirit, and with the Holy Spirit all that makes the Church the Church, and Christians Christians, does not come from any place but only from Christ."[19] This means that all gifts of the Spirit in the Christian community—all speaking, all service—always return to the objective reality of revelation, the incarnate Son, Jesus Christ. As Barth put it, "It means that the Word is His commission. It is constantly applied in new ways, but in content it is always an indication of Him and of Him alone." It is not that the biblical authors have no interest in subjective matters, but Barth was convinced that, even when the biblical authors do take a temporary "detour" from the objective center, "they return to it as it has to be the objective for the sake of the subjective." Thus, Barth understood the New Testament interest in the subjective element of revelation as always leading back again to the objective. Subjective interest, in and for itself, is "only abstract."[20] Or as Busch explains, according to Barth "the work of the Holy Spirit is 'enclosed' in the revelation of Christ."[21]

Barth unabashedly gave the objective element of revelation (Christology) systematic priority over the subjective (pneumatology), but not in such a way as to do away with the subjective altogether. He insisted that a link between

15 *CD* I/2, p. 257.

16 *CD* II/1, p. 101.

17 *CD* II/1, p. 101.

18 Cf. *CD* I/1, p. 481.

19 *CD* I/2, p. 250. Later, Barth would reiterate that it is the Spirit that makes man to be not just any person, but a Christian. Cf. *CD* IV/1, pp. 108, 119; *CD* IV/2, pp. 308-309.

20 *CD* I/2, p. 250.

21 Busch, *Great Passion,* 224, citing *CD* I/2, p. 240.

Christology and pneumatology must be constantly maintained lest pneumatology become released from its moorings in Christology. "If, then, we want truly and properly to understand the Holy Spirit and His work upon us, we can never try to understand them abstractly and in themselves."[22] On the contrary, "[i]f we want truly and properly to investigate the subjective possibility of revelation … [w]e must look rather at the place from which [the Holy Spirit] comes and at what he brings … [i]n other words, we must look at Christ Himself."[23] The Christological import of keeping one's theological eyes fixed on Jesus Christ[24] does not mean that one can ignore the theological reality of the subjective element of revelation (i.e., the work of the Holy Spirit), but one must allow the Spirit to do his work in the human—namely, to bring Jesus Christ ever more clearly into focus as the *object* of faith. This was the reason why, according to Barth, the Western Church thought it necessary to confess that the Spirit proceeds from the Father and the Son; the filioque was thought to underline the objective, Christological center to which the subjective, pneumatological element necessarily leads. He wrote:

> We have here the root of that recognition on whose basis the Western Church assumed into the creed, in relation to the eternal procession of the Holy Spirit, the *Filioque* as well as the *ex Patre*. … Its intention was to recognise the fact that in God's revelation the Holy Spirit is the Spirit of Jesus Christ, that He cannot be separated from Him, that He is only the Spirit of Jesus Christ. And it did it with such definiteness that it found it necessary to confess that he is the Spirit of the Father and of the Son not only here and now and for us, but also from all eternity, in the hidden triune being of God which is revealed to us in revelation. … In respect of revelation the Western Church did not recognise any Spirit to be the Holy Spirit except the Spirit of Christ.[25]

In short, Barth was adamant that the subjective must be understood in light of the objective, and not the other way around.[26]

---

22 *CD* I/2, p. 248. Elsewhere, Barth warned against any such systematic abstraction for the sake of "substantiation" of faith and "confirmation of our systematic deliberations and affirmations in respect of the knowledge of God." Consequently, "we cannot grasp at the Holy Spirit, or the Church, or Christian experience, or the Trinity, or Christ—not to speak of other supports—in order to try to create certainty for ourselves." *CD* II/1, p. 249.

23 *CD* I/2, p. 249. Put more formally, Barth later said, "[W]e cannot discern the being of God in any other way than by looking where God Himself gives us to see, and therefore by looking at His works." *CD* II/1, p. 261.

24 Cf. Heb. 12:2

25 *CD* I/2, p. 250. Similarly, "The Holy Spirit, at least according to the Western understanding of the divine Triunity, cannot be separated from the Word." *CD* I/1, p. 150.

26 Hunsinger argues that this way of putting it (i.e., that pneumatology must be understood in light of Christology) should not be considered definitive for Barth. Had Barth been able to finish his projected fifth volume on "redemption," the relationship may have

The role of the Spirit in drawing the human recipient of revelation back to its objective center, Jesus Christ, had been an important feature of Barth's pneumatology ever since *Romans*, although his terminology there was that it was the Spirit by which Christ is "apprehended." In the *CD*, unlike *Romans*, Barth more clearly indicated that this apprehension of objective revelation is more than a cognitive (noetic) awareness of an otherwise unknown reality (though it certainly includes this awareness); rather, it is an actual entrance of humans into communion with God the Father as the brethren of Christ—a communion made possible only because the Spirit is the eternal communion between the Father and the Son.[27]

> It is because the Holy Spirit is from all eternity the communion between the Father and the Son, and therefore not only the Spirit of the Father but also the Spirit of the Son, that in God's revelation He can be the communion between the Father and those whom His Son has called to be his brethren. … [B]y his Spirit the Father does not call anyone except to His Son.[28]

Barth called the filioque the "root of that recognition" by the Western Church that the Spirit is none other than the Spirit of Christ. It was not as if the confession of the filioque came first and the identification of the Spirit arose in consequence. On the contrary, it was to safeguard against recognizing the Spirit in any other capacity than as the Spirit of Christ that the filioque was upheld. Not any spirit, whether angelic or human, can be trusted to accomplish the necessary task of keeping Jesus Christ at the center. Only Christ's own Spirit—the *Heilige Geist*—is able to accomplish it. But, conversely, because the Spirit is the eternal Spirit of Christ, he is also the Spirit of the Father who is none other than the Father of the Son:

> As the Spirit of Jesus Christ, who, proceeding from Him, unites men closely to Him *ut secum unum sint* ["that they might be one with him"]. He distinguishes Himself from the Spirit of God who lives as *vita animalis* ["animal life"] in creation, nature and history … And just because He is Christ's Spirit, the work

---

also been reversed. "Whereas from the standpoint of reconciliation the work of the Spirit served the work of Christ, from the standpoint of redemption the work of Christ served the work of the Spirit." Consequently, "since [Barth] thought reconciliation was to be fulfilled by redemption, no critique can be very illuminating which presupposes that he saw reconciliation as a whole story in and of itself. Very ambitiously, Barth intended to develop a doctrine of the Holy Spirit's saving work that would be rigorously christocentric yet without becoming deficient in its grasp of essential trinitarian relations." George Hunsinger, "The Mediator of Communion: Karl Barth's Doctrine of the Holy Spirit," in *Disruptive Grace: Studies in the Theology of Karl Barth* (Grand Rapids, 2000), pp. 149-50.

27 In this regard, Hunsinger suggests that Barth essentially understood the Spirit as the "mediator of communion." Ibid., p. 150.

28 *CD* I/2, p. 250.

> of Christ is never done without Him. Nor is it done except by Him. The grace of our Lord Jesus Christ does not exist except in the fellowship of the Holy Spirit (2 Cor. 13[14]), and the love of God is not poured out into our hearts except by the Holy Spirit (Rom. 5[5]).[29]

In short, the work of the Spirit is none other than the work of Jesus Christ.

Barth's way of speaking of the role of the Spirit in relation to the Son raises two important questions. First, how can Barth so closely identify the work of Christ and the work of the Spirit without being opened to the charge of making the Spirit's role in the economy of salvation superfluous? If the Spirit's work is "nothing other" than Christ's work, and if the doctrine of the Trinity is arrived at by analysis of God's revelation of himself in the economy of salvation, how can the claim that the Spirit is a distinct third Person of the Trinity be justified? If it is Christ, even if known and named as the Spirit of Christ, who has been working out salvation in the Church all along, is this not concrete evidence that Barth has severely limited the sense in which one can speak of a "Holy Spirit of God" as a distinct *hypostasis*? Is this not evidence for Christomonism? Does this not negate what Barth spoke of as the eschatological element of pneumatology—the anticipation of the distinct work of the Spirit in redemption? Does this not support Jenson's charge that there is an "impulsion to practiced binitarianism" in Barth?[30]

Barth would have rejected these charges as misunderstandings of his position. In fact, he explicitly denied that an identification of the work of the Spirit and the Son results in an obliteration of the third *Seinsweise*:

> As God, the Holy Spirit is a unique person. But He is not an independent divinity side by side with the unique Word of God. He is simply the Teacher of the Word: of that Word which is never without its Teacher. When it is a matter of instructing and instruction by the Word, that instructing and instruction are the work of the Holy Spirit. Without that work there is no instruction, for the Word is never apart from the Holy Spirit.[31]

Barth's rationale for defending a distinct, third *Seinsweise* was that there can be no Teacher of the Word, the Holy Spirit, without distinguishing it from the Word itself being taught. While it is true that the Word, Jesus Christ, is the objective content of revelation, there is still the need for a divine mode of delivery of the Word in such a way that the human subject is able to receive it. As Barth would put

---

[29] *CD* I/2, p. 241. Torrance puts things similarly: "The Spirit is so intimately one with Christ in his being and activity as the incarnate Son of God that he is, as it were, Christ's *Other Self* through whose presence in us Christ himself is present to us." Thomas F. Torrance, *The Mediation of Christ* (Colorado Springs, 1992), p. 117. Emphasis in original.

[30] Robert W. Jenson, "You Wonder Where the Spirit Went," *Pro Ecclesia* 2/3 (1993): 296-304 at 303.

[31] *CD* I/2, p. 244.

it later, "God in Himself is neither deaf nor dumb but speaks and hears His Word from all eternity, so outside His eternity He does not wish to be without hearing or echo, that is, without the ears and voices of the creature."[32] In contradistinction to proponents of natural theology, Barth did not hold that the human subject is capable of receiving, in and of herself, the Word of God; only the Spirit of Christ can make that reception possible as an event of revelation itself.[33] Or to put it negatively, just because the *work* of the Spirit is none other than the work of Christ[34] does not mean that one can legitimately conclude that the Spirit is therefore none other than Jesus Christ. Rather, Barth's insistence that the work of the Spirit is the work of the Son is a specific and consistent application of *opera Trinitatis ad extra sunt indivisa* ["the external works of the Trinity are undivided"] and the filioque, in this context at least, is a guarantee of the indivisibility of the triune work. The Word is never without its Teacher and the Teacher is never without its Word. The two, though fully and completely unified in their work, are nevertheless distinct in their identity. But as two unique "Persons" of the Trinity, they are never to be understood as "independent" Persons, which would be to engage in a theological abstraction, and to fail to speak faithfully about them in their actual concrete existence in the triune reality. The Word and Spirit, though distinct, are distinct-in-interdependence; they are *perichoretic* Persons.[35]

A second major question also arises: does Barth's filioquist pneumatology still overemphasize the noetic role of the Spirit to the detriment of an ontic role? Rosato thinks so and thus seeks to correct the problem through his own "improvisation" on Barth's otherwise "pneumocentric" thought. As Rosato explains, Barth's pneumatology fulfills "a decidedly noetic function. The Holy Spirit is primarily the divine teacher who transmits the truth revealed by, and

---

[32] *CD* III/1, p. 50.

[33] Busch writes, "As Barth sees it, the Holy Spirit overturns the pillar of the modern doctrine of the spirit, namely, the assertion that there is a capacity for God as a given in the human person. ... Only in the experience of the Holy Spirit does God's Word 'rid him of any idea that he possesses a possibility of his own for such a meeting.'" Busch, *Great Passion,* p. 225.

[34] *CD* I/2, p. 241.

[35] Barth would eventually allude to the unity of the work of the Spirit and the Son in his doctrine of Creation not by speaking of Word and Teacher, but by implying that God both speaks and hears his own Word: "In the same freedom and love in which God is not alone in Himself but is the eternal begetter of the Son, who is the eternally begotten of the Father, He also turns as Creator *ad extra* in order that absolutely and outwardly He may not be alone but the One who loves in freedom. In other words, as God in Himself is neither deaf nor dumb but speaks and hears His Word from all eternity, so outside His eternity He does not wish to be without hearing or echo, that is, without the ears and voices of the creature." *CD* III/1, p. 50. Barth would most certainly view the role of the Spirit as enabling the creature to hear the Word precisely because God's own Spirit is the Eternal Hearer of the Word.

embodied in, Christ."[36] Consequently, Rosato argues, Barth failed to give attention to the ontic role of the Spirit in being the *Spiritus Creator* who continues to play a crucial role in the eschatological thrust of God's salvation.[37] For Barth "[t]here is no new, as yet unrealized future of human nature which man can develop with the aid of God's Spirit; there is only a repetition in the noetic order of what already is a reality in the ontological order eternally grounded in the Logos."[38] In short, Rosato is convinced that "in illumining man's mind, the Holy Spirit constitutes his [i.e., man's] being." But since the Holy Spirit always remains "the transcendent possibility of man's contact with God," Rosato argues, "Barth thus allows pneumatology to replace the entire concept of human nature."[39]

Rosato's anthropological concerns are not entirely unwarranted, and he rightly identifies Barth's application of the filioque, at least as formally presented in *CD* I, as being fundamentally noetic in focus. In this light he asks whether Barth has failed to provide an account of the ontic role of the Spirit precisely because of the way he so consistently speaks of the Spirit as the Teacher of the Word. Unfortunately, Rosato assumes that Barth never attempted to go beyond such a view.[40] In fact, Barth does attempt to open his pneumatology to further development, including locating an ontic role for the Spirit in his procession from Father and Son in the doctrine of creation (i.e., *CD* III). Thus, Rosato's assessment is not so much wrong as it is incomplete. Though Barth does view the role of the Spirit primarily in

36 Philip J. Rosato, *The Spirit As Lord: The Pneumatology of Karl Barth* (Edinburgh, 1981), p. 133. Moltmann's criticism is similar. In reference to Barth's insistence that in the resurrection of Christ one has the self-revelation of God, Moltmann argues that "it becomes almost impossible to see the revelation of the risen Lord as the ground for still speaking of an outstanding future of Jesus Christ. If the idea of self-revelation is not to change tacitly into an expression for the God of Parmenides, then it must have an open eye for the statements of promise in the third article of the Creed. Yet this must not happen in such a way that the future redemption which is promised in the revelation of Christ would become only a supplement, only a noetic unveiling of the reconciliation effected in Christ, but in such a way that it gives promise of the real goal and true intention of that reconciliation, and therefore of its future as really outstanding, not yet attained and not yet realized." See Jürgen Moltmann, *Theology of Hope*, trans. James W. Leitch (New York, 1967), p. 58.

37 Rosato, *Spirit as Lord*, p. 137.

38 Ibid., p. 139.

39 Ibid., p. 131.

40 A similar problem can be observed in Alan Torrance's assessment of Barth's doctrine of Revelation: "The revelation event, so central to Barth's exposition in the first volume of the *Church Dogmatics*, requires us to take more account of these elements than he did—or, indeed, could have done, given the extent to which his whole discussion is locked into certain metaphors and conditioned by too literalistic an interpretation of them." Unfortunately, Torrance's study is itself limited because it focuses almost entirely on *CD* I. See Alan J. Torrance, *Persons in Communion: Trinitarian Description and Human Participation* (Edinburgh, 1996), pp. 223ff.

noetic terms, especially in his doctrine of the Word of God in *CD* I, this is not the end of the story.

A more serious criticism of Rosato is that he assumes that the only way to conceive of a corresponding ontic role for the Spirit is in terms whereby "the free acts of the Spirit … are sparked by the equally free acts of man." [41] However, in putting it this way, Rosato assumes a notion of freedom which is understood univocally to God and the human and which stands logically prior to both God and man. God's freedom and man's freedom must stand on an equal plane if they are both to be "equally free." Consequently, Rosato places Barth on the horns of a false dilemma: either both God the Spirit and the human spirit are unequivocally free, or one or the other (in this case, the human) is not free at all. There is no doubt that Barth accepts the freedom of God, but this does not mean that humans are not free at all. Indeed, Barth insists that they enjoy a "very definite freedom."[42]

Hunsinger and Webster have more recently shown the problems of positing such a concept of freedom against Barth, as Rosato does, if for no other reason than that it is radically inconsistent with Barth's overall thought in which agency in God and the human are always understood in asymmetrical terms[43]—a mere "pneumatological improvisation" on Barth could never bring about that for which Rosato wishes.[44] Spencer also notes, "Contrary to P. J. Rosato's assumption that [the] divine determination of humanity results in a loss of any real status for the human agent, Barth is concerned … with the human as God's covenant partner and thus as an active participant in the grace of God."[45] While Rosato rightly seeks an ontic role of the Spirit in which human freedom is redeemed, he is asking Barth to commit to a theological and ethical view of human freedom which Barth had thoroughly rejected throughout his whole career.

---

[41] Rosato, *Spirit as Lord*, pp. 139-41.

[42] *CD* II/2, p. 585.

[43] George Hunsinger, *How to Read Karl Barth: The Shape of His Theology* (New York and Oxford, 1991), pp. 185-224.

[44] On the matter of human freedom in light of God's freedom, John Webster's work on Barth's moral theology has opened up whole avenues of inquiry that were unfortunately not yet open to Rosato in his account. Unlike Rosato, who sees human freedom in Barth's thought being severely limited, Webster thinks that, for Barth, "freedom in limitation" (especially as developed in *CD* III/4) "*specifies* rather than *hems* in the creature." Consequently, limitation "is not derogation but 'the most positive affirmation'" of the human before God. In this regard, freedom is a "space defined by the action of God and the corresponding acts of God's partners which God's grace evokes." Though Rosato would agree with Barth that human nature is "awakened to its full freedom" by the Spirit, Barth would have serious problems in calling such an awakening a form of "cooperation" between God and the human as if it suggested a cooperation of univocally "free" beings. See John Webster, *Barth's Moral Theology* (Grand Rapids, 1998), p. 115; and Rosato, *Spirit as Lord*, p. 131.

[45] Archibald James Spencer, *Clearing a Space for Human Action: Ethical Ontology in the Theology of Karl Barth* (New York, 2003), p. 288.

Summary and Evaluation

How should the function of the filioque in the *CD* be characterized thus far? Given the context of Barth's concern to guard against what he saw as the dangers of "direct spiritual illumination" and given Barth's concern that the subjective element of revelation be spoken of only in light of its objective Christological focus, the filioque functions for Barth, at least in *CD* I/2, as a theological guarantee of the unity and harmony of the work of Christ and the Spirit. According to Barth, the filioque is an essential dogmatic cue adopted in the West to remind the Church that the work of the Spirit ought not to be spoken of in abstraction from the work of Christ: there is no possibility of an independent pneumatology implying an independent ontic role for the Spirit. An independent pneumatology thus construed would be in danger of confusing and conflating the Spirit of God with the spirit of humanity, or even some other spirit! Rather, Barth argued that the identification of the Spirit as the divine Spirit of God is possible only when one considers from whence the Spirit comes—from Jesus Christ himself. It is in this way that Barth can assert so confidently that the work of the Spirit is the work of the Son. This is not to be understood as confusing the distinction between the hypostases of the Son and the Spirit; it is as much a reiteration of Barth's commitment to the principle of *opera trinitatis ad extra sunt indivisa.* For Barth, the filioque is the Church's way of recognizing, not imposing, a unity of Word and Spirit—a unity that is true *ad extra* because it is antecedently true *ad intra.* Indeed, Barth said as much when he asserted that the filioque *is* "the recognition of the New Testament unity of Christ and Spirit."[46] As a result, Barth fretted that where the filioque is forgotten or downplayed, or where the filioque is said to apply only to revelation, and not to the immanent Trinity itself, there "the Holy Spirit is sundered from Christ, [and] sooner or later He is always transmuted into quite a different spirit, the spirit of the religious man, and finally the human spirit in general."[47] Conversely, the filioque continually reminds the Church of the *deity* of the Holy Spirit in contradistinction from the *created* spirit of humanity. Evidently, then, the filioque can be viewed as one of the tools in Barth's own dogmatic tool-belt by which he could resist what he saw as the crippling effect of the post-Schleiermacherian confusion of the spirit of man and the Spirit of God. Where the filioque is forgotten, to transpose one of Barth's earlier sayings, Schleiermacher is already peeping in the window.[48]

So what can be said by way of evaluation at this point? Positively, one can see in Barth's use of the filioque an important emphasis on the noetic role of the Spirit in bringing about the knowledge of God in Jesus Christ. Even though it is right and

[46] *CD* I/2, pp. 250-51.

[47] *CD* I/2, p. 251.

[48] Barth's original quip, "Feuerbach is again peeping through the window here," belongs to his discussion of the way of eminence as a means of forming concepts of the knowledge of God. Karl Barth, *The Göttingen Dogmatics*, ed. Hannelotte Reiffen, trans. Geoffrey W. Bromiley (Grand Rapids. 1991), pp. 399-400. Hereafter *GD.*

proper to expect Barth to fill out his pneumatology with a clearer articulation of the ontic role of the Spirit, his emphasis on the noetic role should not be downplayed, if for no other reason than Scripture upholds and supports such a noetic role for the Spirit.[49] However, it is also the case that Barth does eventually go on to argue more fully, especially in his doctrine of Creation, that human knowledge of God—a knowledge made possible only in the Holy Spirit—*is* an ontic transformation in humanity: "If man knows God, this includes and primarily implies the fact that God acts towards man as the One who knows. It is thus inevitable that the human knowledge should have a total reference and claim and alter the whole man."[50] To suggest that Barth's view of the knowledge of God in Christ by the Holy Spirit is little more than a shift in cognitive awareness of reconciliation already effected is to separate revelation from reconciliation and redemption in a way that Barth would most certainly resist.[51] In this regard, the criticism that Barth's use of the filioque restricts his pneumatology to being "decidedly noetic"[52] cannot ultimately be sustained when considering further theological development in the *CD*.

Negatively, however, Barth's appeal to the filioque as means of guaranteeing the unity of the work of the Son and Spirit—a laudable theological intention—might very well be asking the doctrine of the filioque to bear a burden too great for it to bear. On the one hand, Barth made use of the filioque to defend the full deity of the Spirit along with the Father and the Son and, in this sense, he was consistent with what appears to be the original Western intention of the filioque clause against all Arian detractors.[53] On the other hand, it is questionable whether upholding the filioque is the only way, let alone the best way, to maintain the theological unity of Word and Spirit. Even if Barth were assumed to be essentially correct that the primary work of the Spirit is to point to the Son as the objective fulfillment of revelation, can this theological assertion only be maintained by affirming the procession of the Spirit from the Father and Son in the immanent Trinity? What makes it theologically necessary that this peculiar work of the Spirit in testifying to the Son is possible only by virtue of recognizing an eternal procession of the Spirit from the Father and Son? Does the monopatrist position effectively deny the noetic role of the Spirit? And is it possible to deduce from the revelation of the Spirit's procession the limits of his work?

---

49 E.g., John 14:26; 15:26; Acts 7:55; 1 Cor. 12:3; Eph. 1:17; 1 John 4:2.

50 *CD* IV/3.1, p. 184. And later Barth could claim that recognition of the resurrection as the revelation of God is a "noetic which has all the force of a divine ontic." *CD* IV/3.1, p. 297.

51 See Hunsinger, "The Mediator of Communion," p. 150.

52 Rosato, *Spirit as Lord*, p. 133.

53 It is noteworthy that some Orthodox theologians fully accept this use of the filioque. For example, Stylianopoulos argues, "the theological use of the *filioque* in the West against Arian subordinationism is fully valid according to the theological criteria of the Eastern tradition." Theodore Stylianopoulos, "The Filioque: Dogma, Theologoumenon or Error?" *Greek Orthodox Theological Review* 31/3-4 (1986): 255-88 at 287.

In conclusion, Barth's appeal to the filioque in *CD* I/2 functions as a means of recognizing and guaranteeing the unity of the work of the Spirit and the Son. As such, Barth was guided by a right theological intention to uphold the objective center of revelation in Jesus Christ as the one in whom the Father is revealed. He was rightly concerned that spiritual knowledge of God the Father comes only in and through the Son, and that any appeal to direct knowledge of the Father apart from the Son is knowledge of "another god." Barth's appeal to the filioque, however, while functioning as a workable reminder of the inseparability of the work of the Son and the Spirit, is not necessarily an essential, irreplaceable, dogmatic safeguard. In this respect, it is unclear why he saw no way of maintaining the unity of the work of the Son and Spirit except by appeal to the filioque, especially since he had already understood that the co-inherence of divine Persons insures that both their essence and their work are shared: the one Being *(Sein)* of God subsists in three distinct modes of being (*Seinsweisen*). In this sense, Barth's rightful concern to safeguard the unity of the Son and the Spirit might have been accomplished through a more thoroughgoing attention to the co-inherence of persons, and more specifically, to the Athanasian emphasis on the *homoousios* of the Spirit, along with the Son, and with the Father. This is not to deny that there might be other sufficient reasons to uphold the filioque—a possibility, for example, that T. F. Torrance does not entertain. Nevertheless, at least in the case of *CD* I/2, we are not convinced that the appeal to the filioque is necessary to maintain the unity of Word and Spirit, and that it could not have been maintained through other theological conceptions such as perichoresis and *homoousia*.

Church Dogmatics III: The Filioque and the Co-inherence of Creation and History

Before moving into an analysis of the next important section where the filioque occurs in Barth's thinking, it might be asked why our analysis fails to mention anything from *CD* II. This is not simply due to space constraint or simple oversight—as if *CD* II were inconsequential!— but because, despite passing allusions to the procession of the Spirit from the Father and the Son in *CD* II,[54] there is no instance where Barth appeals to the doctrine explicitly or seeks to expand or build on it more fully. This is a curious absence from Barth's doctrine of God, to be sure, and it can only be speculated why Barth did not include further discussion of the filioque in *CD* II. However, it is possible that this absence may

[54] E.g., "God is Himself eternally the Holy Spirit, proceeding from the Father and the Son, and of one essence with them both. … in eternity God is also the Holy Spirit proceeding from the Father and the Son, and their unity in love." *CD* II/1, p. 48. "Acts happen only in the unity of spirit and nature. If such a unity is to be denied in regard to God, then … there is no eternal witness of the Son through the Father, no eternal procession of the Holy Spirit from the Father and the Son, no inner life of God." *CD* II/1, p. 267.

be explained as reflecting the pattern already established in the *GD*, where the filioque was understood primarily as a question to be properly dealt with under the doctrine of Revelation rather than under the Doctrine of God proper.

"God's essence and work are not two-fold but one."[55] From this vantage point, *CD* III/1 reveals an important material application of the doctrine of the filioque, unlike its more formal discussions in *CD* I.

Barth's next material application of the filioque occurs in *CD* III/1[56] and emerges in the context of his discussion on "Creation, History and Creation History," the first subsection of §41, "Creation and Covenant."[57] Barth's summary begins, "Creation comes first in the series of works of the triune God, and is thus the beginning of all things distinct from God himself."[58] His doctrine of Creation, then, as a dogmatic response to the "first in the series of [God's] works," is significant because it functions as a testing ground for the theological axiom laid down in the first two volumes: "To the unity of Father, Son and Spirit among themselves corresponds their unity *ad extra*."[59] How did Barth conceive of the "common origin" of the Spirit "from the-Father-and-the-Son" in relation to the unity of God's "first work" in creation? The economic work of the Spirit corresponds to his role in the immanent Trinity in which the Spirit is the communion of the Eternal Father and the Incarnate Son, and Barth arrives at this through a reworked doctrine of Trinitarian appropriations in reference to the doctrine of Creation.[60] In order to accomplish this, he distinguished between three interrelated concepts in his

---

[55] *CD* I/1, p. 371.

[56] Barth apparently approached the task of writing his third volume with a sense of trepidation. He confessed, "In taking up the doctrine of creation I have entered a sphere in which I feel much less confident and sure. If I were not obliged to do so in the course of my general exposition of Church dogmatics, I should probably have not given myself so soon to a detailed treatment of this particular material." *CD* III/1, p. ix. Webster observes, "For all its daring in restructuring the doctrine of creation, and for all that it contains many passages of undoubted intellectual power or sensitivity, in important respects the first part-volume of *Church Dogmatics* III lacks some of the assurance of other parts of the work." John Webster, *Barth* (London and New York, 2000), p. 99.

[57] *CD* III/1, pp. 42-94.

[58] *CD* III/1, p. 42.

[59] *CD* I/1, p. 371.

[60] Hill's explanation of the classical theory of appropriations is helpful: "What is in reality a common prerogative of the trinitarian members is predicated of one alone to manifest his personal uniqueness in the Godhead. But this cannot be done arbitrarily; some mysterious affinity between person and an action *ad extra*, or an essential attribute, lies at the base of this kind of speech." William J. Hill, *The Three-Personed God: The Trinity as Mystery of Salvation* (Washington, DC, 1982), p. 283. Whereas traditionally the Persons of the Trinity have been spoken of as Creator, Redeemer and Sanctifier, Barth, Torrance notes, "restated the doctrine of appropriation, in his radically economic and trinitarian way of appropriating 'creation,' 'reconciliation' and 'redemption' to the hypostatic distinctions between Father, Son and Holy Spirit, in which the order of God's economic self-revelation

doctrine of Creation, as the section title suggests: namely, 1) creation; 2) history; and 3) creation history. In Barth's conception, it is by the Holy Spirit that creation (appropriated to the Father) and history (appropriated to the Son) co-inhere in creation history, even though creation and history continue to remain distinct. This framework, of course, will require some unpacking.

First, Barth pointed out that, in line with the Creed, it is appropriate in particular (*per appropriationem*) to associate God the Father with the work of creation. To confess that the Father is Creator is to testify to the fact that God is not a God who delights in splendid isolation, but a God who freely creates the world as distinct from himself. In this way, for Barth, the doctrine of Creation, taken as a whole, ultimately means that "He who alone is God the Father Almighty is not alone."[61]

But Barth was also quick to point out that the Father is not exclusively the Creator, lest one "make of the triune God a triad of Gods."[62] As he explained, "the proposition that God the Father is Creator and God the Creator [is] the Father can be defended only when we mean by 'Father' the 'Father with the Son and the Holy Spirit.'"[63] In this regard, Barth reminded his readers, "it is not without the Son but in Jesus Christ … that [the Father] makes Himself known as the sovereign Lord of all things and the Creator." And, to be sure, "the Holy Spirit of God is the self-communication of His fatherhood as well as His lordship as Creator, so that without Him God could not partake of the name of Father and Creator."[64]

If creation is properly understood in the fullest sense to be the work of Father, Son and Holy Spirit, what makes it appropriate to speak of the Father, primarily, as the Creator? Barth's answer was that God the Father is known appropriately as Creator not only because he creates the world as distinct from himself, but antecedently because "as the Father, God procreates [*erzeugt*] Himself from eternity in His Son, and with His Son He is also from eternity the origin of Himself in the Holy Spirit."[65] Barth was clear that God's "procreating" *ad intra* is not to be confused with his "creation" *ad extra*:

---

is grounded in the order of the ontological Trinity." Thomas F. Torrance, *The Christian Doctrine of God, One Being Three Persons* (Edinburgh, 1996), p. 200.

61 *CD* III/1, p. 3.

62 *CD* III/1, p. 49.

63 *CD* III/1, p. 49. Once again, though not stated in as many words, the parallel to Torrance's concept of the Monarchy of the Trinity is evident here in Barth. The Father, though appropriately understood as the Monarchy of the Trinity, is not independently so. See Torrance, *Christian Doctrine*, pp. 180-85.

64 *CD* III/1, pp. 49-50.

65 *CD* III/1, p. 49. The dialectical structure in the German is nearly lost in English translation of this passage and the combination of separate sentences in German into compound sentences in English. Barth twice alternates between speaking of God as Father [*Als der Vater*] and God as Creator [*Als der Schöpfer*]. Thus, the structure is: *Als der Vater … Als der Schöpfer… Als der Vater … Als der Schöpfer.* See *KD* III/1, 52.

> The two things are not identical. Neither the Son nor the Holy Spirit is the world; … But between the two, i.e., between the relationship in God Himself and God's relationship to the world, there is an obvious proportion. … It is meaningful and right to designate God the Father in particular (*per appropriationem*) as Creator, and God the Creator in particular (*per appropriationem*) as the Father.[66]

The implication is that the confession of Father as Creator cannot be understood simply to denote "the one who creates the world." Rather, the Father is said to be Creator *ad extra* on the basis that this same Creator is antecedently the Father who generates a distinction within himself *ad intra.* To be Creator, then, is defined as "one who generates that which is distinct from one self." In other words, the creation of the world is not be understood as an absolute first instance in which God generates that which is distinct from himself, even though creation is said to be the first work of God *ad extra;* rather, creation testifies to the fact that God the Father has never been a passive God of isolated solitude, but an active God of eternal positing of "otherness" even within himself. In this way, Barth associated the concept of creation with the Father because God the Father "is in Himself the origin [*Ursprung*] which has no other (not even an eternal and divine) origin, the source [*Quelle*] of the other eternal modes of existence of the divine essence."[67]

If creation is associated in particular with the Father, with what in particular is the Son associated? It is here that Barth introduced the second concept, namely history. Though creation is the first of a series of God's eternally decreed works which is prior to, and the origin of, all other works, history is "the execution of the eternal decision of God's will."[68] Or more simply, history is the "the execution of [God's] activity."[69] In Barth's sense of the term, then, history can be understood only in "indissoluble connexion"[70] with creation, even though history is not identical to creation. History is, in essence, the outworking of God's eternal creative will and must be properly understood in relation to creation as act is to intention. For in God, act and intention are completely unified, and history is the activity of God stemming from his eternal creative intention. As Barth explained:

> In the same freedom and love in which God is not alone in Himself but is the eternal begetter of the Son, who is the eternally begotten of the Father, He also turns as Creator *ad extra* in order that absolutely and outwardly He may not be alone but the One who loves in freedom. … The eternal fellowship between Father and Son, or between God and His Word, thus finds a correspondence in the very different but not dissimilar fellowship between God and His creature.[71]

66 *CD* III/1, p. 49.
67 *CD* III/1, p. 49.
68 *CD* III/1, p. 43.
69 *CD* III/1, p. 59.
70 *CD* III/1, p. 61.
71 *CD* III/1, p. 50.

Though creation and history are unified in intention and act, history is really and truly a *novum*, insofar as it is an "external" actualization of God's will and decree corresponding to an eternal "inner divine reality," the *Realdialektik* that eternally exists as the Father eternally procreates or originates himself in the Son.

Interestingly, Barth found this formal explanation of the relationship of creation to history to be ultimately inadequate on its own. This is because history is an empty concept apart from the incarnation of the Son as "the second mode of existence ('person') of the inner divine reality in itself and as such."[72] It is not as if the Son enters into *a* history—for that would be to make the Son subject to history. Rather, history is possible only as grounded upon the Son, upon Jesus Christ who is "very God and very man." Consequently, it is only in the outworking of God's eternal counsel to differentiate himself from the Son—"the counsel actualised in the manger of Bethlehem, the cross of Calvary and the tomb of Joseph of Arimathea"[73]—that history is said to be simultaneously other than creation, but indissolubly linked. In this sense, it is not merely "possible" for God to be Creator (for that would be to separate creation from history in deistic fashion), nor is it deterministically "necessary" for God to be Creator (for that would be to rob God of his freedom in pantheistic fashion), but it is "essential for God to be Creator." Indeed, Barth argued, the only "genuine necessity" that one can speak of as the basis of creation is God's own free love.[74] That is, Jesus Christ becoming flesh is properly understood not merely as an occurrence or a point in a pre-existing history, nor as one who merely enters into history from without, but, as Barth emphasized, "this history is from the theological standpoint *the* history [*die Geschichte*]."[75] Or in short, the action of God in the man Jesus Christ *is* the history of God's free and loving work to reconcile the world unto himself.[76]

Barth's discussion of creation and history, of course, raises the colossal theological problem of how properly to understand the relationship of eternity and time.[77] If the Father is essentially one who differentiates himself from himself

---

[72] *CD* III/1, p. 50.

[73] *CD* III/1, p. 51.

[74] *CD* III/1, p. 51.

[75] *CD* III/1, p. 59.

[76] Barth explicated this more fully in *CD* IV/2 when he said, "For all its singularity, as His history it was not and is not a private history, but a representative and therefore public[*sic*]. His history in the place of all other men and in accomplishment of their atonement; the history of their Head, in which they all participate. Therefore, in the most concrete sense of the term, the history of this One is world history. When God was in Christ He reconciled the world to Himself (2 Cor. 5[19])." *CD* IV/2, p. 269.

[77] On Barth's dealing with the problem of the relationship of eternity and time, see (in chronological order): A. Bradenburg, "Der Zeit- Und Geschichtsbegriff Bei Karl Barth," *Theologie und Glaube* 45 (1955): 357-78; Robert Jenson, *God After God: The God of the Past and the God of the Future, Seen in the Work of Karl Barth* (Indianapolis and New York, 1969); Colin E. Gunton, *Becoming and Being: The Doctrine of God in Charles*

in the Son, and if the economic manifestation of this divine differentiation is appropriately linked to creation and history respectively, then the question arises how history, as the temporal outworking of God's activity, relates to that which is non-temporal, the first work of the eternal God in his eternal intention to bring about creation.

It comes as no surprise that the relationship of creation to history, or of eternity to time, must be answered in Trinitarian terms for Barth. In this regard, it is of utmost importance to observe that he refused to deal with the problem in the abstract terms of "time and eternity" per se. While such a conceptual abstraction may well be an important philosophical question worth consideration in its own right, Barth is only interested in the question insofar as it can be answered in reference to the doctrine of the Trinity. Thus, the question really and concretely has to do with the relationship of the Creator of all things to his own self-differentiated identity in the one who is to be Incarnate, Jesus Christ of Nazareth.[78] It is evident that Barth's theological strategy for dealing with the problem is simultaneously appreciative and critical of Augustine's treatment of the problem of eternity and time in the *Confessions.*[79] Barth agreed with Augustine that "the Creator is prior to the creature; only the eternity which transcends and includes all time is prior to time." However, he parts company with Augustine and is ultimately critical of his formulation, particularly the way in which Augustine speaks of time and eternity

Hartshorne and Karl Barth (Oxford, 1978); R. H. Roberts, "Karl Barth's Doctrine of Time: Its Nature and Implications," in *Karl Barth—Studies of His Theological Method*, ed. S. W. Sykes (Oxford, 1979); R. D. Williams, "Barth on the Triune God," in S. W. Sykes (ed.), *Karl Barth. Studies of his Theological Method.* (Oxford, 1979); David Ford, *Barth and God's Story: Biblical Narrative and the Theological Method of Karl Barth in the Church Dogmatics* (Frankfurt, 1981); John E. Cowell, *Actuality and Provisionality: Eternity and Election in the Theology of Karl Barth* (Edinburgh, 1989); Douglas Farrow, *Ascension and Ecclesia* (Grand Rapids, 1999), pp. 291ff.; George Hunsinger, "*Mysterium Trinitatis:* Barth's Conception of Eternity," in George Hunsinger (ed.), *For the Sake of the World: Karl Barth and the Future of Ecclesial Theology* (Grand Rapids, 2004); and Adrian Langdon, "God the Eternal Contemporary: Trinity, Eternity, and Time in Karl Barth's *Church Dogmatics*" (PhD thesis, Montreal, 2009).

[78] A particularly thorny problem is the question of whether Barth would posit the concept of a pre-existent *logos asarkos* versus a strict adherence to a *logos ensarkos*. Molnar argues that a *logos asarkos* was retained with "a significant but limited role in Barth's theology," and functioned for Barth as a necessary theological abstraction. See Paul D. Molnar, *Divine Freedom and the Doctrine of the Immanent Trinity* (London and New York, 2002), pp. 64, 71. Others, however, wish to nuance Barth's position. In this regard, see especially Farrow, *Ascension and Ecclesia*, p. 54ff; Edwin Chr. van Driel, "Karl Barth on the Eternal Existence of Jesus Christ," *Scottish Journal of Theology* 60/1 (2007): 45-61; Bruce McCormack, "Seek God Where He May Be Found: A Response to Edwin Chr. van Driel," *Scottish Journal of Theology* 60/1 (2007): 62-79.

[79] Augustine, *Confessions*, XI.

in the abstract and as two concepts in absolute and polar opposition.[80] This is not to say that Barth denied that time and eternity stand in contradistinction to one another; indeed he affirms, as he had ever since *Romans*, that they must not be confused. Though time and eternity continue to be presented dialectically in the *CD*, he now sought a form of relationship between the two that did not result in either a simple negation (which, taken to its logical conclusion, was implied in *Romans*[81]) or in a synthesis of some kind (which might be a capitulation to Hegel, a move that he intentionally wanted to resist[82]). In order to speak of the relationship in such a dialectical form, Barth sought to address the relationship of time and eternity in Trinitarian categories, as the "decisive anchorage" in proposing a solution to the problem.[83] Unlike Augustine, who tended to view God's eternity as an "eternal present" (*nunc aeternitatis*) or "divine timelessness," eternity is, for Barth, the very "source of time … the immediate unity of present, past and future."[84] In this respect, even the eternal God has a temporality of sorts.[85] In contradistinction

[80] Barth's conceptualization of time and eternity in *Romans* was more thoroughly Augustinian.

[81] On Barth's move away from the idea, present in the second edition of *Romans*, that eternity was "equally close and equally far away from every moment in time," see Bruce L. McCormack, *Karl Barth's Critically Realistic Dialectic Theology: Its Genesis and Development, 1909-1936* (Oxford, 1995), pp. 288-90.

[82] See Karl Barth, *Protestant Theology in the Nineteenth Century*, trans. Brian Cozens and John Bowden (London, 2001), pp. 399-400. Cross defines Hegel's dialectic as "a method whereby the reality of truth is exposed and exposited. Through the interplay of contradictory elements, each pole of opposition brings one closer to the truth when it fully passes into its opposite and is canceled, sublimated (*Aufhebung*). However, contradiction never entirely cancels its opponent." Terry L. Cross, *Dialectic in Karl Barth's Doctrine of God* (New York, 2001), pp. 31-32.

[83] Hunsinger's observation here is apt: "If the doctrine of the Trinity is difficult, and the idea of eternity no less difficult, then a trinitarian doctrine of eternity will be doubly difficult." Yet Hunsinger also insists, "Barth makes perhaps the first sustained attempt in history to reformulate eternity's mystery in fully trinitarian terms." Hunsinger, "*Mysterium*," p. 16. Gunton concurs, noting that one of Barth's great achievements was "the restoration of the link between history and the Trinity." Colin E. Gunton, "The Truine [*sic*] God and the Freedom of the Creature," in S. W. Sykes (ed.), *Karl Barth: Centenary Essays* (Cambridge, 1989), p. 47.

[84] *CD* III/1, p. 67.

[85] Later, Barth can claim with even more boldness: "God … is supremely temporal." *CD* III/2, p. 437. However, as Hunsinger notes, Barth's use of the word "time" is often quite ambiguous, possibly reflecting the limitations and vagaries of human language, not to mention the ineffability of God's being. Hunsinger therefore paraphrases Barth's varied use of the word "time" as an attempt to say something like, "God is temporal, and yet God's temporality is unlike any time that we know." Hunsinger, "*Mysterium*," pp. 168-69.

In an earlier parallel section, Barth was even able to maintain, against the concepts of much Western theism, that "God possesses space, His own space and … just because of this spatiality, he is able to be triune." *CD* II/1, pp. 468-69.

to "the time of lost man … lost time," Barth called the temporality of God "the time of the Creator," "a time constituted by God's own presence in Jesus Christ in the world created by Him," "the time of His covenant with man."[86] Christ is thus appropriately spoken of as one who comes in the "fullness of time" and yet who has a "genuine temporal present with a genuine temporal past and future."[87] Jesus Christ is appropriated, therefore, as the very movement (as distinguished from the origin and goal) of God in history.[88] Or, as Jenson has aptly summarized, "[t]he history of man begins (in the most fundamental sense possible) as a progress toward the reconciliation of sinful man in Jesus Christ."[89]

To be sure, Jesus Christ is not to be construed as the entrance of the essential eternal into the relative temporal (as is often understood in classical doctrines of the Incarnation),[90] but as the actualization of the eternal God's *essential* temporality into the relative temporality of the creature in and through the Son, Jesus Christ. In so doing, God condescends to man in Jesus Christ, not by entering history where man is already present, as it were, but by initiating history in Jesus Christ as the "environment" in which reconciliation takes place. It is in and through Jesus Christ, the Son of the Father, the manifestation of God's essential temporality, that humans are themselves located. As Barth asked rhetorically:

> [H]ow can there be any possibility or actuality of the intercourse between God and the creature, and of the establishment and commencement of this intercourse, if not by God's graciousness to His creature, by His condescension to it, by His entrance into its form of existence, by His acceptance of its way, by the utterance of His Word and the accomplishment of His work in time?[91]

To reiterate, Barth was not interested in the question of the relationship between time and eternity considered abstractly; to seek to answer such a question is to speculate on something other than revelation.[92] That is not to say that Barth completely ignored the question as much as he attempted to reframe the question from a Trinitarian perspective. Instead of the abstract question, "What is the

---

86 *CD* III/1, pp. 72-73.

87 *CD* III/1, p. 73.

88 *CD* III/1, p. 68.

89 Robert W. Jenson, *Alpha and Omega* (reprint, Eugene, 2002), p. 28.

90 Jenson has aptly observed that any characterization of the incarnation as "[God's] decision … to send His Son as a man to restore order and to open the way for the realization of God's original plan, whatever that may be" would "infuriate Barth." Ibid., p. 21.

91 *CD* III/1, pp. 68-69.

92 It is interesting how Barth identified the problem as he did in *CD* III, but even here his wrestling with it still appeared to be laboring under the philosophical weight of the abstractions of time and eternity. It is not until *CD* IV that Barth boldly admitted that it is not merely a philosophical problem with which human minds grapple, but "a spiritual problem, characterized as the problem of God Himself." *CD* IV/2, p. 344.

relationship of eternity to time?" Barth asked the concrete question, "What is the relationship of Jesus Christ of Nazareth to the eternal God?" That question can only be answered in light of the doctrine of the Incarnation, that Jesus Christ *is* Immanuel. It is in Jesus Christ that eternity and temporality meet most fully and completely.

Barth also recognized that however neatly he might appeal to the incarnation as the solution to how divine and human are to be related, there are still some particularly thorny problems. Most significantly, if God is both essentially eternal *and* essentially temporal in himself, and if the true and real distinction between the temporal and the eternal is to be maintained even in the incarnation, is there not a danger that the temporal might be overcome or obliterated by the eternal? If, in fact, both the terms of the problem and the solution to the problem are grounded in Jesus Christ, is there not a danger that the eternity of the Son of the Father might overshadow the historical temporality of Jesus of Nazareth? Or to use the terminology that Barth himself would eventually use: in what way can the eternal God *tolerate* the distinctly "other" temporal creature? Even apart from the great problem of sin that plagues humanity, the question highlights the need to understand how to speak of a God who allows the presence of another that is both essentially unified in essence and genuinely distinct from him without allowing the glory of the eternal to overwhelm the created Other, not to mention providing genuine freedom for the created Other to be other than eternal.

Pneumatology holds the key here for Barth. Drawing upon a suggestive turn of phrase in Calvin,[93] Barth argued that the Holy Spirit is to be understood as the "divine *virtus* [power] poured out on all things and supporting, sustaining and quickening all things."[94] In this light, he adds, "the Holy Spirit is in some sense the necessary divine justification and sanctification of the creature as such, and therefore, if not the ground, at least the fundamental condition of its existence."[95] Assuming that God is antecedently in himself that which he reveals himself to be, this implies to Barth that "in some sense it is a matter of the self-justification and self-sanctification of God without which He could not have loved the creature nor willed or actualized its existence."[96] For Barth, this "self-justification" and "self-sanctification" is identified with none other than the Holy Spirit. Here it is necessary to cite Barth at length:

> The fulfillment of this presupposition, the eternal accomplishment of this divine self-justification and self-sanctification, is the Holy Spirit of the Father and the

---

[93] Though the concept goes back at least to Irenaeus. See, for example, Irenaeus, *Against Heresies*, v. 12, in *Ante-Nicene Fathers,* vol. 1, ed. Alexander Roberts and James Donaldson (Peabody, 1994), pp. 537-39.

[94] *CD* III/1, p. 58. Cf. John Calvin, *Institutes of the Christian Religions*, ed. John T. McNeil, trans. Ford Lewis Battles (Louisville, 1960), I, 13, 14 at pp. 138-41.

[95] *CD* III/1, p. 58.

[96] *CD* III/1, pp. 58-59.

> Son *qui procedit ex Patre Filioque,* who in his common origin in the Father and the Son not only does not hinder their fellowship but glorifies it; in whom God does not restrict His deity but causes it to overflow even in the decree of grace and His creative will. In this way the Holy Spirit is the inner divine guarantee of the creature. If its existence were intolerable to God, how could it be loved and willed and made by Him? How could it emerge and be? That its existence should not be intolerable to God but destined to serve His greater glory—the creation of this essential condition of its existence is the peculiar work of the Holy Spirit in creation.[97]

In other words, God would not *tolerate* the creature, the one created distinct from himself, lest there was something presupposed *in himself* that made this toleration possible, some form of what Barth called a "self-justification" and "self-sanctification" that made creaturely existence, particularly creaturely existence in the incarnation of the Son, possible.

It is especially noteworthy how Barth conceived of the work of the Spirit in this context. Without the Spirit, there would be an insurmountable obstacle to fellowship between the eternal and the temporal, between the Father and the Son, and, more importantly, between the Father and the incarnate Son of God, Jesus Christ, despite their indissoluble shared essence. It is because of the Spirit that a living fellowship and co-inherence and coincidence of time and eternity, creation and history, Father and Son, is not only possible, but glorified. Without the Spirit, the utterly overwhelming eternal and glorious essence of divinity would obliterate the lowly creature. With the Spirit, the eternal essence of divinity is not only appropriately restricted, but allowed to overflow into the temporal realm precisely by enabling the creature—and, for Barth, this is first and foremost true in the man Jesus Christ—to live and to move and to have its being. This is what Barth called the "inner divine guarantee of the creature," namely the Holy Spirit, who proceeds from the Father and the Son. It is the peculiar work of the Spirit, Barth said, to make the creature tolerable—tolerable to God, and beyond that, to make the creature able to bring glory to God himself. In this regard, Jesus Christ is understood to share fully both in divinity and humanity by virtue of the Holy Spirit who maintains this union without dissolving their difference. The Holy Spirit is therefore not to be understood as being appropriated either particularly to creation or to history per se, but is the eternal, ontological bond, the "indissoluble connexion" or "communion" of creation and history, such that history is neither confused with, nor separated from, its origin in creation. In Barth's terminology, the Holy Spirit is the creator and sustainer of the possibility of "Creation History" whereby the Creator God enacts his eternal will and decree for his Son among his temporally located creatures not by overwhelming them in their creatureliness, but by providing through his Spirit the guarantee of their real, though not independent, ontological existence, even in the face of God's Eternal Glory.

---

97 *CD* III/1, p. 59.

It is important to note the significant development in Barth's own thinking on the Spirit at this point, and specifically, how he appealed to the filioque. Whereas in earlier volumes, Barth had spoken of the Spirit primarily in his noetic role as the "Teacher of the Word," in *CD* III/1 Barth readily saw the Bible attributing to the Holy Spirit the ontic role of being the "*conditio sine qua non* of creaturely existence."[98] Though Barth admitted that the Bible does not explicitly say that the world was created *by* the Spirit, it does say, "that it is only through Him that the creature has its indispensable life; only through Him that it has continued enjoyment and exercise of the existence loaned to it in creation."[99] But most important to this study is that Barth appealed to the filioque as the eternal ground by which it is possible for the Spirit to be the "indissolubly real connexion" between God and the creature, between the Father and his Son, and between the divine and the human in Jesus Christ.[100]

From *Romans* on, Barth had struggled to speak of the ontological continuity between Creator and creature,[101] but to speak of this relationship in such a way that, paradoxically, an ontological distinction could also be maintained. The solution, for Barth, is not to seek a continuity of being (*analogia entis*) between the divine and the human, but to identify the Holy Spirit as the agent of continuity. It is the Spirit who is (or more properly, who acts as) the *conditio sine qua non* of creaturely existence; ontological continuity is therefore a *relation* between God and creature which is utterly dependent on the continuous free act of the Holy Spirit.[102]

In light of this real, enduring and continuous creative activity of the Holy Spirit, Barth conceived of a correspondence between the eternal and the temporal, between the inner divine relationships and God and creation. Whereas creation appropriately corresponds to the Father, and history to Jesus Christ the Son, it is in the Holy Spirit that creation and history are appropriately related in what Barth calls "creation history" (or the "history of creation"). As Barth explained, "the history of creation is at one and the same time both the originating divine activity and the originated creaturely occurrence. And, in it, the two are not only coincident but (for all their difference in dignity and power) co-inherent."[103]

Barth's concept appears to take a cue from how the relationship of the human and divine in Christ is delineated at Chalcedon. In a similar way to how the

98 *CD* III/1, p. 58.

99 *CD* III/1, p. 57. Barth's principal text here is Psalm 104:29ff.

100 Cf. *CD* I/1, p. 481.

101 See pp. ??? above.

102 Though he does not explicitly mention the pneumatological aspect, Torrance's explanation is apt: "There certainly is an ontological continuity, Barth argued, but it derives from the *Creator-creature* relation which by its very nature is contingent and which, while stable and continuous, [is] unceasingly sustained in the faithfulness of God." Thomas F. Torrance, "Karl Barth and Patristic Theology," in John Thompson (ed.), *Theology Beyond Christendom* (Allison Park, 1986), pp. 215-39 at p. 235.

103 *CD* III/1, p. 71.

human and divine in Christ are spoken of as being related in a union without confusion, separation, division, or change, "creation" and "history" are related in such a way that there is no confusion, separation, division, or change; they are co-inherent, but never conflated. To put it yet another way, the human, while ontologically distinct from God and residing in the temporal realm of history, cannot be understood in isolation from the Creator God from whom he has his being and in whose covenant he lives. Likewise, God is understood as a covenant-making God who, by creating, covenants from all eternity to be a God who dwells with his creation (cf. Lev. 26:11-12).[104] In this regard, Barth resisted speaking of God strictly *a se,* but instead sought to speak of God only as the one who reveals himself as Immanuel, God with us.

Furthermore, in introducing the concept of "creation history," Barth intended to demonstrate the simultaneity of creation and time in revelation. While it is true that God the Father's "eternity is itself revealed in the act of creation as his readiness for time, as pre-temporal, supra-temporal (or co-temporal) and post-temporal, and therefore as the source of time, of superior and absolute time," it is also the case that "His revelation, the act of creation, is simultaneous with the emergence of the creature and the commencement of time."[105] Whereas prior to the actual creation of the world, creation took place in the "sphere of God's pure, inner being … (as an *opus ad extra internum*)," it now "(as an *opus ad extra externum*) takes place outside this sphere, where over and against and distinct from it the creature comes into being in the new sphere posited by it and arising from the fact that it takes place."[106] Even though the creation of the world is external to God, it is by the Holy Spirit that the creation and history are united, that the Creator Father unites himself with creation in Jesus Christ by the Holy Spirit who proceeds from Father and Son.

Summary and Evaluation

The third volume of the *CD* marks an important material advance in Barth's application of the doctrine of the filioque. According to Barth, the Spirit who proceeds from Father and Son is to be understood as the third divine mode of being who unifies in coincident and co-inherent manner both the originating Father and originated Son *ad intra* and creation and history in the history of creation *ad extra*. Barth attempted to demonstrate how each mode of being is intimately involved in creation by seeking to redefine the question of the relationship of eternity to time in a Trinitarian framework. Because the Spirit holds together creation and history in the history of creation, Barth interpreted this as a sign of the Spirit as the mediator of communion in God. Consequently, the Spirit is to be viewed, in terms of the doctrine of Creation, as the divine mode of being by which the eternal

104 Cf. Lev. 26:11-12.

105 *CD* III/1, p. 70.

106 *CD* III/1, pp. 70-71.

God's relationship to the temporal creature is made possible; this is most fully exemplified in the union of divine and human in Jesus Christ as the outworking of God's eternal creative intent, without denigrating the ontological distinction between the two. Since the Spirit is understood to be the *conditio sine qua non* of the creaturely existence of humans in relation to God, it is therefore possible, in Barth's estimation, to understand the Spirit to be likewise the *conditio sine qua non* of the divine existence of Father and Son in eternity. Thus, for Barth, the Spirit, as the third *Seinsweise* of the Triune God, is antecedently responsible for maintaining the unity and difference between Father and Son in the immanent Trinity and is therefore the ground by which the unity and difference between the eternal God and the temporal creature is maintained, first in Jesus Christ and second to all creatures in Christ in the economy of creation.

At this juncture at least, Barth's view of the procession of the Spirit from the Father and the Son should not be understood as something passive, as if the Spirit merely receives from the Father and the Son. On the contrary, it is precisely because the Spirit proceeds from the common origin of the shared being of the Father and the Son that the Spirit is to be understood as the active divine agent who, to use Rosato's terms, "unites the nonidentical, qualitatively different beings of God and man."[107] In other words, the Spirit does for the creature what he does eternally in God.

How should Barth's use of the filioque in *CD* III be evaluated? Positively, it should be maintained that Barth's filioquist pneumatology, as delineated in his doctrine of Creation, resists three significant criticisms often lodged against it. First, if there has been any suggestion that Barth's pneumatology tends toward being "merely noetic," it is in the doctrine of creation that Barth found room for, and insisted upon, an ontic role for the Spirit. Indeed, it is in the doctrine of Creation that the Spirit is presented by Barth as being not only an enabler or completer of creation *post facto*, but is the very *conditio sine qua non* of creaturely existence. Because the Spirit is the eternal divine agent by which the Father eternally originates himself in the Son, so also the Spirit is the eternal divine agent, the Giver of Life, to the human creature, first and foremost in Jesus of Nazareth, but also to all other human creatures. According to Barth, this union of the Creator and the created is possible only because the Spirit is antecedently the Spirit of the Father and the Son and proceeds from their unity. In this regard, the Spirit is not only the mediator of communion, but is also the justification and sanctification of the creature in the face of the eternal glory of God.

Second, critics commonly suggest the filioque inevitably subordinates the Holy Spirit to the Father and the Son. However, given his view of the ontic role of the Spirit both in the internal divine relations and relative to creation, it would be difficult to see how such a charge could be applied to Barth. This is because the filioque functions for Barth not only to safeguard the divinity of the Spirit (as it has generally functioned in traditional Western formulations), but also because Barth

[107] Rosato, *Spirit As Lord*, p. 20.

interpreted the filioque in such a way that the Spirit is given a much more active role in the inner divine reality than the traditional language of procession tends to imply. In fact, if there is a *tendency* in Barth's use of the filioquist pneumatology as presented in his doctrine of Creation, it is actually less toward the subordination of the Spirit and more toward a *superordination* of the Spirit to the Father and the Son. This is because it is by the Holy Spirit that the Father and Son are eternally (not inevitably, as in Hegel) maintained and upheld (*Aufhebung*) in their distinct modes of being. This is not to say that Barth should be accused formally of a form of pneumatological superordination over Father and Son; however, given the crucial role the Spirit plays in the structure of the eternal divine relations, it is difficult to see how the charge of the Spirit's subordination to the Father and Son could legitimately be sustained, particularly *after* the completion of Barth's doctrine of Creation. For whatever incipient subordinationism could be detected in Barth's formal defense of the filioque in *CD* I/1 is now counterbalanced by the heightened ontic role given to the Spirit in *CD* III.

Third, Barth's use of the filioque in *CD* III represents an important corrective to his own theology insofar as he succeeded in better relating the work of the Spirit to the humanity of Jesus. Whereas in *CD* I, Barth had insisted that the Spirit's role in bringing about the humanity of Jesus in the Virgin birth has nothing whatsoever to do with the procession of the Spirit, in *CD* III he partly modified his position. Here, he recognized that the Holy Spirit who proceeds from the Father and the Son is the one who upholds and maintains in union the "Otherness" of the Father and Son, and therefore is also the Spirit who brings together the Creator and the created in the Incarnate Son without thereby diminishing the ontological distinction between the divine and the human. While he did not explicitly negate his own position outlined in *CD* I, Barth did bring the humanity of Jesus into closer connection with his divinity by arguing the Spirit is the *conditio sine qua non* of creaturely existence, and most specifically, of Jesus' human existence. If the Spirit "makes the existence of the creature as such possible, permitting it to exist, maintaining it in its existence, and forming the point of reference of its existence," he can only do this because "He is the communion and self-impartation realised and consisting between [Father and Son] from all eternity; the principle of their mutual love proceeding from both and equal in essence."[108] In short, the union of human and divine in Christ is possible only because the Spirit is antecedently the Spirit of union between Father and Son in all eternity.

Though Barth took important pneumatological steps forward in *CD* III, particularly relative to the ontic role of the Spirit, there are least two major criticisms that need to be highlighted. First, Barth's attempt to deal with the question of the relationship of time and eternity in a thoroughly Trinitarian manner is to be lauded as the correct way forward on the problem, but his construal of creation, history, and creation history on the basis of a reworked doctrine of Trinitarian appropriations ends up being admittedly formalistic. Indeed, Barth's way of lining

108 *CD* III/1, p. 56.

up creation, history and creation history with Father, Son and Spirit respectively looks strikingly similar to the formal structural analogy he used when speaking in the *GD* about the inner structural relationships of the threefold Word of God. However, the same weakness of the structural analogy between the threefold form of the Word of God and the triune Persons carries forward to how Barth posits a structural similarity between God and the whole created order—namely that Barth sets aside his own rule that there is no analogy to the Trinity but the Trinity itself. Thus, for Barth, to view creation, history and creation history as a structural analogy to the divine Persons is to posit a version of the *analogia entis* (or is it a *vestigium Trinitatis?*) of his own, his resistance to such a concept notwithstanding.[109]

Second, it is questionable whether in Barth's doctrine of Creation he has actually allowed the economic Trinity to inform the immanent Trinity. While Barth's theological ingenuity once again shines through as he sought to provide a Trinitarian solution to the problem of time and eternity, his appeal to the concepts of creation, history and creation history, appropriated respectively to Father, Son and Holy Spirit, relies on seeking a relationship between three theological abstractions, none of which can be concretely located in the biblical narrative itself. Consequently, Barth tended to theorize from a concept presupposed in the immanent Trinity (i.e., the Spirit as the communion between the Father and the Son by virtue of his eternal procession from both) to the economic Trinity rather than vice versa. In other words, it is not clearly evident that Barth found a filioquist structure displayed in the relationship of creation and history, but rather that he sought to relate creation and history on the basis of a doctrine of the filioque already presupposed. In this regard, Barth is likely more susceptible to the charge of systematic overuse of the filioque in his doctrine of Creation than anywhere else in the entire *CD*. Though Barth seems to have been intuitively aware of the kinds of corrections he needed to make after *CD* I/1 and begins to make them, is also apt to recall that his own reservations and lack of confidence expressed at the outset of *CD* III were probably appropriate. In this regard, the "weak link" in Barth's chain of use of the filioque has to be *CD* III.

Church Dogmatics IV: Dialectical Filioquist Pneumatology

There are two passages in which Barth appeals explicitly to the filioque in *CD* IV. The first reference is found in §64 "The Exaltation of the Son of Man" in *CD* IV/2, and most specifically section 4 entitled "The Direction of the Son." It is here that the "dialectical" element of Barth's filioquist pneumatology comes out most clearly. The second reference is found in *CD* IV/3.2 in §72 "The Holy Spirit and the Sending of the Christian Community." This reference can be understood as a clear application of the dialectical filioquist pneumatology as it pertains to the

---

[109] *CD* I/1, p. 239; *CD* II/1, pp. 79-84.

relationship of Jesus and the Church. The remainder of this chapter will consist of an examination of these two final passages.

CD *IV/2: The Filioque and the Problem in God*

Though there is great scholarly interest in Barth's fourth volume as a whole,[110] it is very unfortunate that the first passage in *CD* IV/2 has rarely been examined carefully in reference to the filioque, even though it represents Barth's most mature and most sophisticated attempt to explicate the significance of the doctrine in the entire *CD*. This is because Barth appeared finally to return with greater clarity to some of the dialectical themes evident some four decades earlier in the writing of his commentary on *Romans*, and some decades since the beginning of the *CD*.[111] Barth's material application of the filioque in *CD* IV thus simultaneously reveals an *advance* in his thought and a marked *return* to a motif already evident in *Romans*—that God is one who is marked in his own being as displaying a *Realdialektik* such that it is appropriate not only to confess that "God is God"[112] but that, within his own triune being, "God confronts God"!

Barth noted in his "retrospective" at the outset of *CD* IV/2 that the first part of the doctrine of Reconciliation (*CD* IV/1) is concerned with the initial movement of God from above to below, from God to man, and, as such, as the affirmation of the covenantal promise of God: "I will be your God."[113] But the second part of the doctrine (*CD* IV/2) is concerned with man reconciled with God in Jesus Christ. This is the second movement of God—a movement portrayed as being from man to God, from below to above, and represented by the renewal of the covenantal promise: "Ye shall be my people."[114] Together, the two sides of the covenant and the work of atonement are that:

---

[110] Some scholars argue that a reading of Barth's theology requires allowing *CD* IV a particularly important interpretative position. E.g., Richardson argues that a priority must be given to *CD* IV "because Barth allowed himself to be constrained by increased understanding, we too are constrained by his constraint—at least in the matter of reading him." Thus, Richardson argues, a regular front-to-back reading of the *Dogmatics* can also benefit from a back-to-front reading. That is, *CD* IV often sharpens and clarifies that which is sometimes ambiguous or not fully worked out in the earlier Barth. Kurt Anders Richardson, *Reading Karl Barth* (Grand Rapids, 2004), pp. 9-10.

[111] Barth can confidently claim in the "Preface" to *CD* IV/2 that "in the twenty-three years since I started this work I have found myself so held and directed that, as far as I can see, there have so far been no important breaks or contradictions in the presentation; no retractions have been necessary (except in detail)." However, "only the angels in heaven do actually know in detail what form the material will take." *CD* IV/2, p. xi.

[112] For an insightful interpretation of this phrase, see Eberhard Busch, "God Is God: The Meaning of a Controversial Formula and the Fundamental Problem of Speaking About God," *Princeton Seminary Bulletin* 7/2 (1986): 101-13.

[113] *CD* IV/2, p. 4. Cf. Exod. 6:7; Lev. 26:12.

[114] *CD* IV/2, p. 5.

> … as God condescends and humbles Himself to man and becomes man, man himself is exalted, not as God or like God, but to God, being placed at His side, not in identity, but in true fellowship with Him, and becoming a new man in this exaltation and fellowship.[115]

Thus, while it is true that God elected himself in the Son to take up the cause and the judgment of humanity, it is also true that "in and with His own abasement God has elected and achieved man's exaltation" and that the *telos* of God's judgment "can only be the redemption of man."[116] Despite the incumbent dangers he himself pointed out,[117] Barth nevertheless embarked on a journey of seeking to answer a "line of thought from below to above."[118] This second movement is what he called "The Direction of the Son," or as he puts it more fully, "the power of the existence of the one man Jesus Christ for all other men."[119] The central question, therefore, that occupies Barth for many, many pages is:

> [W]hat is the meaning, or better the power, of the existence of the one man Jesus Christ for those among whom and for whom as Reconciler, He, the Son of God, became also the Son of Man and one of them, their Brother; for us other men in our anthropological sphere which He also made His own when He became man?[120]

Put another way, the question of the direction of the Son for Barth is a question that moves from the particular to the general: how does *this* specific man, Jesus Christ, in whom time and eternity co-inhere, become a reality for the many persons for whom pure temporality is the sphere in which they find themselves existing?

On the one hand, Barth suggested, it is possible to view the biblical account of the exaltation of the Son of Man, Jesus Christ, to the right hand of God as but an isolated history that has no connection whatsoever to other humans. "What took place and has to be noted as this communication between divine and human being and activity in this One was and is only, as the reconciliation of man with God by God's own incarnation, His own history, and not that of any other man."[121] On the other hand, Barth insisted that Christ's exaltation cannot be isolated from the rest

---

115 *CD* IV/2, p. 6.

116 *CD* IV/2, p. 6.

117 As Barth aptly put it, "The *theologia crucis*, in which the true *theologia gloriae* has its roots, may easily be destroyed by a false *theologia gloriae*. This has happened time and again on the way which we are now entering, in the attempt to unfold the problem of the reconciled man. We have every reason to consider ourselves warned in this respect." *CD* IV/2, p. 9.

118 *CD* IV/2, p. 8.

119 *CD* IV/2, p. 265.

120 *CD* IV/2, pp. 264-65.

121 *CD* IV/2, p. 269.

of humanity. "[F]or all its singularity, as His history it was not and is not a private history, but a representative and therefore a public [history]. … When God was in Christ He reconciled the world to Himself (2 Cor. 5^{19}), and therefore us, each one of us."[122] But if this is the case—that in Christ Jesus the whole world is reconciled to God—then the question remains: how is such reconciliation accomplished? What is the power by which it is actualized? Or to use the repeated terminology of Barth himself, what is the "power of transition from Christ to us Christians"?[123]

Barth went on to expand greatly upon the meaning of the power of transition of the Son for others. According to Barth's reading of the New Testament, the power of transition is the power of light,[124] liberation,[125] knowledge,[126] peace,[127] and, most importantly, life eternal,[128] arising, as it does, as the "absolutely unique … power of the resurrection of Jesus Christ."[129] In all this, Barth sought continually to avoid speaking of this power in Gnostic terminology which emphasizes a "spiritual" aspect to the detriment of human existence as it actually is—bodily and in this time and place on earth. As he insists, "[t]he work of this power is not to destroy our earthliness, but to give to it a new determination."[130] In this sense, the power of transition of the Son to humans is a power to redeem humans in their current existence *as* humans, not a transubstantive power which changes humans into a "higher" non-human reality other than they are. In other words, the power of transition is a power to redeem humans to be human as Christ is fully human.

However, the extent to which Barth held back from identifying or naming this power is intriguing, even though it is plainly evident for pages on end that he was speaking about the operation of the Holy Spirit. In such cases, Barth's critics aptly "wonder where the Spirit went,"[131] or they are prone to observe an "eclipse" of the Spirit by the Son.[132] But it is arguable that Barth's reluctance to identify openly and forthrightly the Spirit, even in a context where such identification would surely be appropriate, is neither accidental nor a theological "compulsive" fear of Schleiermacherian pneumatology (*pace* Rogers). Instead, Barth, in seeking to be faithful to the New Testament witness to the Spirit, hoped to allow his own

122 *CD* IV/2, p. 269.

123 *CD* IV/2, p. 309.

124 *CD* IV/2, p. 310.

125 *CD* IV/2, pp. 311-12.

126 *CD* IV/2, pp. 312-24.

127 *CD* IV/2, pp. 314-15.

128 *CD* IV/2, pp. 315-17.

129 *CD* IV/2, p. 310.

130 *CD* IV/2, pp. 318-19.

131 Cf. Jenson, "You Wonder Where," pp. 296-304.

132 As Rogers has quipped, "Karl Barth allows the Son to eclipse the Spirit, when he allows his fear of Schleiermacher to overshadow his admiration for Athanasius." Eugene F. Rogers, Jr., "The Eclipse of the Spirit in Karl Barth," in John C. McDowell and Mike Higton (eds), *Conversing with Barth* (Aldershot, 2004), p. 173.

speech to be conformed to the New Testament manner of speaking in which the Holy Spirit's operation (and therefore, his presence) is more often *presupposed* than *presented*:[133] "In the New Testament sphere there never seems to have been any uncertainty or disquietude or anxiety at this vital point … In this sphere there is no one who finds any difficulty in the invisibility of the Spirit." Yet the New Testament gives every indication that "[t]here is no one who hesitate[d] to entrust himself wholly and exclusively to [the Spirit's] guidance and impulsion."[134]

Nevertheless, Barth finally succumbed in his exposition to the weight of the Spirit's reality and makes that which is implicit explicit: "The power whose operation is presupposed in the New Testament is the outgoing and receiving and presence and action of the Holy Spirit."[135] This marks a significant turning-point in his exposition.

Barth then turned to the questions of how and why this power of transition from Christ to Christians, the Holy Spirit, is spoken of *as* "Holy." According to Barth, the Spirit is confessed to be holy precisely because of his essential difference from humanity, his utter "Otherness." It is not just that the Holy Spirit is different from humans, for in this respect so are the Father and the Son; rather, the Spirit is holy because it is of his *essence* to be separate and to separate. "We are speaking of the Holy Spirit, and therefore, if we are to do justice to the meaning of the term, of a Spirit who is separate, and who separates, in the supreme sense. No other spirit is separate, or separates, in the same way."[136] In the second instance, on the question of why, Barth asked: "Why is it that He is the Holy Spirit *per definitionem?*"[137] He then noted that the answer is "staggering in its simplicity": "He is the Holy Spirit in this supreme sense—holy with a holiness for which there are no analogies—because He is no other than the presence and action of Jesus Christ himself: His outstretched arm; He Himself in the power of His resurrection."[138] Or even more succinctly, "The Spirit is holy in the New Testament because He is the Spirit of Jesus Christ."[139]

Barth went on to argue that the Spirit is "the history which takes place between the existence of the man Jesus and that of other men."[140] This Spirit is the power of the resurrected Christ, the one who is outpoured upon all humans as an "effect of

---

133 *CD* IV/2, p. 319. Later Barth will say, "[T]he Spirit who makes Christians Christians is the power of this revelation of Jesus Christ Himself—His Spirit." *CD* IV/2, p. 323.

134 *CD* IV/2, p. 320.

135 *CD* IV/2, p. 319.

136 *CD* IV/2, p. 322.

137 *CD* IV/2, p. 322.

138 *CD* IV/2, pp. 322-23.

139 *CD* IV/2, p. 325. Barth made this claim repeatedly in the following pages. See *CD* IV/2, pp. 331-33.

140 *CD* IV/2, p. 333.

[Christ's] resurrection, of His life in His death and in the conquest of His death."[141] It is the history of the Spirit which constitutes

> … the secret of all secrets which we have come up against at every point; the beginning and end and centre in our consideration of it on this level. It is the Christian thought of God which, when it is rightly thought, is kindled from the very outset in the history whose origin is the man Jesus, whose goal is Christendom, and whose centre is the Holy Ghost as the living transition from the one to the other.[142]

In attempting to conceptualize the history of the Spirit as the "living transition" from Christ to all other humans, Barth identified what he called the three decisive factors that must be considered. The first factor is the existence of the man Jesus: "The existence of the man Jesus … coincides with the history of God himself."[143] The second factor (which Barth also said "is really the third in order") is the existence of the community, of Christians, of Christendom: "The man Jesus does not exist only for their sake, but He does exist in the first instance for their sake."[144] However, it is the third factor which is of central concern to him:

> The third factor is the one which links the first and second. It is the power of transition, the downward movement, from the one to the other, from Christ to Christendom. It is the power which overcomes their distance between that one man and these many, between His height and their depth. What takes place in this history is that this distance is overcome. The man Jesus Christ is not alone, nor are these other men. There takes place His disclosure to them, and their disclosure to Him.[145]

Barth admitted that this way of putting it can only be viewed as a formal outline suggesting that the Triune God is present and active in history, and no attempt should be made to discern in the outline a *vestigium trinitatis* simply because there can be no analogy to God, no correspondence to God except the analogy of God to himself. Nevertheless, Barth does venture that, of the three decisive factors, "one … coincides with one of the three modes of being (or 'persons') of God, … [and] in this case the coincidence is quite unequivocal, the third and middle power, the divine power of the transition from Christ to Christendom, being identical with God in the mode of being of the Holy Spirit."[146] In other words, for Barth, the

---

141 *CD* IV/2, p. 333.
142 *CD* IV/2, p. 336.
143 *CD* IV/2, p. 336.
144 *CD* IV/2, p. 337.
145 *CD* IV/2, p. 337.
146 *CD* IV/2, pp. 338-39.

event of Pentecost—the post-resurrection giving of the Spirit by Christ—stands as the most important economic indicator of the reality of the Holy Spirit.

Despite Barth's unequivocal declaration that the Spirit is the power of transition from Christ to Christians, he was immediately forced to grapple with two extremely important questions. First, if indeed one insists that the Spirit *is* the power of the resurrected and ascended Christ poured out on many, if indeed it is the role of the Spirit in the economy to communicate the one man, Jesus Christ, to many humans, then how can one speak of this same Spirit in ways appropriate to (to follow Barth's own maxim) his antecedent identity as the eternal Spirit of the Triune God? In other words, how does one continue to speak of the distinction between the economic and immanent Trinity without, on one hand, collapsing the two, or on the other hand, without putting a conceptual wedge between the two? Second, if the Spirit is the one who intervenes in such a way that he creates and maintains fellowship "as a mediator between Jesus and other men,"[147] then does this not imply that there is a distance that needs to be overcome within God himself? If, in Christ, those who are far are brought near[148] by the work of the Spirit, does this not imply that there is antecedently nearness *and* farness in God? Or in negative terms, how might the Spirit be understood as doing something for humans in their unreconciled state unless the Spirit was also in some way, antecedently in God's own eternal relations, doing something similar *in God*? Does this mean that there is something in God's eternal being that needs to be reconciled? Does this not introduce something that can only be understood as alienation within God—the need for a divine intervention or reconciliation in God's own eternal being?

Barth did not shy away from these difficult questions, and what is most germane to the inquiry of this study is the way in which he sought to answer them both by an appeal to the doctrine of the filioque. Though the answers he gave have formal similarity to Hegel's doctrine of the Trinity, it is also the case that Barth attempted to avoid falling into what he saw as Hegelian determinism. To hear Barth on this point, an extended citation is necessary:

> The divine intervention which creates fellowship reveals itself and takes place, not as something which is alien to God, but as a mediation which is most proper to Him, which takes place first in Himself, in His divine life from eternity to eternity, in His fellowship and inward peace, in the love which is primarily and properly in Him. What is revealed and represented and active is the unity of the Father and the Son in the Holy Spirit, who like the Father and the Son, as the Spirit of the Father and the Son, is the one true God, *qui ex Patre Filioque procedit, qui cum Patre et Filio simul adoratur et conglorificatur* ["who proceeds from the Father and the Son, and who with the Father and the Son is worshiped and glorified"]. ... In what takes place between the man Jesus and us when we may become and be Christians, God Himself lives. Nor does He live

[147] *CD* IV/2, p. 341.

[148] Cf. Eph. 2:13.

> an alien life. He lives His own most proper life. The Father lives with the Son, and the Son with the Father, in the Holy Spirit who is Himself God, the Spirit of the Father and the Son. It is as this God that God is the living God.[149]

It is highly significant here that Barth "reads back," in all its radical implications, the problem of alienation that is readily apparent between Jesus and all other humans into the "proper life" of God himself. This problem expresses itself between Jesus and other humans as "the problem of distance and confrontation, of encounter and partnership." If one wants to continue to affirm the way in which the incarnate Jesus Christ wholly and completely *identifies* with humans in their state, then the problem itself cannot be viewed as "primarily our own problem, a human problem of earthly history," but can only be viewed "spiritually, i.e., in the light of its solution in the Holy Spirit." In a startling way, to be sure, Barth argued that the human need of reconciled fellowship is only secondarily a manifestation of a human problem; on the contrary, it is primarily "a divine problem—the problem of God's own being." As Barth summarized it:

> It is not the case, then, that we have here something which is really not applicable to God, but which is in a sense alien to Him. ... The Holy Spirit is not a magical third between Jesus and us. God Himself acts in His own most proper cause when in the Holy Spirit He mediates between the man Jesus and other men.[150]

Unlike the problem in its human form, the divine form of the problem brings with it "the answer and solution in and with which, by His own personal intervention in the Holy Spirit, He also answers and solves our problem."[151]

It is also important to observe Barth's repeated use of two pairs of terms: 1) distance and confrontation; and 2) encounter and partnership. The first pair of terms—distance and confrontation—represents for Barth "the eternal form of the problem" as posed in God himself. They speak in human terms of that which can only be described as antitheses: the antitheses of "here and there," "before and after," and "above and below." Even though these antitheses are commonly ascribed as problems proper only to the world—antitheses that must be overcome in some way—these dialectical antitheses, Barth insisted, "were and are already, in their original and proper form, quite apart from us and before the world was, the antitheses in God's own being and life—antitheses which are eternally fruitful, which cannot be overcome as such ... but which stand always in a mutual relationship of self-opening and self-closure."[152] On the other hand,

---

149 *CD* IV/2, pp. 341-42.

150 *CD* IV/2, p. 343.

151 *CD* IV/2, p. 343.

152 *CD* IV/2, p. 343. Barth clearly wanted to resist coming to a Hegelian conclusion. While he continued to use the Hegelian concept of *Aufhebung*, a simultaneous cancelation and upholding of the antithesis, Barth refused to recognize in his doctrine of God any form

however, these antitheses do not stand alone as a problem in God. The second pair of terms—encounter and partnership—indicates that there is also in God "the eternal form of the answer and solution," an answer and solution given only by the Holy Spirit:

> God is in Himself—and here we have the distance and confrontation, the encounter and partnership, which are first in Him—Father and Son. He is both in equal Godhead, so that He is Father and Son without any abstraction or contradiction. But He is really both, and therefore not merely Father or merely Son. As Father and Son He is twice ineffaceably the one God, twice the same. This is His divine here and there, before and after, above and below. This is the problem which with its answer and solution is primarily His own, so that we are not alien to Him, nor He to us, when in the Holy Spirit he intervenes with the solution and answer for the problem of these antitheses before and in which we also stand. He knew this problem long before we did, before we ever were and before the world was. For He knew Himself from all eternity, the Father the Son and the Son the Father.[153]

Though it is a common assumption that by *CD* IV Barth has ceased to deal with matters from a dialectical perspective,[154] it is evident here that Barth's doctrine of the procession of the Spirit from the Father and the Son in *CD* IV can only be described as dialectically structured. Indeed, the similarity to Barth's halting descriptions in *Romans* can hardly be ignored. However, the dialectic of *CD* IV, while similar to the dialectic at work in *Romans,* is engaged in a different key or with different emphases. Whereas in *Romans* the dialectical confrontation that Barth emphasized is that of the confrontation (*Krisis*) between God and the world—a confrontation that only partially recognized the confrontation within God—in *CD* IV Barth reversed the emphasis and sought to understand the confrontation between God and the world by reference to the antecedent confrontation that takes place eternally within God. In other words, the solution to the confrontation

---

of development in God. In this regard, he did not see the Spirit as a higher synthesis in God in history. Rather, in God there is an eternally existing, but eternally fruitful, relationship between the Father and the Son in the Holy Spirit whereby the distinction of the Father and Son is upheld in their difference but simultaneously united in their difference, a union-in-distinction and distinction-in-union.

153 *CD* IV/2, pp. 343-44.

154 "The first volume of the *Church Dogmatics* was still speaking of the 'contrast,' the 'contradiction,' between the Word of God and its configuration in the Bible, between proclamation and theology. But this thought is now [in the latter volumes of the *CD*] completely jejune, overtaken along with all theological methodologies built atop such contrasts. Now the thought of the Incarnation takes over and determines all questions of method." Hans Urs von Balthasar, *The Theology of Karl Barth: Exposition and Interpretation* (San Francisco, 1992), p. 114. Or does it? It is apparent that Barth's reasoning, even as late as 1958, could still make use of dialectic contrasts.

between God and the world is by way of a posited problem and solution in the eternal triune nature of God himself.

Further, it is helpful to think about the dialectic at work in *CD* IV in terms of a problem and solution whereby God is understood both to be the eternal ground of the problem of confrontation between "others" and the eternal provision of a reconciliatory solution appropriate to that problem. More concretely, at the same time that there is the problem of the distance and confrontation of the identities of Father and Son as distinct "Others," there is also the solution of encounter and partnership[155] whereby Father and Son come together in a divine encounter and together enjoy fellowship with one another as they work in complete unity, in a truly united partnership. To be sure, Barth continued to be wary of allowing the dialectic to be construed merely as a see-saw, a pendulum, or two sides of a scale.[156] It is not that sometimes the distance and confrontation in God is pre-eminent while equally at other times the encounter and partnership gains pre-eminence. On the contrary, together the distance-confrontation/encounter-partnership dialectic is eternally balanced yet moving, as it were—a *Realdialektik* in God, in which there is "transition in distance, mediation in confrontation, and communication in encounter." Similarly, the dialectic is not to be understood in successive or linear terms such that the problem in God is followed in the second instance, either logically or chronologically, by the solution. Rather, "there is only the being of God the Father and the Son with the Holy Spirit who is the Spirit of both and in whose eternal procession they are both actively united." As Barth went on to insist, "[t]he history between the Father and the Son culminates in the fact that in it God is also *Spiritus Sanctus Dominus vivificans, qui ex Patre Filioque procedit* ["the Holy Spirit, the Lord, the giver of life, who proceeds from the Father and the Son"]." Most importantly, Barth insisted:

> The Father and the Son are not two prisoners. They are not two mutually conditioning factors in reciprocal operation. As the common source of the Spirit, who Himself is also God, they are the Lord of this occurrence. God is the free Lord of His inner union. Concretely, He is Spirit.[157]

By now it should be evident that Barth has enacted a material application of the filioque, hinted at in *CD* I, but which only takes on a heightened significance in *CD* IV. This is not to say that Barth has left behind the noetic and ontic functions of the filioque as demonstrated in *CD* I and III. Rather, in some respects, his use

---

[155] "God was always a Partner. The Father was the Partner of the Son, and the Son of the Father." *CD* IV/2, p. 345.

[156] *CD* IV/2, p. 272.

[157] *CD* IV/2, p. 345. The Hegelian parallels here can hardly be ignored, though we judge there to be significant differences. However, rather than get sidetracked from the present exposition, we will address the comparison to Hegel briefly at the outset of the next and final chapter.

of the filioque is really a new application of the filioque based on a much older dialectical methodology originally exercised in the *Romans* period and hinted at in the earlier volumes of the *CD*. It will be recalled that in *CD* I/2 Barth could write:

> The Holy Spirit puts God on the one side and man on the other. And then He calls this God our Father and man the child of this Father. He brings God straight to those eyes and ears and hearts of ours which are so utterly unfitted for Him. And He takes us straight to the reality of God's action, the God who so utterly does not need us. Therefore the line is really drawn about which the agnostic wisdom of this world can never even dream, let alone perceive. And this line is not expunged or removed in the Holy Spirit. It remains drawn. The miracle does not cease to be a miracle. It will remain a miracle to all eternity of completed redemption. The children of God are those in whom the miracle of their sonship persists, and with it free grace ... There is no other knowledge apart from this. We cannot pull down God from His throne and set man over against Him in a kind of fore-heaven. There is no synthesis than that which is achieved solely in the Word of God and in His Holy Spirit ... In the Holy Spirit we know the real togetherness of God and man ... We know, therefore, that we cannot ascribe to man any freedom of his own for God, any possibility of his own to become the recipient of revelation. And we know it in a way which does not admit of any question. For the Holy Spirit is not a dialectician. And the negation is not our own discovery. Unlike our own positive or negative discoveries, it is not open to revision.[158]

This passage indicates, among other things, that early on, Barth was grasping for words to express the mystery of the work of the Holy Spirit, especially in a role "between" God the Father and the Son of Man, Jesus Christ. Nevertheless, it is also true that in speaking about the communion that exists between God and humanity in Jesus Christ, Barth was continually insuring that his pneumatology guarded the essential divinity of the Holy Spirit. The Spirit remains on the divine side of the ontological line drawn between God and the world while enabling a "real togetherness of God and man." Thus, looking at *CD* I in retrospect, it appears that Barth knew intuitively, at least, that the Spirit's work could only be construed in a dialectical manner, even if the Holy Spirit himself is not to be regarded as a dialectician![159] Furthermore, true to his own methodological conviction, Barth knew that the Spirit had to be understood economically in a manner consistent with his eternal existence as the third Person of the Trinity. He perceived that, in doing all this, the demarcation between God and man, and even between Father

---

158 *CD* I/2, pp. 245-46.

159 Though it is not immediately clear from the context, Barth's comment that "the Holy Spirit is not a dialectician" almost certainly has to be Barth's veiled rejection of Hegel's notion of *Geist* as the end-product of the historical Trinitarian dialectic.

and Son, could in no way be erased, lest talk of the triune being of God fall into Unitarianism, and the infinite qualitative distinction between God and man gave way to pantheism. Yet it also appears that it is only in *CD* IV/2 that Barth is willing to take that final step and more radically and consistently apply the method of reading the economy of salvation back into the immanent Trinity, going so far as to identify the human problem of distance from Christ as being antecedently grounded in an eternal dialectic of problem and solution in the inner divine reality between Father and Son in the Spirit. What is unclear, however, is the nature of the human problem itself: is it because the human is a created being that there is a distance that needs transition? Or is it because of the fallenness of the human that a transition is necessary? As will be noted shortly, this is a significant problem inherent to Barth's application of the filioque in *CD* IV.

CD *IV/3.2: Filioque, the "Whole Christ," and the Church*

The very last explicit reference to the filioque occurs in *CD* IV/3.2 near the end of the section entitled "The People of God in World-Occurrence." The appeal to the filioque pertains specifically to the question of how it is that Christ is present in the midst of the Christian community (i.e., the Church),[160] even though he had now ascended to the right hand of the Father. For Barth, this "christo-ecclesiological" question has a "pneumatologico-ecclesiological" answer.[161] What is of most interest, however, is the dialectical nature of the answer which he provides.

On the one hand, Barth insists that "the Holy Spirit is the enlightening power of the living Lord Jesus Christ in which He confesses the community called by Him as His body, i.e., as His own earthly-historical form of existence."[162] Or put another way, the "Holy Ghost calls, gathers, enlightens and sanctifies all Christians on earth, keeping them in the true and only faith in Jesus Christ."[163] What is crucial here is that, for Barth, for the Church to be truly confessed to be "in Christ" and to have its existence as Christ's own "earthly-historical form," the presence of Christ must be a *real* presence in the Church, so much so that the "*unus Chrisus* [*sic*]" ["one Christ"] is said to be "*solus,* yet also *totus*" ["alone, yet also whole"]. Consequently, Barth insists that Jesus Christ be understood as the "basis and secret of its existence."[164]

---

160 Barth consistently uses the terminology of "Christian community" [*christliche Gemeinde*] more often than "Church" [*Kirche*]. However, for the sake of simplicity, we will hereafter use the English term "Church" in the exposition. For the most current recent definitive work on Barth's ecclesiology, see Kimlyn J. Bender, *Karl Barth's Christological Ecclesiology* (Aldershot, 2005).

161 *CD* IV/3.2, p. 758.

162 *CD* IV/3.2, p. 681.

163 *CD* IV/3.2, p. 758.

164 *CD* IV/3.2, p. 758.

On the other hand, Barth is also concerned not to allow statements about the Church to become swallowed up by statements about the divine reality of Christ such that it is rendered superfluous. "Neither [Christology or ecclesiology] can be reduced to the other. Hence neither is dispensable. Again, neither can be separated from the other. Neither can be understood to be true except as elucidated by the other."[165] Here the dialectical nature of Barth's expected solution to Christ's real presence becomes clearly evident, for the answer cannot be one of "either/or" but only a rightly ordered and rightly related "both/and." Of course, the concrete question to be answered is: how can the Church have Christ as the basis and secret of its existence without allowing him to overshadow and overpower the Church with his glorious presence? Or, to put it in Pauline terms,[166] how can the body of Christ *be* the presence of Christ in the world without thereby erasing the distinction that continues between the Head and the Body?

Barth's answer, not surprisingly, is that it is only by the power of God that the "world-occurrence" [*Weltgeschehen*] of the people of God can occur, with the "power of God" being understood by Barth as none other than "the act of the Holy Spirit."[167] As Barth explains, "In the power of [God's] Holy Spirit as the creative power of the Word which calls it, it takes place that the [Church] exists as He, Jesus Christ, exists."[168] In what manner, then, does Jesus Christ exist? According to Barth, Christ has "primary and secondary dimensions and forms of existence or His being." That is, Jesus Christ is properly understood to be both "the heavenly Head with God" (the primary dimension) and the "earthly body with His community" (the secondary dimension).[169] But clearly both primary and secondary dimensions of Christ's existence must be ontologically related in such a way that the primary dimension does not swallow up the secondary dimension into a form of Christomonism, or cause the primary and the secondary dimensions to become an unrelated ontological dualism, or lose the asymmetrical relation that exists between primary and secondary dimensions. Such a task of rightly ordering and coordinating these primary and secondary dimensions of Christ, according to Barth, is the work of the Holy Spirit. As he explains:

> The Holy Spirit is the power, and His action the work, of the co-ordination of the being of Jesus Christ and that of his community as distinct from and yet enclosed within it. Just as the Holy Spirit, as Himself an eternal divine "person" or mode of being, as the Spirit of the Father and the Son (*qui ex patre Filioque procedit*), is the bond of peace between the two, so in the historical work of reconciliation He is the One who constitutes and guarantees the unity of the *totus Christus* ["whole Christ"), i.e., of Jesus Christ in the heights and in the depths,

165 *CD* IV/3.2, p. 759.

166 Cf. 1 Cor. 12:27; Eph. 5:23.

167 *CD* IV/3.2, p. 759.

168 *CD* IV/3.2, p. 759.

169 *CD* IV/3.2, p. 760.

> in His transcendence and in His immanence. He is the One who constitutes and guarantees the unity of the first and the second predicates, of the primary and secondary dimensions and forms of existence of His being.[170]

It is little surprise that, in the crucial moment of explanation, Barth appeals to the filioque as illustrating how the Spirit works alike in both economic and immanent Trinity. In so doing, he provides additional evidence that he understands the filioque to be an important doctrinal testimony to the work of Holy Spirit in binding together Christ and the Church in the economy of salvation in a manner antecedently to what the Holy Spirit does in the immanent Trinity in binding together the Father and Son as the bond of peace.

Perhaps there is no better representative sample of Barth's dialectical filioquist pneumatology than his own description of the work of the Holy Spirit which follows his ecclesiologico-pneumatological description of the Church as the secondary dimension of the *totus Christus*. The explanation is worth citing at length:

> The work of the Holy Spirit … is to bring and to hold together that which is different and therefore, as it would seem, necessarily and irresistibly disruptive in the relationship of Jesus Christ to His community, namely, the divine working, being and action on the one side and the human on the other, the creative freedom and act on the one side and the creaturely on the other, the eternal reality and possibility on the one side and the temporal on the other. His work is to bring and to hold them together, not to identify, intermingle nor confound them, not to change the one into the other nor to merge the one into the other, but to co-ordinate them, to make them parallel, to bring them into harmony and therefore to bind them into a true unity. In the work of the Holy Spirit there takes place that which is decisive for the calling and therefore the existence both of the individual Christian and of the Christian community, namely, that the light of the crucified and risen and living Jesus Christ does not merely shine objectively, but shines subjectively into fully human eyes and is seen by them; that His Word as the Word of God does not only go out into all lands and even to the ends of the world (Ps. 19:4), but here and now is heard by very human ears and received and understood by very human reason; that God's revelation of His accomplished act of reconciliation has its counterpart here and now in human faith and love and hope and knowledge, its echo in human confession at this specific time and place; that its creative freedom finds an equivalent in real creaturely freedom.[171]

In the same way, then, that the Spirit's role in the immanent Trinity is to be both "bond and boundary" between the Father and the Son, and so is called the Spirit who proceeds from the Father and the Son, so, too, Barth argues, the Holy Spirit

170 *CD* IV/3.2, p. 760.

171 *CD* IV/3.2, p. 761.

is the "bond and boundary" between Christ's primary ecclesiological dimension as divine Head of the Church and his secondary ecclesiological dimension as the earthly-historical Body. Both dimensions of the *totus Christus* must be confessed, Barth insists, but both can only be confessed as one recognizes this possibility in and through the work of the Holy Spirit who proceeds from Father and Son.

Summary and Evaluation

In what turns out to be Barth's last two (and, we would add, most profound) applications of the filioque, Barth spoke in *CD* IV of how the Holy Spirit works as the power of transition in distance, the mediation in confrontation, and the communication in encounter, between Jesus and all other humans (*CD* IV/2) and, more specifically, as the divine active power of meditation between the primary and secondary dimensions of the *totus Christus* (*CD* IV/3.2). In order to fulfill this important task, which, from the human perspective, can be viewed only as a problem of distance and confrontation, the Spirit can only be conceived as doing economically between Jesus and humans what he does eternally between the Father and Son. As the Spirit re-establishes fellowship between Christ and humans, and establishes an ontologically real relationship between Christ and the earthly-historical community called by the Spirit, so, too, the Spirit is the eternal solution to the eternal "problem" that is not alien to God but essential to God's eternal triune being. In this respect, Barth conceives the relationship of the Father and the Son dialectically as an eternally fruitful antithesis of concrete (rather than abstract) personal Others, who are never overcome one by the Other, and who never succumb to a higher synthesis (as in Hegelian thought). Rather, Father and Son are maintained dialectically as eternal Persons in union with one another in their distinction, as Persons who exhibit a unity-in-distinction and a distinction-in-unity, by the Holy Spirit who alone can unite and differentiate only because he is common to both (filioque).

How should these latter uses of the filioque in *CD* IV be evaluated? On the basis of the evidence adduced, it would be very difficult to sustain the charge that the Spirit is subordinated to the Father and Son in Barth's theology because of the filioque. On the contrary, Barth's filioquist pneumatology of *CD* IV actually serves to demonstrate his heightened awareness of the Spirit's vital role in the inner divine relationship that exists between the Father and the Son. If anything, it is evident that Barth's use of the filioque in the doctrine of Reconciliation has a tendency to move not in a *subordinationist* direction, as is commonly argued, but instead toward seeing the Spirit in a *superordinationist* direction as related to the Father and the Son. This is because of the way in which Barth construes both Father and Son as "depending" on the Spirit to maintain their fellowship with one another and to prevent them from becoming lost in an undifferentiated unity of the divine essence. In this sense, Barth views the Spirit as the Spirit of reconciliation between Father and Son—a reconciliation that anticipates the problem of sin in humanity, and is fully realized in the Son taking up humanity and reconciling it to God in the Spirit. In addition, it would be difficult to see the Spirit as one who is subject to ecclesiological subordination in Barth. On the contrary, for Barth, the Holy Spirit is to be understood as being the active agent of God's power in ensuring that Jesus Christ is really and fully present in the Church, all the while preventing the loss of distinction between the primary and secondary dimensions in speaking of the Christian community or Church as the *totus Christus*.

Furthermore, Barth's application of the filioque in *CD* IV must be judged to be closer in content and structure to the pneumatology espoused in his *Romans* period than perhaps even the earlier volumes of the *CD*. It will be recalled that it was in *Romans* that Barth spoke of a "confrontation in God" between the Father and the Son, and that the Spirit was understood not only as a "bond" of love between the two, but also as a "boundary" which prevents the Father and Son from canceling each other out. Interestingly, it is as if Barth had held himself back for many decades from speaking again of the Spirit in such a way, as if he were consciously resisting his old dialectical ways of speaking. But when the mature Barth was faced with the problem of how humans benefit from the union of human and divine in Christ, it is as if his only way through was to speak once again of the dialectic that exists eternally between the Father and the Son in the Spirit. The filioquist dialectic was also helpful to Barth in providing an account of the real presence of Christ in the Church, without breaking down the distinction between the two.

However, in the end it is evident that the problem of the relationship of the economic and the immanent Trinity continues to haunt Barth (and other theologians), and it is precisely in his use of the filioque in *CD* IV that the problem becomes especially acute. Despite the fact that *CD* IV displays Barth's greatest ingenuity in his application of the filioque, it also raises the question yet again of the criteria he used to "read back" into the immanent Trinity that which he discerned in the economy. Unfortunately, there is some ambiguity here and it is difficult to deny that Barth practically conflated the economic and immanent Trinity, his own stated attempts to maintain a "deliberate and sharp distinction" between the two notwithstanding. He earlier had argued that it is necessary to distinguish between that which may be said for a "strict doctrine of the Trinity … [which] must speak of God in Himself, in isolation from man" and that which may be said for the "step which God takes [freely] towards man."[172] However, in locating a problem in God himself—the problem of the confrontation between the Father and the Son—that the Holy Spirit who proceeds from both is called upon to answer, Barth failed to show how the confrontation of "Otherness" that takes place between the Father and the Son who are one in divine essence (*homoousia*) is qualitatively different from the confrontation that takes place between the humanity and divinity of Christ, or, more seriously, the confrontation that takes place between God in Christ and all other humans as a result of sin. Barth equivocated on the meaning of the various kinds of confrontation and distance which the Holy Spirit is called upon to

[172] *CD* I/1, p. 172.

mediate. Thus, what is missing is an account of how the Spirit deals with human sin in relationship to his role in upholding the union-in-distinction of the Father and the Son in the eternal Trinity and his role in upholding the union-in-distinction of the humanity and divinity in Jesus Christ. Perhaps this is something that Barth intended to clarify in *CD* V, but, without this account, it is difficult to see how one can avoid reading back the origin of human sin into the immanent Trinity, even though it is clearly something Barth did not want to do.

Chapter Five

Conclusion: The Filioque in Karl Barth's Theology

Concluding Summary

The foregoing account of Barth's doctrine of the filioque has covered, in a representational way, nearly the full theological career of Karl Barth from his pastoral beginnings in Safenwil to his senior years writing the *Church Dogmatics* in Basel. Following the lead of Bruce McCormack's seminal genetic-historical study of the early development of Karl Barth's theology, the study has assumed that Barth's doctrine of the filioque cannot properly be understood apart from close consideration of his earlier theology. Much of the scholarly literature reviewed in Chapter One tended to deal with Barth's defense of the filioque in the first half-volume of the *Church Dogmatics* as if this were the sum total of what he had to say about it, or as if the *CD* were a closed system impervious to previous or later theological influence and development. It is hoped that this study has shown that, though Barth remained consistent in his defense of the filioque, his reasons for doing so continued to change and develop over the course of his entire life.

Furthermore, most scholarly critiques of Barth's doctrine of the filioque assume that his position is typical of traditional Western defenses of the filioque and therefore subject to the same persistent criticisms. Consequently, many critics fail to differentiate Barth's position sufficiently from other Western proponents of the filioque and to discern how the doctrine functions systematically within his overall thought. While the value of exegetical, comparative, and intrasystemic analysis of the filioque in Barth should not be underestimated, it was suggested that a genetic-systemic examination of Barth's doctrine of the filioque was needed, which would take into account its origin in his earlier thought and which would analyze how he actually defended and used the doctrine throughout his career. It was this methodology that informed the direction and content of this study.

Chapter Two identified the origin of the filioque in Barth's theology antecedent to the beginnings of the *Church Dogmatics.* Analysis of the second edition of *Romans* (1921) revealed an underlying Christocentric dialectical pneumatology in which the Holy Spirit was understood to be the one who simultaneously highlights the infinite qualitative distinction between God and humanity, eternity and time, while binding God and humans together by "dissolving their duality" in union with Christ. This ontic union in Christ reflects that which existed originally between God and humans in creation but which has since degenerated into a false human perception of ontological dualism which the Spirit of God in the resurrection of Christ now overcomes. Barth grounds the role of the Spirit between God and humans in his view of the Spirit as the one who simultaneously and eternally distinguishes and upholds Father and Son in a "union-in-distinction" and a "distinction-in-union." Thus, Barth spoke of the Spirit as the Spirit of the Father and of the Son, and, as such, the Spirit is both the bond and boundary between Father and Son.

The filioque was not explicitly mentioned at all in *Romans,* but it was argued that the emerging dialectical pneumatology in *Romans* provided the material theological support for it. Thus, it was in the *Göttingen Dogmatics* (1924), the record of Barth's first cycle of lectures in dogmatics, that the filioque first formally appears. Barth's pre-eminent pastoral concern in Göttingen was to provide a theological (and distinctly Reformed) ground for the task of preaching. This led him to a renewed doctrine of the Word of God in which the filioquist structure of revelation is first manifest, namely in Barth's doctrine of the threefold form of the Word of God: preaching proceeds from revelation and Scripture as the Holy Spirit proceeds from the Father and the Son. In other words, the interrelationship of the three forms of the Word of God—preaching, revelation and Scripture—constitutes a formal structural analogy to the relationships the Triune God has in himself. It is only after Barth identified this formal structural correspondence to the Trinity that he briefly introduced, in a later lecture, the problem of the filioque as a dogmatic and ecumenical problem. Thus it is evident that the filioque arose in Barth's theology not as a metaphysical *a priori* speculation on the ontology of the eternal Trinity, but in consideration of the nature and structure of God's revelation of himself. It was in the *GD* that Barth's theological strategy of speaking of the immanent Trinity only on the basis of reading back from the economy is first clearly established. However, at this stage of his development, Barth had a very limited understanding of the broader historical, ecumenical, and dogmatic issues surrounding the filioque controversy itself, as his discussion of the problem clearly attests.

The third chapter focused on Barth's defense of the filioque in the crucial first half-volume of the *Church Dogmatics.* It was noted that his doctrine of the filioque needs to be understood, as in the *GD*, against the backdrop of the continuing development of his doctrine of the threefold form of the Word of God. Though Barth continued to speak of the threefold Word as a theological analogy to the triune relations, he made important modifications to how he spoke of the "schedule of relations" that existed between the three forms. The geometric characterization of the interrelationships of the *GD* in which revelation has priority over Scripture and preaching gave way in the *CD* to speaking of the complete co-inherence of preaching, Scripture and revelation. Though not explicitly negating the geometric relations expressed in the *GD*, Barth's shift to speaking of the threefold form of the Word in perichoretic terms served to downplay the structure of the threefold Word as an analogy to the intra-Trinitarian relations per se. While this was an important corrective in Barth's thinking over the more problematic way of construing the three forms of the Word in the *GD*, it was also the case that Barth continued to uphold the filioque in the *CD*, despite the fact that he increasingly appeared to have left behind the very ground upon which he originally adopted the filioque.

Chapter Three went on to analyze Barth's actual defense of the filioque. It was noted how few scholars have discerned that Barth refused to speak of the filioque as if it denoted a "double" procession of the Spirit in terms of its eternal origin. Rather, Barth spoke consistently of the Spirit's procession in terms of a "common origin" from the being of the modes of being of the Father and the Son—a theological recognition of the eternal communion of the Father and the Son in the Holy Spirit. By putting it this way, Barth indicated a procession of the Spirit neither from the being (*Sein*, or *ousia*) of God alone, nor from the distinct modes of being (*Seinsweisen*, or *hypostases*) of the Father and the Son. Rather, in order to avoid giving ontological precedence to either the being (*Sein*) or the modes of being (*Seinsweisen*), Barth sought to maintain a delicate dialectical unity of the *Sein* and the *Seinsweisen* as the common origin of the Spirit. Barth, it was argued, understands the filioque to affirm that the Spirit proceeds *from the-common-being-of-the-modes-of-being-of-Father-and-Son.*

Chapter Three concluded by comparing Barth's and T. F. Torrance's positions on the procession of the Spirit not only to show their similarity, but also to seek to delineate why Barth continued to hold to the filioque when Torrance did not. Both Barth and Torrance emphasized, following the lead of Athanasius, that the Holy Spirit is to be spoken of as *homoousios* with the Father and the Son. Torrance felt that the twin doctrines of *homoousia* and *perichoresis* were sufficient to safeguard the full divinity of the Holy Spirit and the communion of the Father and the Son in the Spirit. However, Barth continued to uphold the filioque in order to safeguard the unique dialectical relationship that exists between the Father and the Son—a concept which had been present in his thought ever since *Romans*. Barth thus insisted that the filioque needed to be retained, lest one fail to recognize the unique dialectical relationship of Father and Son spoken of in Scripture. To speak rightly of God in his self-revelation is to affirm the eternal union-in-distinction and distinction-in-union of the Father and Son in the Holy Spirit, who is the mediation of communion. This, according to Barth, is what it means for the Spirit to proceed from the common essence or being of the two modes of being, Father and Son.

Barth's dialectical view of the filioque makes it difficult to categorize him neatly under either classical Western or Eastern positions. Unlike most Western proponents of the filioque, Barth refused to speak of the procession of the Spirit as a "double procession," as if the Spirit had two origins in God—a notion Barth clearly rejected along with the Eastern critics. Unlike most Eastern monopatrists, Barth insisted that the procession of the Spirit cannot be spoken of in isolation from the fact that the Spirit is antecedently and eternally the Spirit of the Father and the Son: to speak of the Spirit of the Father and the Son in the economy without affirming that the Spirit also proceeds from the Father and the Son is to posit a gap between the God revealed and the God who reveals. Consequently, Barth's continued insistence on the filioque is entirely wrapped up with the principle of the identity of the economic and immanent Trinity.

The task of Chapter Four was to analyze Barth's application of the filioque beyond his initial defense in the first half-volume of the *CD* in order to appreciate more fully the systematic function the doctrine played in his theology. Barth's consistent filioquist grammar throughout the *CD* functions primarily to uphold the divinity of all three modes of being of the Trinity—a way of speaking consistent with what appears to be the original intentions of the filioque doctrine in the Western tradition. Beyond that, Barth's explicit appeals to the filioque reveal several distinctive systematic functions of the doctrine in Barth's thought.

First, the filioque represents an affirmation of the unity and indivisibility of the work of the Son and the Spirit (*CD* I/2). The Son and the Spirit do not work independently to bring about God's purposes, and the Spirit comes from the Father and Son to actualize the work of the Son. In this regard, Barth was adamant that because the Spirit is the Teacher of the Word, pneumatology needs to be understood in light of Christology.

Second, Barth appealed to the filioque in his doctrine of Creation (*CD* III) as properly pointing to the Spirit as the ontic ground for a real connection between God and the creature, precisely because the Spirit is antecedently the ontic ground of communion between the Father and his Son, and between the divine and the human in Jesus Christ. The Creator Father unites himself with creation in Jesus Christ in the history of creation by the Holy Spirit—the Holy Spirit who proceeds eternally from Father and Son.

Third, and perhaps most importantly, in Barth's doctrine of Reconciliation the Spirit is spoken of as the power of transition in distance, the mediation in confrontation and the communication in encounter between Jesus and all other humans, and between Christ and the earthly-historical form of his existence, the Church. This is possible only because the Spirit is antecedently the eternal power of transition, mediation, and communication between the Father and the Son. In this regard, Barth's pneumatology is such that the Spirit is understood as a living *boundary* that prevents the two persons (*Seinsweisen*) of Father and Son from collapsing into undifferentiated oneness; and simultaneously a living *bond* that maintains the unity of being (*Sein*) of the Father and the Son. That the Spirit is to be understood as both "bond and boundary" is predicated upon the Spirit being related internally to both Father and Son. That is, the Spirit is technically not an external "third agent" to the Father and Son, but is internally related to Father and Son as the one who proceeds eternally from their shared being as the Father of the Son, and the Son of the Father. Such a procession for Barth cannot be spoken of as if it were two parallel acts from two other independent "sending" agents, but only as a common procession from the Father and Son, who themselves are to be understood dialectically as wholly united yet wholly differentiated by the Spirit who proceeds from them. This is why the *Holy* Spirit can neither be wholly identified with Father or Son and must therefore be considered as a third *Seinsweise*; it is also why the Spirit is not an "independent" third, but is rightly and consistently spoken of in Scripture as the Spirit of the Father and the Spirit of the Son.

On the basis of this framework, then, Barth made the bold suggestion that the confrontation between God and the world that is reconciled in Jesus Christ is eternally anticipated because of the dialectic of confrontation and fellowship that exists between the Father and the Son, mediated by the Spirit. In other words, the procession of the Spirit represents the upholding in eternally fruitful antitheses of personal Others who are never overcome by one another, or who do not succumb to a higher synthesis or *tertium quid*. Rather, the Spirit insures that the Father and Son are maintained in a unity-in-distinction and a distinction-in-unity; it is only the Spirit who can unite and differentiate because he is common to both Father and Son as one who proceeds from both. Thus, for Barth, to affirm the filioque is to affirm the eternally fruitful dialectic that exists between the Father and the Son in the Holy Spirit. Or, to put it yet another way, the filioque for Barth is dialectical shorthand for speaking after God as he has revealed himself to be in his eternal dialectical structure (*Realdialektik*).

It is significant that Barth's last applications of the filioque in *CD* IV have formal and material parallels to the dialectical pneumatology latent in *Romans*. However, it was also argued how in Barth the economic Trinity and the immanent Trinity have become so conceptually close that they are in danger of being conflated. If the problem of confrontation between God and humans is already anticipated in the confrontation (and fellowship) between the Father and the Son in the Spirit, might this imply that God himself supplies the ground for the breach of fellowship between God and humans? Does Barth fail to make a distinction between the "difference" that subsists between God and humanity as to their ontological constitution and the "difference" that arises as a result of the fallenness of humanity? This will be further addressed shortly.

Assessing the Filioque in Karl Barth's Theology: Questions and Implications

There is no evidence either in the *Church Dogmatics* or other literature written later in his life to suggest that Karl Barth ever considered abandoning the doctrine of filioque. This has been troubling to some theologians, especially those who see great promise in Barth for ecumenical solutions to some of the great problems that still divide the churches. Consequently, even sympathetic readers of Barth occasionally speak of his continued defense of the filioque as evidence that even great theologians have their points of blindness! However, this study demonstrates that Barth's doctrine of the filioque must be taken more seriously than many have chosen to take it, even if one is not ultimately convinced that he made the definitive case for continuing to confess the filioque. Nevertheless, this study makes the modest claim that even though Barth fails to make a watertight case for the filioque, his defense and use of the filioque give good reason to consider its continuing dogmatic significance. In other words, it would not be wise to abandon the filioque too quickly, as some (mainly Protestant) ecumenical strategists seem to think is necessary. Indeed, Barth's defense and use of the filioque, more fully considered, continues to function as a critical pointer to some of the perennial theological problems that theologians in both Eastern and Western traditions will need to continue to debate.

Before concluding, however, it will be helpful to explore some of the implications of the study by posing a series of questions to Barth, pertaining to the filioque and its theological significance. Though none of these questions could possibly be answered definitively in the brief space remaining, each will serve to highlight not only problems that remained in Barth's defense and systematic use of the filioque, but also the promise his work might have in future debate concerning it.

Does Barth have an Ecumenical Contribution to Make on the Filioque Debate?

Many scholars continue to view Barth's defense of the filioque as an example of his well-known theological stubbornness, analogous perhaps, to the hard-nosed stance he took against the analogia entis and the possibility of natural theology: once he had set course, he found it difficult, if not impossible, to change direction. However, such a psychologization of scholarly intent can hardly be called upon to explain the matter without simultaneously running roughshod over other legitimate theological reasons that Barth had for holding as firmly as he did to the filioque. If nothing else, this study shows that Barth's view of the need to continue to defend the filioque was more sophisticated than most have been willing to concede.

But the question must be asked: can Barth's defense of the filioque contribute anything significant to the contemporary ecumenical debate? Of course, the answer to that question will depend in large part on how one wants to use Barth. If Barth is sought as an ally in bringing about an ecumenical solution to the filioque debate, it must be borne in mind that his contribution will at best be indirect. Barth can no more be viewed as successfully or singlehandedly solving the age-old dispute between East and West on the filioque than anyone else to this point, not to mention that he clearly had no intentions of wanting to "solve" a puzzle he did not think needed to be solved. He did not seek an apologetic for the filioque that would convince Orthodox or Old Catholic theologians regarding its acceptability. Nor did he seek a synthetic solution that would be acceptable to both Eastern and Western churches. Nor did he seek to encourage the churches in the Western tradition (the Reformed churches in particular) to move toward a theological and historical repristination of the Creed whereby the original form of the Nicaeno-Constantinopolitan Creed was set over against subsequent Western Trinitarian thinking. Nevertheless, Barth's "failure" in this regard can hardly be counted against him; each of these options has been attempted since Barth's death without resulting in full *rapprochement* between East and West, even if some of the results are showing some signs of being encouraged.

However, if Barth is heard on his own terms and from within his own systemic logic, even while acknowledging that his position *prima facie* has close affinity to the Western tradition, it becomes clear that Barth was less interested in defending the Western filioquist argument and more interested in better understanding what was dogmatically at stake if the filioque were denied, regardless of what might eventually take place at a formal ecumenical level. Rather than falsely claiming to understand the Eastern rejection of the filioque (which he apparently did not ponder for any significant length of time), Barth wanted to think through the meaning of the doctrine of the filioque as a Western, Reformed theologian. As he sometimes argued, it is pointless to denounce another tradition without first unpacking the internal dogmatic logic of one's own tradition. Certainly, Barth could have arguably provided a better defense had he investigated the Eastern position more closely. Yet that is to criticize his position for what he did not do—a common critique, to be sure. However, this study has tried to take Barth seriously on the filioque and to hear him from within his own systemic theo-logic. In this regard, we are confident that such careful listening has been fruitful in delineating some of the finer nuances of his position.

This book has also sought to show that Barth's doctrine of the filioque is not wholly typical of historic Western defenses. Most specifically, a dogmatic adherence to the filioque does not necessitate holding the notion of a "double procession" of the Spirit, despite the fact that this is how it has been described typically by Western proponents and Eastern critics alike. Rather than speaking of a double procession of the Spirit from the modes of being (or hypostases) of the Father and Son, Barth sought to preserve in this matter a delicate dialectic between the essence (*Sein*) and the Persons (*Seinsweisen*) of the Trinity without giving ontological priority to one or the other.[1] It is thus arguable that Barth was at least partly responsible for pointing ecumenically-oriented scholarship in this direction during the later quarter of the twentieth century. Consequently, more research needs to be undertaken in comparing Barth with contemporary ecumenical scholars for whom the filioque is still a live issue. In particular, it is evident that careful consideration of the Athanasian parallels in Barth's thought is needed, for Athanasius appears increasingly to be viewed as the common theological denominator by Western and Eastern theologians alike.

On the other hand, this study has also pointed out the ambiguity in Barth's way of speaking of the filioque in relationship to "origin" in God and in the doctrine of perichoresis.[2] Though Barth did speak of the origin of the Spirit from the Father

[1] Indeed, this appears to be the direction in which some Reformed scholars (such as T. F. Torrance) have been headed, not to mention the Vatican's so-called "Roman clarification" of the filioque.

[2] It should be noted that some scholars are beginning to raise critical questions about how the doctrine of perichoresis continues to be used in contemporary Trinitarian thought. See, for example, Karen Kilby, "Perichoresis and Projection: Problems with Social Doctrines of the Trinity," *Blackfriars* 81/956 (October 2000): 432-45.

and the Son, he also increasingly linked the filioque to the doctrine of perichoresis without delineating how perichoresis and origin are themselves to be related. Indeed, both Barth and Torrance ultimately speak of the procession of the Spirit in terms of perichoresis, even though both Eastern and Western traditions have normally spoken of the procession in terms of origin. More work must be done in order to disentangle these concepts.

Does the Filioque Result in a Subordinationist Pneumatology in Barth?

Historically, a general theological criticism of the filioque is that doctrinally it results in some form of pneumatological subordinationism. Consequently, it is appropriate to ask whether Barth's adherence to the filioque results in some form of dogmatic subordination of the Spirit. Of course, the answer depends on what is meant by the "subordination of the Spirit." If the phrase means that the filioque leads one to view the Holy Spirit as ontologically less than divine, then this study demonstrates Barth would answer with a resounding "No!" Barth repeatedly reinforced that the Spirit is fully divine—*homoousios* with the Father and the Son. Indeed, part of his theological rationale for upholding the filioque was to defend the full divinity of the Holy Spirit. For that which proceeds from God can be nothing less than God Himself. Furthermore, that Barth continued to resist the Schleiermacherian conflation of the Spirit of God and the spirit of man should be evidence enough that he would have never spoken of the Spirit in any other way but as fully divine.

Few of Barth's critics have been bold enough to suggest that the filioque compromises his recognition of the full deity of the Holy Spirit. More commonly, it is supposed that Barth's loyalty to the filioque doctrine results in denying an independent ontic role to the Spirit in the work of salvation. Barth's pneumatology, it is argued, ends up emphasizing almost exclusively the noetic work of the Spirit to the denigration of his ontic role.

It is understandable why critics perceive that the filioque is connected in the first volume of the *CD* to a particularly strong emphasis upon the noetic role of the Spirit. Taken on its own, the defense of the filioque in *CD* I/1 could justifiably be viewed as restricting the work of the Spirit to making Christ known. However, the foregoing has shown that one must continue reading, for Barth went on to argue, especially in *CD* III, that the noetic work of the Spirit must be understood to include the ontic transformation of humanity. Though Barth continued to speak in filioquist terms in his doctrine of Creation, he also insisted that the Spirit is the *conditio sine qua non* of creaturely existence and, as such, is worshiped as the Spirit of Life, *Spiritus Creator.* Indeed, only a selective and narrow reading of Barth could conclude that the filioque is directly connected in a systematic way to a subordinationist and strictly pedagogical pneumatology. However, even if Barth is cleared of charges of pneumatological restriction and subordinationism, there is need for continued research on the relationship of Barth's pneumatology to other aspects of his theology. Two of the most pressing areas are in the intersection of Barth's pneumatology with his Christology and anthropology.

On the anthropological front, the sympathetic critic P. J. Rosato insists that Barth is first and foremost a pneumatologist, but that it is precisely the strength of Barth's pneumatology that results in denigration and overshadowing of the freedom of the human. In contrast, recent research into Barth's moral theology has suggested the need to read the *CD* as setting forth a pneumatological framework that makes room for a genuinely free humanity. The Spirit does not merely replace the human recipient as the subjective side of revelation, but actually re-creates and restores humanity in Jesus Christ to fulfill, through grateful obedience, the covenant God has made with it. This debate is just beginning to gain momentum, but further study of Barth's dialectical pneumatology in reference to anthropology and ethics would be justified.

In terms of Christology, the present study notes some ambiguities in Barth's theology about the relationship of the Spirit to Christ's humanity. Though Barth must be read as one who continually sought to "begin again at the beginning," and who demonstrated an unusual self-awareness and ability to correct what may have been a Nestorian or even Apollinarian tendency in *CD* I, it is arguable that his adherence to the filioque is not so much a formal cause of the dogmatic marginalization of the work of the Spirit upon the human Jesus, as it is a result of Barth's tendency to overidentify the economic activity of the Holy Spirit with the outpouring of the Spirit in the event of Pentecost. In other words, all other activity of the Spirit upon Jesus spoken of in Scripture (e.g., his conception and baptism) is read retrospectively by Barth through the lens of the post-resurrection, post-ascension giving of the Spirit—the Spirit who proceeds from the Father (John 15:26) and is sent by the Son. Thus, a close analysis of how Barth's Pentecostally-centered pneumatology informs (and perhaps restricts) his pneumatology in relation to the humanity of Jesus would certainly be worthwhile. This is also a pressing question in light of a concern (reviewed below) respecting the criteria Barth uses to select what it is that he does and does not read back from the economic Trinity into the immanent Trinity.

Is Barth's Doctrine of the Filioque Hegelian After All?

From the start, this study has cautioned against making abstract generalizations about the systematic implications of the filioque without considering the concrete defense and use of the filioque in a particular theologian's work. Grandiose assertions made by both Eastern and Western critics about the deleterious effect the filioque has had upon Western theology should be viewed with a healthy dose of hermeneutical suspicion. The example just given is a case in point. There is a lack of hard evidence that the filioque can be linked with any degree of certainty to a subordination of the Spirit in Barth's theology. In this regard, it was argued in Chapter Four that, if anything, Barth has a tendency—especially as one reads his comments on the filioque in *CD* IV—toward a *superordinationist*, rather than a *subordinationist*, pneumatology. The word "tendency" has deliberately chosen here in recognition of the fact that it may be no more helpful to accuse Barth at any one point of overtly espousing a superordination of the Spirit than it is helpful to suggest that he holds to an overt subordination of the Spirit. If in fact there have been formal elements of pneumatological subordination in the earlier parts of the *CD*, such a reading needs to be counterbalanced by what appears to be elements of pneumatological superordination in *CD* IV. As is so often the case with Barth, one must try to get the full picture of his theology before making a generalization about theological tendencies in his work. Indeed, it is his dialecticism that demands that one reads Barth always *on the one hand*, and then *on the other*.

Such a dialectical understanding of Barth's filioquist pneumatology is vitally important to understanding his pneumatology more broadly. Barth has consistently spoken of the Spirit ever since *Romans* as the one in whom the Father and Son are eternally constituted in their union and differentiation. Scholars such as Jenson detect a "two-sidedness" in Barth's doctrine of God, a two-sidedness which Jenson suggests results in a "practiced binitarianism." Jenson is not wrong to see the way in which the dyad of the Father and the Son is pre-eminent in the *CD*, but he fails to recognize that that this two-sided dialectic between Father and Son is itself upheld and maintained by the third *Seinsweise*, the Spirit of the Father and the Son. Failure to perceive this by Jenson and others has likely been due in large part to how far the von Balthasarian "dialectic to analogy" reading of Barth has prevailed, preventing scholars from seeing dialectic elements still present in Barth's way of speaking about God even late in the *CD*. In this regard, a great debt is owed to McCormack for opening up new avenues of inquiry into Barth's later thought, based on continuities with his earlier dialecticism.

Structurally speaking, the analysis of Barth's doctrine of the filioque in a dialectical framework also reveals close affinities to Hegel's Trinitarianism, and it would be absurd to deny the obvious similarities between Barth and Hegel. Thus, it is important to ask: is Barth's dialectical doctrine of the filioque evidence that he has succumbed to Hegel after all?

It is clearly not coincidental that Barth unabashedly used the Hegelian terminology of *Aufhebung* to underscore the fact that the Spirit simultaneously upholds both the unity and differentiation of the Father and Son. This is especially evident both in *Romans* and in Barth's doctrine of Reconciliation, where he posited the "problem and solution" in God's own eternal being as mediated by the Spirit.

However, two crucial differences between Barth and Hegel need to be briefly noted, both of which are suggestive of the need for further research on the Hegelian roots of Barth's pneumatology. First, in his doctrine of Reconciliation Barth insisted, without explicitly mentioning Hegel, that:

> [God] does not lack in Himself either difference or unity in difference, either movement or stillness, either antitheses or peace. In the triune God there is no

> stillness in which He desires and seeks movement, or movement in which He desires and must seek stillness. This God has no need of us.[3]

Or more explicitly, "There is no rigid or static being which is not also act. There is only the being of God as the Father and the Son with the Holy Spirit who is the Spirit of both and in whose eternal procession they are both actively united."[4] In short, *Geist* is not the final culmination of God's positing of himself in an active, self-manifestation in history. Rather, "God the Holy Spirit,"[5] according to Barth, is none other than the *Eternal Spirit*.[6] This Spirit is the sovereign free Lord who is none other than the Holy Spirit who proceeds *eternally* (and not just as the culmination of the historical procession of God) from the Father and Son. Thus, unlike Hegel, Barth refused to contemplate any notion of "development" in God; the Triune God acts in the world in accordance to his own self-sufficient eternal triune essence *ad intra*, and the Spirit is the "basis of [God's] whole will and action .... *ad extra*."[7]

Second, Barth continued to differentiate himself from Hegel by asserting that God's economic action has nothing to do with the development (or the becoming) of God into God, but is the *revelation* of God as God is antecedently and eternally in himself. "In what [God] does on earth He reveals himself as the One He is in heaven, so that not only on earth but in heaven we have no reason to expect anything higher or better or more."[8] In other words, Barth consistently sought to maintain a distinction between the economic and immanent Trinity—a distinction Hegel apparently was not overly concerned to make. Whatever one makes of how well Barth succeeded in his resistance to what might ultimately be considered a Hegelian position, it is evident that there is still great room in the literature to explore the close similarity, reliance, appreciation, and criticism that Barth had of Hegel. For example, greater attention needs to be given to Barth's extensive review of Hegel in his *Protestant Theology in the Nineteenth Century*,[9] and to trace how Barth sought to incorporate both his appreciation and criticism of Hegel in the *Church Dogmatics* and, more specifically, in his resistance to the conclusions of Hegel's pneumatology.[10]

---

3 *CD* IV/2, p. 346.

4 *CD* IV/2, p. 345.

5 Cf. §12 "God the Holy Spirit," *CD* I/1, pp. 448ff.

6 Cf. section 2 "The Eternal Spirit" under §12 "God the Holy Spirit." *CD* I/1, pp. 466ff.

7 *CD* IV/2, p. 345.

8 *CD* IV/2, p. 345.

9 Karl Barth, *Protestant Theology in the Nineteenth Century*, trans. Brian Cozens and John Bowden (London 2001).

10 Webster notes that "one consequence of the relatively recent publication of [Barth's] historical lectures from the 1920s has been to stimulate a fresh appreciation of the fact that Barth's work on the history of theology cannot simply be treated as a *violon d'Ingres*, but

Does the Filioque Contribute to a Conflation of the Economic and Immanent Trinity?

If Barth tried to distinguish himself from Hegel by positing the necessity of a dogmatic distinction between the economic and immanent Trinity, it is also the case that he was most susceptible to the charge of failing to escape Hegel by virtue of his commitment to "the rule, which we regard as basic, that statements about the divine modes of being antecedently in themselves cannot be different in content from those that are to be made about their reality in revelation."[11] That Barth was indeed consistent in applying this rule became increasingly evident as closer attention was paid to his use of the filioque in the *CD*. In his doctrine of Creation, Barth posited that the Spirit is responsible for binding creation and history together, without loss of distinction, in the history of creation. But this is possible only because the Spirit is antecedently the Spirit of the Creator Father and the Incarnate Son. Likewise, in his doctrine of Reconciliation, Barth spoke of the Spirit as the mediator of communion between God and humanity in Jesus Christ, and between Christ and the Church; the Spirit is able to do this, however, only because he is antecedently the Spirit who proceeds eternally from the Father and the Son. That is, reconciliation is grounded by reading back into the immanent Trinity how the "problem" of the confrontation between God and humanity is anticipated by an eternal "problem and solution" located within God himself: the problem of the distance and confrontation of the Father and Son as distinct "Others" is "overcome" (*Aufhebung*) by the Holy Spirit who upholds in a union-in-distinction and a distinction-in-union of the Father and the Son.

It is noteworthy that Barth insisted that certain limits needed to be observed in speaking of the correspondence between the economic and immanent Trinity. In *CD* I/1 he cautions:

> In these analogies, which are not present in the world like the alleged *vestigia trinitatis* but which have been set up in the world by revelation, and by which the mystery is not as it were abandoned and solved but rather denoted, and denoted precisely as a mystery, we have the truth of the triunity as it is assigned and appropriate to us. We shall not overestimate this truth. If we did, if we confused the analogy with the thing itself, if we equated the distinctions that are comprehensible to us with those that are not, in other words, if we thought we had comprehended the essence of God in comprehending His word, we should be plunged at once into the error of tritheism.[12]

---

has to be seen as integral to his overall project as a biblical, Reformed dogmatician." John Webster, "'There is No Past in the Church, so There is No Past in Theology': Barth on the History of Modern Protestant Theology," in John C. McDowell and Mike Higton (eds), *Conversing with Barth* (Aldershot, 2004), pp. 14-39 at p. 15.

[11] *CD* I/1, p. 479.

[12] *CD* I/1, pp. 372-73.

Thus, in both instances of the application of the filioque noted above, Barth appeared quite confident that he had not transgressed the analogical limits imposed by revelation itself. Rather, he readily discerned in the economy filioquist structures that he unhesitatingly read back into the immanent Trinity. However, in so doing, it is as if Barth had discerned in revelation a set of analogies which practically end up sounding very much like the very *analogia entis*, or perhaps even a *vestigium Trinitatis*, between God and the world that Barth so vehemently opposed. Consequently, one is forced to consider whether he had overestimated the extent to which he could read back from the economy into the immanent Trinity. This is an especially pronounced problem in Barth's doctrine of Reconciliation, where he does not clearly or definitively differentiate between the kind of confrontation and union that occurs between the Father and the Son and the confrontation that occurs between fallen humanity and God. Despite the fact that Barth insisted that one must maintain a distinction between the economic and immanent Trinity, and that one can only speak of the relationship of the economic to the immanent in terms of analogy, one must ask whether he was successful in maintaining strictly enough the limits of the analogy itself. That he was able to read the filioque so readily in both the economy and the immanent Trinity is, at the very least, symptomatic of the greater problem that Barth (and, indeed, Western theology as a whole) had in maintaining a distinction between economic and immanent Trinity. But if that distinction is not properly maintained, it appears that Hegel's conclusion becomes increasingly inevitable, as is evidenced by how many post-Barthian (and, for that matter, post-Rahnerian) theologians have balked at speaking of the immanent Trinity altogether. Rahner's rule states that the economic Trinity is the immanent Trinity and vice versa.[13] In this regard, it is evident that Barth would have agreed with the first half of Rahner's rule, but probably not the second. Yet it appears that, even if Barth began by reading the filioque back into the immanent Trinity from the structure of revelation, he slipped all too easily into the "vice versa" mode and sought to find in the economy additional theological analogies that lined up and corresponded with the filioque.

Barth believed that one ought to uphold a principle of correspondence between the economic and immanent Trinity, lest one be forced to admit that an "unknown God" might stand behind the back of Jesus of Nazareth, who reveals God fully and truly. However, as this study has sought to show, the genesis and systematic function of the filioque in Barth highlights the need to pay much closer attention to the question of how one appropriately "reads back," and by what criteria, from the economic to the immanent Trinity without transgressing the analogical limits that Barth wanted to maintain. Barth insisted that evangelical dogmatics must not "invent freely" an appropriation of the triunity of God in treating the economy, but that all Trinitarian appropriations of the immanent Trinity must be "taken literally or materially or both from Holy Scripture."[14] The question is: did Barth

[13] Karl Rahner, *The Trinity* (New York, 1970), p. 22.

[14] *CD* I/1, p. 374.

take liberties in inventing a bit too freely his own Trinitarian appropriations in his doctrines of Creation and Reconciliation, as outlined in the chapters above? It is not as if Barth's reading of the economy is fanciful or completely disconnected from Scripture, but it might be questioned how materially it has arisen from Scripture. This remains a problem that is unresolved, not only in Barth but in Western theology as a whole. It is also why ongoing attention both to Barth and to the filioque debate may well need to continue to stand near the heart of debates concerning Trinitarian theology in years to come.

Bibliography[1]

Primary Sources

Books

Barth, Karl, *Anselm: Fides Quaerens Intellectum*, reprint edn, London: SCM Press, 1960; reprint, Pittsburgh: The Pickwick Press, 1975.

________, *Die christliche Dogmatik im Entwurf: Die Lehre vom Worte Gottes. Erster Band,* ed. Gerhard Sauter, Zürich: Theologischer Verlag Zürich, 1982.

________, *Church Dogmatics,* 4 vols in 13 parts, trans. Geoffrey Bromiley and T. F. Torrance, Edinburgh: T & T Clark, 1936-1962.

________, *Dogmatics in Outline*, New York: Harper Torchbooks, 1959.

________, *The Epistle to the Romans*, 6th edn, trans. Edwyn C. Hoskyns, London: Oxford University Press, 1933, 1968.

________, *The Göttingen Dogmatics,* ed. Hannelotte Reiffen, trans. Geoffrey W. Bromiley, Grand Rapids: Wm. B. Eerdmans Publishing, 1991.

________, *The Humanity of God*, Richmond: John Knox Press, 1960.

______, *How I Changed My Mind*, ed. John D. Godsey, Richmond: John Knox Press, 1966.

________, *Die Kirchliche Dogmatik,* 4 vols in 14 parts, Zurich: EVZ Verlag, 1932 70.

________, *Letters, 1961-1968*, ed. Jürgen Fangmeir and Hinrich Stoevesandt, trans. Geoffrey W. Bromiley, Grand Rapids: Eerdmans, 1981.

________, *Protestant Theology in the Nineteenth Century*, trans. Brian Cozens and John Bowden, Zürich: Evangelischer Verlag, 1952; reprint, London: SCM Press, 2001.

________, *Der Römerbrief*, Munich: Chr. Kaiser, 1926.

________, *The Theology of the Reformed Confessions*, ed. and trans. Darrell L. Guder and Judith J. Guder, Zürich: Theologischer Verlag Zürich, 1923; reprint, Louisville: Westminster John Knox Press, 2002.

________, *The Word of God and the Word of Man*, trans. Douglas Horton, New York: Harper & Row, 1957.

[1] Excluding references to classical sources.

Articles

Barth, Karl, “Concluding Unscientific Postscript on Schleiermacher,” in Dietrich Ritschl and Geoffrey W. Bromiley (eds), *The Theology of Schleiermacher*, trans. Geoffrey W. Bromiley, 261-79. Grand Rapids: Wm. B. Eerdmans Publishing, 1982.

________, “Jesus Christ and the Movement for Social Justice,” in George Hunsinger (ed.), *Karl Barth and Radical Politics*, 19-45, Philadelphia: The Westminster Press, 1976.

________, “Karl Barth’s Foreword,” in Heinrich Heppe (ed.), *Reformed Dogmatics*, rev. and reprinted edn, ed. Ernst Bizer, Grand Rapids: Baker Book House, 1978, pp. v-vii.

________, “A Thank You and a Bow: Kierkegaard’s Reveille: Translated by H. M. Rumscheidt,” *Canadian Journal of Theology* 11 (1965): 3-7.

________, “A Theological Dialogue,” *Theology Today* 19/2 (July 1962): 171-77.

Secondary Sources

Adeney, Walter F., *The Greek and Eastern Churches*, New York: Charles Scribner’s Sons, 1939.

Almond, Philip C., “Karl Barth and Anthropocentric Theology,” *Scottish Journal of Theology* 31/5 (1978): 435-47.

Anselm, “The Procession of the Holy Spirit,” in Jasper Hopkins and Herbert Richardson (eds), *Anselm of Canterbury,* trans. Jasper Hopkins and Herbert Richardson, Vol III of IV, Toronto and New York: Edwin Mellen Press, 1976.

Andrews, Isolde, *Deconstructing Barth: A Study of the Complementary Methods in Karl Barth and Jacques Derrida*, Frankfurt: Peter Lang, 1996.

Augustine, *On the Holy Trinity*, in *Nicene and Post-Nicene Fathers,* first series, vol 3, ed. Philip Schaff (Peabody: Hendrickson, 1994),

Badcock, Gary D., *Light of Truth & Fire of Love: A Theology of the Holy Spirit*, Grand Rapids: Wm. B. Eerdmans, 1997.

Baillie, D. M., *God Was in Christ*, New York: Charles Scribner’s Sons, 1948.

Barbour, R. S., “Biblical Classics: X. Karl Barth: The Epistle to the Romans,” *The Expository Times* 90/9 (June 1978): 264-68.

Barnes, Michel René, “De Régnon Reconsidered,” *Augustinian Studies* 26/2 (1995): 51-79.

Beintker, Michael, *Die Dialektik in der “Dialektischen Theologie” Karl Barths*, Munich: Chr. Kaiser Verlag, 1987.

Bender, Kimlyn J., *Karl Barth’s Christological Ecclesiology*, Aldershot: Ashgate, 2005.

Berkouwer, G. C., *The Triumph of Grace in the Theology of Karl Barth*, Grand Rapids: Wm. B. Eerdmans Publishing, 1956.

Berthold, George C., "Saint Anselm and the Filioque," in *Faith Seeking Understanding: Learning and the Catholic Tradition*, Manchester: Saint Anselm College Press, 1991.

Bobrinskoy, Boris, "The Filioque Yesterday and Today," in *La Signification et l'Actualité du IIe Concile Oecumenique pour le Monde Chrétien d'Aujourd'hui*, Chambesy: Du Centre Orthodoxe du Patriarcat Oecumenique, 1982, pp. 275-87.

________, *The Mystery of the Trinity: Trinitarian Experience and Vision in the Biblical and Patristic Tradition*, trans. Anthony P. Gythiel, Crestwood: St Vladimir's Seminary Press, 1999.

Boff, Leonardo, *Trinity and Society*, Marknoll: Orbis, 1988.

Boyd, Ian R., *Dogmatics among the Ruins: German Expressionism and the Enlightenment as Contexts for Karl Barth's Theological Development*, Religions and Discourse, no. 21. ed. James M. M. Francis, Bern: Peter Lang, 2004.

Bradenburg, A., "Der Zeit- Und Geschichtsbegriff Bei Karl Barth," *Theologie und Glaube* 45 (1955): 357-78.

Bradshaw, Timothy, *Trinity and Ontology: A Comparative Study of the Theologies of Karl Barth and Wolfhart Pannenberg*, Edinburgh: Rutherford House Books, 1988.

Bray, Gerald, "The *Filioque* Clause in History and Theology," *Tyndale Bulletin* 34 (1983): 91-144.

Bromiley, Geoffrey W., *An Introduction to the Theology of Karl Barth*, Grand Rapids: Wm. B. Eerdmans Publishing, 1979.

Burnett, Richard E., *Karl Barth's Theological Exegesis*, Grand Rapids: Wm. B. Eerdmans Publishing, 2004.

Busch, Eberhard, *The Great Passion: An Introduction to Karl Barth's Theology*, Grand Rapids: Wm. B. Eerdmans, 2004.

________, "God Is God: The Meaning of a Controversial Formula and the Fundamental Problem of Speaking About God," *Princeton Seminary Bulletin*, NS 7 (1986): 101-13.

________, *Karl Barth: His Life from Letters and Autobiographical Texts*, trans. John Bowden, Munich: Christian Kaiser Verlag, 1975; reprint, Grand Rapids: Wm. B. Eerdmans Publishing, 1976.

Calvin, John, *Institutes of the Christian Religions* ed. John T. McNeil, trans. Ford Lewis Battles (Louisville: Westminster John Knox Press, 1960).

Clark, Gordon H., *Karl Barth's Theological Method*, Philadelphia: Presbyterian and Reformed Publishing, 1963.

Cobb, John B. Jr., *God and the World*, Philadelphia: Westminster Press, 1969.

Coffey, David, "The Roman 'Clarification' of the Doctrine of the Filioque," *International Journal of Systematic Theology* 5/1 (March 2003): 3-21.

Colle, Ralph Del, "Reflections on the *Filioque*," *Journal of Ecumenical Studies* 34/2 (Spring 1997): 202-17.

Collins, Paul M., *Trinitarian Theology West and East: Karl Barth, the Cappadocian Fathers, and John Zizioulas*, Oxford: Oxford University Press, 2001.
Colyer, Elmer M., *How to Read T. F. Torrance*, Downers Grove: InterVarsity Press, 2001.
Congar, Yves, *I Believe in the Holy Spirit*, 3 vols, trans. David Smith, London: Geoffrey Chapman, 1983; reprint, New York: The Crossroad Publishing Company, 2001.
Cortez, Marc, "What Does It Mean to Call Karl Barth a 'Christocentric' Theologian?" *Scottish Journal of Theology*, 60/2 (2007): 127-43.
Cowell, John E., *Actuality and Provisionality: Eternity and Election in the Theology of Karl Barth*, Edinburgh: Rutherford House Books, 1989.
Cross, Terry L., *Dialectic in Karl Barth's Doctrine of God*, New York: Peter Lang, 2001.
Daley, Brian E., "Revisiting the 'Filioque': Roots and Branches of an Old Debate, Part One," *Pro Ecclesia* 10/1 (Winter 2001): 31-62.
Dalferth, Ingolf U., *Theology and Philosophy*, Oxford: Basil Blackwell, 1988.
Dawson, R. Dale, *The Resurrection in Karl Barth*, Aldershot: Ashgate, 2006.
Deddo, Gary, "The Holy Spirit in T. F. Torrance's Theology," in Elmer M. Colyer (ed.) *The Promise of Trinitarian Theology*, Lanham: Rowman & Littlefield Publishers, 2001.
de Halleux, André, "Towards an Ecumenical Agreement on the Procession of the Holy Spirit and the Addition of the Filioque to the Creed," in Lukas Vischer (ed.), *Spirit of God, Spirit of Christ: Ecumenical Reflections on the Filioque Controversy*, London: SPCK, 1981, pp. 69-84.
Dorrien, Gary, *The Barthian Revolt in Modern Theology: Theology Without Weapons*, Louisville: Westminster John Knox Press, 2000.
Duke, James O. and Robert F. Streetman (eds), *Barth and Schleiermacher: Beyond the Impasse?*, Philadelphia: Fortress Press, 1988.
Dvornik, Francis, *The Photian Schism: History and Legend*, Cambridge: Cambridge at the University Press, 1948.
Farrow, Douglas, *Ascension and Ecclesia*, Grand Rapids: Wm. B. Eerdmans, 1999.
________, "Karl Barth on the Ascension: An Appreciation and Critique," *International Journal of Systematic Theology* 2/2 (July 2000): 127-50.
Fatula, Mary Ann, "The Council of Florence and Pluralism in Dogma," *One in Christ* 19/1 (1983): 14-27.
________, "The Holy Spirit in East and West: Two Irreducible Traditions," *One in Christ* 19/4 (1983): 379-86.
________, "A Problematic Western Formula," *One in Christ* 17/4 (1981): 324-34.
Ford, David, *Barth and God's Story: Biblical Narrative and the Theological Method of Karl Barth in the Church Dogmatics*, Frankfurt: Verlag Peter Lang, 1981.

Fouyas, Methodius, *Orthodoxy, Roman Catholicism and Anglicanism*, London, New York and Toronto: Oxford University Press, 1972.

Frei, Hans, "The Doctrine of Revelation in the Thought of Karl Barth, 1909 to 1922," PhD thesis, Yale University, 1956.

Gemeinhardt, Peter, *Die Filioque-Kontroverse zwischen Ost- und Westkirche im Frühmittelalter*, Berlin and New York: de Gruyter, 2002.

Gill, Joseph, *The Council of Florence*, Cambridge: Cambridge University Press, 1959.

Gockel, Matthias, *Barth and Schleiermacher on the Doctrine of Election: A Systematic-Theological Comparison*, Oxford and New York: Oxford University Press, 2006.

"The Greek and Latin Traditions about the Procession of the Holy Spirit," in *L'Osservatore Romano,* 38 (September 20, 1995): 3, 6.

Gregory of Nazianus, "Third Oratorical Oration," in William G. Rusch (ed.), *The Trinitarian Controversy*, Philadelphia: Fortress Press, 1980.

Gunton, Colin E., *Becoming and Being: The Doctrine of God in Charles Hartshorne and Karl Barth*, Oxford: Oxford University Press, 1978.

________, "The Truine [*sic*] God and the Freedom of the Creature," in S. W. Sykes (ed.), *Karl Barth: Centenary Essays*, Cambridge: Cambridge University Press, 1989, pp. 46-68.

Guretzki, David, "The *Filioque:* Assessing Evangelical Approaches to a Knotty Problem," in Stanley E. Porter and Anthony R. Cross (eds), *Semper Reformandum: Studies in Honour of Clark H. Pinnock*, Carlisle: Paternoster Press, 2003, pp. 183-207.

________, "The Function of 'Mediator' in St. Augustine's *De Civitate Dei*, Book IX," *Hirundo: The McGill Journal of Classics,* 1 (Fall 2001): 62-75.

Haddad, Robert M., "The Stations of the Filioque," *St. Vladimir's Theological Quarterly* 46/2-3 (2002): 209-68.

Hart, Trevor, *Regarding Karl Barth*, Downers Grove: InterVarsity Press, 1999.

Haugh, Richard, *Photius and the Carolingians: The Trinitarian Controversy*, Belmont: Nordland Publishing Company, 1975.

Healy, Nicholas M., "Communion Ecclesiology: A Cautionary Note," *Pro Ecclesia* 10/4 (Fall 1995): 442-53.

Heath, R. G., "The Western Schism of the Franks and the 'Filioque,'" *Journal of Ecclesiastical History,* 23.2 (April 1972): 97-113.

Hendry, George S., "From the Father and the Son: The *Filioque* after Nine Hundred Years," *Theology Today* 11 (January 1955): 449-59.

________, *The Holy Spirit in Christian Theology*, London: SCM Press, 1957.

________, "Review of *The Spirit as Lord: The Pneumatology of Karl Barth* by P. J. Rosato", *Theology Today* 43/3 (October 1986): 419-23.

Heppe, Heinrich, *Reformed Dogmatics,* rev. and reprinted edn, ed. Ernst Bizer, Grand Rapids: Baker Book House, 1978.

Heron, Alasdair I. C., "'Who Proceedeth from the Father and the Son': The Problem of the Filioque," *Scottish Journal of Theology* 24/2 (May 1971): 149-66.

________, "The Filioque in Recent Reformed Theology," in Lukas Vischer (ed.), *Spirit of God, Spirit of Christ: Ecumenical Reflections on the Filioque Controversy*, London: SPCK, 1981, pp. 110-17.

________, *The Holy Spirit*, Philadelphia: The Westminster Press, 1983.

Hill, William J., *The Three-Personed God: The Trinity As Mystery of Salvation*, Washington, DC: Catholic University of America Press, 1982.

Hunsinger, George, "The Mediator of Communion: Karl Barth's Doctrine of the Holy Spirit," in *Disruptive Grace: Studies in the Theology of Karl Barth*, Grand Rapids: Wm. B. Eerdmans Publishing, 2000.

________, *How to Read Karl Barth: The Shape of His Theology*, New York; Oxford: Oxford University Press, 1991.

________, "Karl Barth's *The Göttingen Dogmatics*," *Scottish Journal of Theology* 46/3 (1993): 371-82.

________, "*Mysterium Trinitatis:* Barth's Conception of Eternity," in George Hunsinger (ed.), *For the Sake of the World: Karl Barth and the Future of Ecclesial Theology*, Grand Rapids: Wm. B. Eerdmans Publishing, 2004.

Hwang, Jae-Bum, "The Trinitarian Logics of St. Augustine and Karl Barth: With Special Reference to their Respective Pneumatologies and *Filioque*-Positions," PhD thesis, Union Theological Seminary, 1998.

Irenaeus, *Against Heresies*, in *Ante-Nicene Fathers,* vol. 1, ed. Alexander Roberts and James Donaldson (Peabody: Hendrickson, 1994), pp. 537-39.

Jehle, Frank, *Ever Against the Stream: The Politics of Karl Barth, 1906-1968*, trans. Richard and Martha Burnett, Zürich: Theologischer Verlag, n.d.; reprint, Grand Rapids: Wm. B. Eerdmans, 2002.

Jenson, Robert W., *Alpha and Omega*, Nashville: Thomas Nelson & Sons, 1963; reprint, Eugene: Wipf and Stock Publishers, 2002.

________, *God After God: The God of the Past and the God of the Future, Seen in the Work of Karl Barth*, Indianapolis and New York: The Bobbs-Merrill Company, 1969.

________, "Jesus, Father, Spirit. The Logic of the Doctrine of the Trinity," *Dialog* 26/4 (Fall 1987): 245-49.

________, "Karl Barth," in D. F. Ford (ed.), *The Modern Theologians*, Vol. 1, Oxford: Oxford University Press, 1989, pp. 21-36.

________, *Systematic Theology,* Vol. 1, New York and Oxford: Oxford University Press, 1997.

________, *The Triune Identity*, Philadelphia: Fortress Press, 1982.

________, "You Wonder Where the Spirit Went," *Pro Ecclesia* 2/ 3 (1993): 296-304.

Jüngel, Eberhard, "Von der Dialektik zur Analogie: Die Schule Kierkegaards und der Einspruch Petersons," in *Barth Studien: Ökumenische Theologie*, Zurich: Benziger Verlag, 1982, pp. 127-79..

Kelly, J. N. D., *The Athanasian Creed*, London and New York: A. and C. Black Ltd, 1964.

________, *Early Christian Creeds*, 3rd edn, London: Longman, 1972.

Kilby, Karen, "Perichoresis and Projection: Problems with Social Doctrines of the Trinity," *Blackfriars* 81/956 (October 2000): 432-45.
Laats, Alar, *Doctrines of the Trinity in Eastern and Western Theologies: A Study with Special Reference to K. Barth and V. Lossky*, Studien zur Interkulturellen Geschichte des Christentums [Studies in the Intercultural History of Christianity], Vol. 114, Frankfurt am Main and New York: Peter Lang, 1999.
LaCugna, Catherine Mowry, *God for Us: The Trinity & Christian Life*, San Francisco: HarperSanFrancisco, 1991.
Langdon, Adrian, "God the Eternal Contemporary: Trinity, Eternity, and Time in Karl Barth's *Church Dogmatics*," PhD thesis, McGill University, 2009.
Letham, Robert, The *Holy Trinity: In Scripture, History, Theology, and Worship*, Phillipsburg: P&R Publishing, 2004.
Lindbeck, George, "Barth and Textuality," *Theology Today* 43/3 (October 1986): 361-72.
Link, Hans G., *One God, One Lord, One Spirit: On the Explication of the Apostolic Faith Today*, Faith and Order Paper No. 139, Geneva: WCC Publications, 1988.
Lossky, Vladimir, *In the Image and Likeness of God*, Paris: Aubier-Montaigne, 1967; reprint, London and Oxford: Mowbrays, 1975.
________, *The Mystical Theology of the Eastern Church*, London: J. Clarke, 1957.
________, *Orthodox Theology: An Introduction*, trans. Ian and Ihita Kesarcodi-Watson, Crestwood: St Vladimir's Seminary Press, 1989.
MacDonald, Neil B., *Karl Barth and the Strange New World within the Bible: Barth, Wittgenstein, and the Metadilemmas of the Enlightenment*, Carlisle: Paternoster Press, 2000.
Marshall, Bruce D., "The Defense of the *Filioque* in Classical Lutheran Theology: An Ecumenical Appreciation," *Neue Zeitschrift für Systematische Theologie und Religionsphilosophie* 44/2 (2002): 154-73.
McIntyre, John, *The Shape of Pneumatology*, Edinburgh: T & T Clark, 1997.
McLelland, Joseph C., "Philosophy and Theology—A Family Affair (Karl and Heinrich Barth)," in H. Martin Rumscheidt (ed.), *Footnotes to a Theology: The Karl Barth Colloquium of 1972*, Waterloo: Corporation for the Publication of Academic Studies of Religion in Canada, 1974, pp. 30-52.
McCormack, Bruce L., "Dankeswort," *The Princeton Seminary Bulletin* 21/2 (2000): 211-19.
________, "The End of Reformed Theology? The Voice of Karl Barth in the Doctrinal Chaos of the Present," in Wallace M. Alston, Jr. and Michael Welker (eds), *Reformed Theology: Identity and Ecumenicity*, Grand Rapids and Cambridge: Wm. B. Eerdmans Publishing, 2003, pp. 46-64.
________, *Karl Barth's Critically Realistic Dialectic Theology: Its Genesis and Development, 1909-1936*, Oxford: Clarendon Press, 1995.
________, "Seek God Where He May Be Found: A Response to Edwin Chr. Van Driel," *Scottish Journal of Theology* 60/1 (2007): 62-79.

________, "The Unheard Message of Karl Barth," *Word & World* 14/1 (Winter 1994): 59-66.

McDonald, William, "Søren Kierkegaard," *The Standford Encyclopedia of Philosophy* (Summer 2005 Edition), ed. Edward N. Zalta, available from http://plato.stanford.edu/archives/sum2005/entries/kierkegaard.

Metaxas-Mariatos, Ioannes, "The Filioque Controversy: Chapters from the Eastern Orthodox Reaction," MA thesis, University of Durham, 1988.

Metzger, Paul Louis, "Introduction: What Difference Does the Trinity Make?" in Paul Louis Metzger (ed.), *Trinitarian Soundings in Systematic Theology*, London and New York: T&T Clark, 2005.

Meyendorff, John, *The Orthodox Church: Its Past and its Role in the World Today*, trans. John Chapin, London: Darton, Longman & Todd, 1962.

Migliore, Daniel I., "Karl Barth's First Lectures in Dogmatics: Instruction in the Christian Religion," in Hannelotte Reiffen (ed.), *The Göttingen Dogmatics: Instruction in the Christian Religion*, trans. Geoffrey W. Bromiley, Grand Rapids: Wm. B. Eerdmans Publishing, 1991, pp. xv-lxii.

________, "Vinculum Pacis: Karl Barths Theologie des Heiligen Geistes," *Evangelische Theologie* 60/2 (2000): 131-52.

Minear, Paul S., "Barth's Commentary on the Romans, 1922-1972: Or Karl Barth vs. The Exegetes," in Martin Rumscheidt (ed.), *Footnotes to a Theology: The Karl Barth Colloquium of 1972*, Waterloo, ON: Canadian Corporation for Studies in Religion, 1974, pp. 8-29.

Molnar, Paul D., *Divine Freedom and the Doctrine of the Immanent Trinity*, London and New York: T & T Clark, 2002.

________, "Toward a Contemporary Doctrine of the Immanent Trinity: Karl Barth and the Present Discussion," *Scottish Journal of Theology* 49/3 (1996): 311-57.

Moltmann, Jürgen, *The Spirit of Life: A Universal Affirmation*, trans. Margaret Kohl, Minneapolis: Fortress Press, 1992.

________, "Theological Proposals Towards the Resolution of the Filioque Controversy," in Lukas Vischer (ed.), *Spirit of God, Spirit of Christ: Ecumenical Reflections on the Filioque Controversy*, London: SPCK, 1981, pp. 164-73.

________, *Theology of Hope*, trans. James W. Leitch, New York: Harper & Row, 1967.

________, *The Trinity and the Kingdom*, trans. Margaret Kohl, London: SCM Press, 1981; reprint, Minneapolis: Fortress Press, 1983.

Ngien, Dennis, *Apologetic for Filioque in Medieval Theology*, Milton Keynes: Paternoster Press, 2005.

Nodes, Daniel J., "Dual Processions of the Holy Spirit: Development of a Theological Tradition," *Scottish Journal of Theology* 52/1 (1999): 1-18.

O'Carroll, Michael, *Veni Creator Spiritus*, Collegeville: The Liturgical Press, 1990.

Oberdorfer, Bernd, *Filioque: Geschichte und Theologie eines ökumenisches Problems*, Göttingen: Vandenhoeck & Ruprecht, 2001.

O'Donovan, Oliver, *On the Thirty Nine Articles: A Conversation with Tudor Christianity*, Exeter: Paternoster Press, 1986.

Olson, Alan M., *Hegel and the Spirit*, Princeton: Princeton University Press, 1992.

Orphanos, Markos A., "The Procession of the Holy Spirit According to Certain Later Greek Fathers," in Lukas Vischer (ed.), *Spirit of God, Spirit of Christ: Ecumenical Reflections on the Filioque Controversy*, London: SPCK, 1981, pp. 21-45.

Osborne, Catherine, "The *Nexus Amoris* in Augustine's Trinity," in Elizabeth A. Livingstone (ed.), *Studia Patristica Vol. XXII: Proceedings of Tenth International Conference on Patristic Studies in Oxford 1987*, Leuven: Peeters Press, 1989, pp. 309-14.

Pannenberg, Wolfhart, *Systematic Theology,* 3 vols, vol. I, trans. Geoffrey W. Bromiley, Grand Rapids: Wm. B. Eerdmans, 1991.

Papadakis, Aristeides, *Crisis in Byzantium: The* Filioque *Controversy in the Patriarchate of Gregory II of Cyprus (1283-1289)*, rev. edn, Fordham University Press, 1983; reprint, Crestwood: St Vladimir's Seminary Press, 1997.

Parker, T. H. L., *Karl Barth*, Grand Rapids: Wm. B. Eerdmans, 1970.

Pelikan, Jaroslav, *The Christian Tradition*, Vol. 3: *The Growth of Medieval Theology (600-1300),* Chicago: University of Chicago Press, 1978.

________, "The Doctrine of the Filioque in Thomas Aquinas and Its Patristic Antecedents," in Etienne Gilson (ed.), *St. Thomas Aquinas, 1274-1974: Commemorative Studies*, Toronto: Pontifical Institute of Mediaeveal Studies, 1974, pp. 315-36.

Pépin, Jean, "Theories of Procession in Plotinus and the Gnostics," in Richard T. Wallis and Jay Bregman (eds), *Neoplatonism and Gnosticism*, Albany: State University of New York Press, 1992, pp. 297-335.

Photius I., *Mystagogia Spiritus Sanctus*, trans. Holy Transfiguration Monastery, Astoria: Studion Publishers, 1983.

Pinnock, Clark H., *Flame of Love: A Theology of the Holy Spirit*, Downers Grove: InterVarsity Press, 1996.

Pius XI., *Mortalium Animos,* available from http://www.vatican.va/holy_father/pius_xi/encyclicals/documents/hf_p-xi_enc_19280106_mortalium-animos_en.html.

Powell, Samuel M., *The Trinity in German Thought*, Cambridge: Cambridge University Press, 2001.

Prestige, G. L., *God in Patristic Thought*, 2nd edn, William Heinemann Ltd, 1936; reprint, Guildford and London: SPCK, 1952.

Prestige, Leonard, "ΠΕΡΙΧΩΡΕΩ and ΠΕΡΙΧΩΡΗΣΙΣ in the Fathers," *Journal of Theological Studies* XXIX [Old Series] (1928): 242-52.

Rahner, Karl, *The Trinity*, trans. Joseph Donceel, New York: Herder & Herder, 1970.

Rauser, Randal, "Rahner's Rule: An Emperor without Clothes?" *International Journal of Systematic Theology* 7/1 (January 2005): 81-94.

Reid, Duncan, *Energies of the Spirit: Trinitarian Models in Eastern Orthodox and Western Theology*, Atlanta: Scholars Press, 1997.

Richardson, Kurt Anders, *Reading Karl Barth*, Grand Rapids: Baker Academic, 2004.

Ritschl, Dietrich, "Historical Development and Implications of the Filioque Controversy," in Lukas Vischer (ed.), *Spirit of God, Spirit of Christ: Ecumenical Reflections on the Filioque Controversy*, London: SPCK, 1981, pp. 46-65.

________, "The History of the Filioque Controversy," in Hans Küng and Jürgen Moltmann (eds), *Conflicts About the Holy Spirit*, New York: The Seabury Press, 1979, pp. 3-14,.

Roberts, R. H., "Karl Barth's Doctrine of Time: Its Nature and Implications," in S. W. Sykes (ed.), *Karl Barth—Studies of His Theological Method*, Oxford: Clarendon Press, 1979.

Rogers, Eugene F. Jr., "Eclipse of the Spirit in Karl Barth," in John C. McDowell and Mike Higton (eds), *Conversing with Barth,* Aldershot: Ashgate Publishing, 2004.

Rosato, Philip J., *The Spirit As Lord: The Pneumatology of Karl Barth*, Edinburgh: T & T Clark, 1981.

Runciman, Steven, *The Eastern Schism: A Study of the Papacy and the Eastern Churches during the 11th and 12th Centuries*, Oxford: Clarendon, 1955.

Rusch, William G. (ed.), *The Trinitarian Controversy*, Philadelphia: Fortress Press, 1980.

Sanders, Fred, *The Image of the Immanent Trinity: Rahner's Rule and the Theological Interpretation of Scripture*, New York: Peter Lang, 2005.

Schaff, Philip (ed.), *The Creeds of Christendom*, reprint edn, Vol. 2: *The Greek and Latin Creeds*, Grand Rapids: Baker Books, 1993.

Schlitt, Dale M., "The Whole Truth: Hegel's Reconceptualization of Trinity," *The Owl of Minerva* 15/2 (Spring 1984): 169-82.

Smail, Thomas A., "The Doctrine of the Holy Spirit," in John Thompson (ed.), *Theology Beyond Christendom*, Allison Park: Pickwick Publications, 1986, pp. 87-110.

________, "The Filioque in Recent Theological Discussion,", unpublished MS, June 1986.

________, *The Giving Gift*, London: Hodder and Stoughton, 1988; reprint, London: Darton, Longman & Todd, 1994.

________, "The Holy Spirit in the Holy Trinity," in Christopher Seitz (ed.), *Nicene Christianity: The Future for a New Ecumenism*, Grand Rapids: Brazos Press, 2001, pp. 149-65,.

Sokel, Walter H., *The Writer in Extremis, Expressionism in Twentieth-Century German Literature*, Stanford: Stanford University Press, 1959.

Spencer, Archibald James, *Clearing a Space for Human Action: Ethical Ontology in the Theology of Karl Barth*, New York: Peter Lang, 2003.

Stalder, Kurt, "The Filioque in the Old Catholic Churches: The Chief Phases of Theological Reflection and Church Pronouncements," in Lukas Vischer

(ed.), *Spirit of God, Spirit of Christ: Ecumenical Reflections on the Filioque Controversy*, London: SPCK, 1981, pp. 97-109.
Steiner, George, *Martin Heidegger*, 2nd edn, New York: Viking Press, 1978.
Stewart, Jon, *Kierkegaard's Relations to Hegel Reconsidered*, Cambridge: Cambridge University Press, 2003.
Stratoydaki-White, Despina, "Photios and the Filioque Controversy," *The Patristic & Byzantine Review* 2/2 (1983): 246-50.
Stylianopoulos, Theodore, "The Filioque: Dogma, Theologoumenon or Error?" *Greek Orthodox Theological Review* 31/3-4 (1986): 255-88.
Swete, H. B., *On the History of the Doctrine of the Procession of the Holy Spirit from the Apostolic Age to the Death of Charlemagne*, Cambridge: Cambridge University Press, 1876.
Sykes, S. W., "The Study of Barth," in S. W. Sykes (ed.), *Karl Barth: Studies of his Theological Method*, Oxford: Clarendon Press, 1979, pp. 1-16.
Taylor, Iain, "In Defence of Karl Barth's Doctrine of the Trinity," *International Journal of Systematic Theology* 5/1 (March 2003): 33-46.
Thompson, John, *The Holy Spirit in the Theology of Karl Barth*, Allison Park: Pickwick Publications, 1991.
________, *Modern Trinitarian Perspectives*, New York and Oxford: Oxford University Press, 1994.
Torrance, Alan J., *Persons in Communion: Trinitarian Description and Human Participation*, Edinburgh: T & T Clark, 1996.
Torrance, Thomas F., *The Christian Doctrine of God, One Being Three Persons*, Edinburgh: T & T Clark, 1996.
________, *Karl Barth: An Introduction to His Early Theology, 1910-1931*, London: SCM Press, 1962.
________, "Karl Barth and Patristic Theology," in John Thompson (ed.), *Theology Beyond Christendom*, Allison Park: Pickwick Publications, 1986, pp. 215-39.
________, *Karl Barth, Biblical and Evangelical Theologian*, Edinburgh: T & T Clark, 1990.
________, *The Mediation of Christ*, Colorado Springs: Helmers & Howard, 1992.
________, *Theology in Reconciliation*, London: Geoffrey Chapman, 1975.
________, *Trinitarian Perspectives: Toward Doctrinal Agreement*, Edinburgh: T & T Clark, 1994.
van Driel, Edwin Chr., "Karl Barth on the Eternal Existence of Jesus Christ," *Scottish Journal of Theology* 60/1 (2007): 45-61.
Vischer, Lukas (ed.), *Spirit of God, Spirit of Christ: Ecumenical Reflections on the* Filioque *Controversy*, London: SPCK, 1981.
Visser 't Hooft, W. A., "Karl Barth and the Ecumenical Movement," *Ecumenical Review* 32 (April 1980): 129-51.
von Balthasar, Hans Urs, *The Theology of Karl Barth: Exposition and Interpretation*, trans. Edward T. Oakes, Cologne: Jakob Hegner, 1951; reprint, San Francisco: Ignatius Press, 1992.

Ware, K and C. Davey (eds), *Anglican-Orthodox Dialogue. The Moscow Agreed Statement. Anglican-Orthodox Joint Doctrinal Commission 1976*, London: SPCK, 1977.

Watson, Gordon, "The Filioque—Opportunity for Debate?" *Scottish Journal of Theology* 41 (1988): 313-30.

Webb, Stephen H., *The Divine Voice*, Grand Rapids: Brazos Press, 2004.

________, *Re-Figuring Theology: The Rhetoric of Karl Barth*, Albany: State University of New York Press, 1991.

Webster, J. B., "'On the Frontiers of What Is Observable': Barth's *Römerbrief* and Negative Theology," *Downside Review* 105 (July 1987): 169-80.

Webster, John, *Barth*, London and New York: Continuum, 2000.

________, *Barth's Moral Theology*, Grand Rapids: Wm. B. Eerdmans Publishing, 1998.

________, "'There is No Past in the Church, so There is No Past in Theology': Barth on the History of Modern Protestant Theology," in John C. McDowell and Mike Higton (eds), *Conversing with Barth,* Aldershot: Ashgate, 2004, pp. 14-39.

________, "Translator's Introduction," in Eberhard Jüngel, *God's Being is in Becoming: The Trinitarian Being of God in the Theology of Karl Barth*, Grand Rapids: Wm. B. Eerdmans Publishing, 2001, pp. ix-xxiii.

Widmer, Gabriel, "La Théologie Réformée et le 'Filioque'," in *La Signification et l'Actualité du IIe Concile Oecumenique pour le Monde Chrétien d'Aujourd'hui*, Chambesy: Du Centre Orthodoxe du Patriarcat Oecumenique, 1982, pp. 319-37.

Williams, R. D., "Barth on the Triune God," in S. W. Sykes (ed.), *Karl Barth. Studies of his Theological Method*, Oxford: Clarendon Press, 1979, pp. 147-93.

Willis, Robert E., *The Ethics of Karl Barth*, Leiden: E. J. Brill, 1971.

Winter, Mary Corinne, "Ecclesiological Implications of the Current *Filioque* Discussion," PhD thesis, University of Notre Dame, 1995.

Yong, Amos, "A Theology of the Third Article? Hegel and the Contemporary Enterprise in First Philosophy and First Theology," in Stanley E. Porter and Anthony R. Cross (eds), *Semper Reformandum: Studies in Honour of Clark H. Pinnock*, Carlisle: Paternoster Press, 2003, pp. 208-31.

Zizioulas, John D., *Being As Communion*, Crestwood: St Vladimir's Seminary Press, 1985.

________, "One Single Source: An Orthodox Response to the Clarification on the Filioque," 2002, available from: http://www.orthodoxresearchinstitute.org/articles/dogmatics/john_zizioulas_single_source.htm.

________, "The Teaching of the Second Ecumenical Council on the Holy Spirit in Historical and Ecumenical Perspective, Vol. 1." in *Credo in Spiritum Sanctum*, Vatican City: Libreria Editrice Vaticana, 1983, pp. 29-45.

Secondary Uncited Sources

de Margerie, Bertrand, *The Christian Trinity in History*, trans. Edmund J. Fortman, Still River: St Bede's Publications, 1982.

Godsey, John, "The Architecture of Karl Barth's Church Dogmatics," *Scottish Journal of Theology,* 9 (1956): 236-50.

Jugie, Martino, "Origine de la Controverse sur l'Addition du Filioque au Symbole," *Revue des sciences philosophiques et théologiques* 28 (1939): 369-85.

Jülicher, Adolf, "A Modern Interpreter of Paul," in Keith R. Crim and Louis De Grazia (eds), *The Beginnings of Dialectic Theology*, vol. I, Richmond: John Knox Press, 1968, pp. 72-81.

Jüngel, Eberhard, *God's Being Is in Becoming*, trans. John Webster, Tübingen: J. C. B. Mohr, 1986; reprint, Grand Rapids: Wm. B. Eerdmans Publishing, 2001.

Körtner, Ulrich H. J., "Der Göttliche Ursprung des Geistes das Filioque im Ökumenischen Gespräch," in *Die Gemeinschaft des Heiligen Geistes*, 47-62, Neukirchener: Neukirchen-Vluyn, 1999.

Letham, Robert, "East is East and West is West? Another Look at the *Filioque*," *Mid-America Journal of Theology* 13 (2002): 71-86.

Myers, Bernard S., *The German Expressionists, A Generation in Revolt*, New York: Frederick A. Praeger, 1956.

Needham, Nick, "The *Filioque* Clause: East or West?" *Scottish Bulletin of Evangelical Theology* 15/2 (Autumn 1997): 142-62.

Rawlinson, Alfred E. J., "The *Filioque* Clause," *Scottish Journal of Theology* 10 (June 1957): 166-73.

Rawlinson, Alfred E. J., "The *Filioque* Clause," *Scottish Journal of Theology* 10 (June 1957): 166-73.

Roberts, R. H., "The Reception of the Theology of Karl Barth in the Anglo-Saxon World: History, Typology, and Prospect," in S. W. Sykes (ed.), *Karl Barth: Centenary Essays*, Cambridge: Cambridge University Press, 1989, pp. 115-71.

Scheffczyk, Leo, "The Meaning of the 'Filioque,'" *Communio* 13/2 (Summer 1986): 125-38.

Smolík, Josef, "Filioque in the Reformed Tradition," *Communio Viatorum* XXIV (1981): 219-22.

Subject and Name Index

Scripture Index